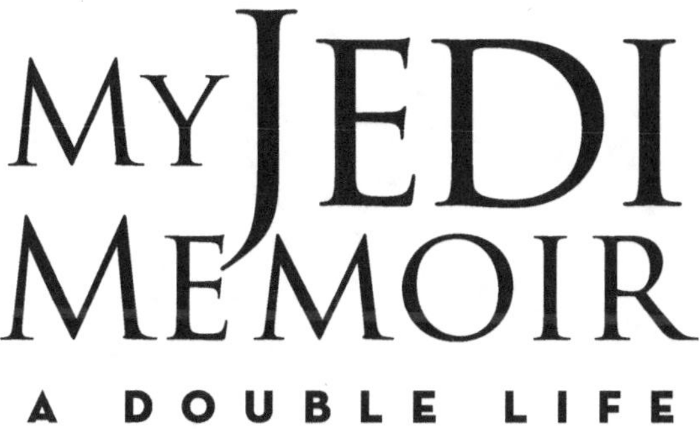

My Jedi Memoir

A Double Life

By James Kahn

My Jedi Memoir: A Double Life
By James Kahn
Copyright © 2025 James Kahn

Published in the USA by:
BearManor Media
1317 Edgewater Dr #110
Orlando, FL 32804
www.bearmanormedia.com

Perfect ISBN 979-8-88771-730-2
Case ISBN 979-8-88771-731-9
BearManor Media, Orlando, Florida
Printed in the United States of America
Book design by Robbie Adkins, www.adkinsconsult.com

TABLE OF CONTENTS

THE INCITING INCIDENT

ST. JOHN'S HOSPITAL, SANTA MONICA, CALIFORNIA, Thursday, October 29, 1981

"St. John's Emergency Room, how can I help you?"

"I need someone to resuscitate an alien."

"Have you called 911?"

"No, no, he doesn't need it now. Early next week."

"If he's so sick you think he'll need it next week, maybe you should bring him in now. If he's undocumented, we don't call Immigration, you don't have to worry about that."

"No, not that kind of alien. I'm talking about an extraterrestrial. You know, from outer space."

"Hold, please."

Croon, the Ward Clerk, thought: So it was going to be one of those kind of days. Full moon, maybe, or Santa Ana winds making people crazy, or aerosolized toxins from a wildfire in the hills, or close to Halloween. It wasn't near Christmas yet, the season that typically saw the most psychoses roll in through the ER doors like a red tide. Just a random yahoo, maybe.

That's when she saw Murphy walking out of the Break Room. This was definitely a call for Murphy, who'd been known to reduce telemarketers to tears by pretending to be a homicide detective. "Murph!" Croon called out, "Line 4, question for a doctor."

Murphy was manic on his slowest days, and game for anything that came his way. A Viet Nam vet with stories he mostly didn't talk about, nothing in this civilian life threw him. He walked to a phone, grabbed up the receiver, and punched Line 4. "This is Dr. Murphy, what's on your mind?"

"Hi, Dr. Murphy, I won't take much time out of your busy day, but we're making a movie about a space creature that lands on earth and has a cardiac arrest – or something like that – and I wonder if you, or anybody there, could tell us how you might approach resuscitating him."

Murphy looked at Croon, who was eavesdropping on the extension, stifling laughter. But now this sounded like a serious call. Making a movie. This was Hollywoodland, after all. He put on his doctor voice. "Yeah, we know how to do that. Why don't you come down to the ER tomorrow, and we'll show you."

"Great. Thank you so much. Would 1 be a good time?"

"Sure. What's your name, so the front desk will let you in?"

"My name is Kathleen Kennedy, and I'll be with the writer, Melissa Matheson."

"Okay, I'll leave your names on the list." He hung up.

Croon looked at him. "What list?"

"Figure it out. I gotta tell Lampone."

Lampone was the guy who ran the ER. Murphy knew he – Murphy – was out of his depth with this kind of mission. Needing some backup, he found Lampone suturing a skateboarder's scalp, and brought him up to speed on the extraterrestrial problem.

Lampone was a problem solver. He nodded at Murphy's story, took a moment with needle holder poised in his right hand, forceps in the left, and said, "Call Kahn. He wants to be in the movies."

That's how it started.

But First, A Little Backstory

That was the nexus moment, when my career as an emergency room doctor collided with what was about to become my Hollywood writing career. I called that moment the Inciting Incident because in The Hero's Journey, the Inciting Incident is the event that kicks off the story, and I like to think of myself as the hero in my own life's journey. So what follows – if you're a student of Joseph Campbell – is my Call to Adventure, Refusal of the Call, Acceptance of the Call, Obstacles and Allies, Midpoint Crisis, Rising Stakes, Collapse of the Hero's Plan, Triumph, and Bringing the Jewels Back Home. All those stations of the cross that filmmakers use to mark the narrative structure of their movies. I can certainly see some of those landmarks showing up in my life.

But life is messier than art, and things don't always go according to plan, or even logic; or even movie logic. Less of a Hero's Journey than a series of short jaunts, or overlapping stutter-steps, an unfinished Venn Diagram, with random discontinuities in the arcs. Like the Hero's Gap Year. Or the Hero's Road Trip.

My life does have recurring themes, however. Everyone's life does.

One time while in the Writer's Room on a series called *Doc*, the showrunner said that in his opinion, every writer has a personal theme that's at the core of, or at least makes its way into, every script that writer writes. A theme that can usually be distilled into a phrase in three to six words.

The reaction in the room ranged from scoffing to endorsement to bemusement. But within five minutes, everyone there had come up with a facsimile of their own personal theme, an idea that resonated with them, and had cropped up in at least some of their scripts. These are a few I remember:

I've got a secret.
You owe me!
Life changes in a hurry.

Where do I fit in the world?
Who am I?
And the phrase I thought most often informed my writing? *The masks we wear.*

In fact, I think I've felt masked most of my life. I was an only child, well loved by my proud parents, who also loved to parade me in front of relatives at family gatherings to show off how great I was at singing, doing impressions, telling jokes – all to my great discomfort and embarrassment. What my wife, Jill, later called "The Dancing Bear Syndrome." Like the poor bear in the circus, chained at the ankle and wearing a tutu, looking like he feels kind of foolish, prodded by his handler into dancing for the crowd.

But I was also the only Jewish kid in school, experiencing a fair number of antisemitic taunts, insults, and occasional assaults – which served to keep me isolated, and made me want to stay below the radar as much as possible, to not let kids know I was Jewish.

I think being told how great I was by my parents, being embarrassed by all that attention, and simultaneously ashamed of who I was in public, and trying to hide it – these irreconcilable forces forged who I became. Forever trying to mask my shame with hubris, and masking my hubris with self-deprecation. The mask of the Dancing Bear Below the Radar.

The first way I dealt with these confusions was to seek solace in imaginary worlds. And sometimes playing in these worlds together with the few friends I did have – Cops and Robbers, monsters and ghouls on the loose – all of us playing roles, wearing masks, and creating these fantasy scenarios, hiding in empty lots and excavations, escaping dangers, inventing weapons and shields. "You're dead!" "No I'm not, you missed me!"

When I was around nine, I remember watching *Flash Gordon* on TV. And *Captain Video and his Video Rangers*. I used to read *Superman* and *Batman* comics, as well as *Strange Tales, Tales from the Crypt, Amazing Stories, Weird Tales* – lots of sci-fi/fantasy/horror/sorcery pulp. But here's the thing: I used to think of different plot twists or endings for the stories I read – so I'd rewrite them in my nine-year-old scrawl, in my spiral notebooks. I was novelizing comic books for my own amusement in 4th grade. I added *Mad Magazine* to my booklist, as well, which taught me about life's absurdity and the pompous bluster of the ruling classes, while its segment "Scenes We'd Like to See" was my first instruction in movie tropes.

My inclination to write got a boost from my 7th grade English teacher, Mr. Meisterheim. The assignment was to write a four page essay on the origin of Thanksgiving. Instead, I turned in a four page short story. Meisterheim gave me a B+ because it was such an entertaining read, but he couldn't give me an A because it failed the assignment so miserably.

A couple high school English teachers gave me encouragement, as well, though overall high school was a pretty mixed bag. On the one hand, I continued to be intimidated by anti-Semitic attacks – one guy in my homeroom saluted me with a Heil Hitler every morning for four years – on the other hand I made friends: kids I played music with (Al Ripperger, Brian Dole and I formed the rock group Lord Kelvin and the Absolute Zeros); kids I played poker and bridge and ping-pong with, and joined theater with, and laughed with, girls I had crushes on, science nerds and band-mates and English classmates. I even had a girlfriend, Dawn.

In retrospect, I took for granted my place in an extremely privileged environment. Maine West had an orchestra, a band, a marching band, a stage band, a theater, chem and physics labs, language lab, auto shop, wood shop, metal shop, swimming pool, track, basketball courts, baseball field, radio station, newspaper, library… so I don't know that I have all that much to gripe about. Compared to most kids around the world, I think I won the lottery.

My father was a doctor, a GP, and his office was in the downstairs den of our split-level house. I grew up thinking it was normal to have a lot of coughing, sneezing strangers sitting in your basement. Occasionally I was awakened in the middle of the night by the telephone in the other room, and vaguely aware of my father getting dressed to go out and make a house call. And once I was roused by a pounding on the front door. I walked out of my 2nd floor bedroom and stood on the landing to see some guy with a gashed, bleeding hand, being ushered downstairs by my father in his bathrobe.

Medicine, it seemed to me from my little boy fantasy/sci-fi bubble, was a kind of sorcery, and doctors were wizards, pulling people back from the clutches of death and dismemberment. Like my father fixing up the guy with the gory hand at midnight. So I ultimately went into Emergency Medicine, which was the most sorcery-like specialty I could imagine. People would literally be brought in to me dead, and I would literally make them alive again. How cool would that be?

I'd always wanted to write, too – ever since rewriting those pulp comic books at age nine. So I took a year off after my medical internship – my first gap year – got married to Jill, lived in France for a season, and wrote my first novel – titled *Oculus Sinister*, the medical term for "left eye," but also a bilingual pun for "evil eye." I got an agent, who sold it on the 20th submission, to Carlyle Press. They barely even edited it, but only insisted I retitle it, because nobody had any idea what my title meant. So I retitled it *Diagnosis: Murder*, about this crime-solving doctor. (It of course had no relationship to the TV series of the same name, about a doctor who solves crimes, and produced by a company I'd once pitched my book to. No relationship whatsoever.)

My first book! Very exciting. On the day it was shipped I drove to the warehouse in L.A., near the Fairfax ramp off the 10, where the publisher said it was being housed. I found the floor supervisor – a 60-year-old, working-class guy – told him my name, and the title of my book, and the publisher, and asked if he could tell me which bookstores it was being distributed to, so I could tell my friends where to go buy it.

He gave me a kindly, if weary, smile. "I don't want to break your bubble, kid, but we don't distribute Carlyle Press by the title, we ship 'em by the pound." Mostly porn, it turned out, but a smattering of potboilers, gothic romances, and thrillers. I thanked him, and vowed never to tell anyone that story. Maybe it meant I wasn't really an author at all. Even the guy in the warehouse saw through my mask.

The only person who saw clearly through all my masks was the woman I married, artist Jill Littlewood. We got hitched right at the transition from Chicago to L.A., where we moved for me to start my Emergency Medicine Residency at USC/LA County Hospital. Jill was the only person who knew the real me – whoever that was.

The LA County experience was kind of insane. Around 1000 patients/day came through the ER, so I saw and trained on just about every possible medical disaster. Collected a lot of stories there, too, which kept my creative juices going. It was during this period that I started writing a science-fiction/fantasy novel, the first of a sci-fi trilogy. The book was called *There's a New Animal in the South*, and my agent, Jane Jordan Browne, eventually sold it to Judy Lynn Del Rey, the editor/publisher of Del Rey Books. A real publishing house! Again, they did very little editing, except to insist I change the title, which I did, to *World Enough, and Time.* What is it with publishers and titles?

It took a few years to get written and sold, though – during which time I left LA County Hospital, helped create the ER Residency at UCLA, finished the Residency at UCLA, helped create the emergency room at St. John's Hospital in Santa Monica, and began working there full time as an ER Doc. That's when Del Rey bought my novel.

Judy Lynn flew out to L.A. from New York to meet me, but when she got to town, she called to say she had to cancel because her nose was bleeding and wouldn't stop. No problem, I told her.

I was working at St. John's Hospital Emergency Room at the time, but I got one of the other docs there (Bob Murphy – the same guy who later took the alien resuscitation call) to cover for me. I gathered up a bag full of ENT tools, and made a house call to Judy Lynn's room at the Beverly Hills Hotel. A nasal speculum, some Gelfoam, a long forceps, *et voila!* I stopped her nosebleed. It was the beginning of a beautiful friendship, and the first crossing of my doctoring with my writing.

Over the next couple years, I kept working emergency rooms around L.A., as I continued writing – and eventually, as Jill and I started raising a family together. So if this memoir sometimes comes off as feeling a little disjointed, it's because that's how my life felt, pulled in three different directions. I had my own Three Body Problem, unpredictably pulled into differing orbits by the influence of rising and falling gravities.

And once the L.A. Residency started, I began writing screenplays as well as novels – for who doesn't come to Los Angeles to be discovered by Hollywood, and swept up in the movie industry?

I provide a little more context to my backstory at the end of this book, in the section titled Afterthoughts. But when you tell a tale, as I am telling you now, you don't want to get too bogged down with backstory at the top of the narrative; you want to dive in to the action. So let's go.

Chapter One
My First Taste

In late October, 1981, I was working the ER at St. John's Hospital. St. John's was on the West Side of L.A., at that point kind of a chichi, boutique ER that I'd helped create a couple years earlier with a few other recent graduates of the Emergency Medicine Residency at USC/LA County Hospital.

I was off-duty the day the call from Kathleen Kennedy came in, asking about how to resuscitate an alien. Lampone had told Murphy to call me, which he did. But I didn't answer Murphy's message to call him right back, because I figured the only reason he'd be calling me was to ask me to take one of his shifts, and I just wanted to lay low.

Later that day, after I hadn't returned Murphy's call, Lampone called me – Caller ID on my answering machine, if anybody remembers those – and I had to take that call, because Lampone was the boss. He told me the story about the alien movie, and us being part of it, and I thanked him profusely for including me. On a movie set! I was going to get to be on a movie set!

I went in to the ER the next day, where I met Kathleen Kennedy and Melissa Mathison, the screenwriter of *ET: The Extraterrestrial.* We gave them a demonstration, I took the part of the cardiac arrest patient, Murphy pounded on my chest – a little too hard, Murphy often got carried away – shouting out orders… and they must have liked the performance, because we got the gig.

Lampone rounded up a few nurses, and the next day we all went down to the set of *ET*, being shot at Laird Studios, then a satellite of MGM, but once housing the sound stages where *Gone With the Wind* was filmed. Film history! To say I was excited to walk the ground where Scarlett O'Hara once swooned, and to meet Steven Spielberg, would be a vast understatement. To get to be in the movie was unbelievable. And to watch him direct was awe-inspiring.

But of course, I had a hidden agenda, too. I wanted the great director to read my sci-fi novel and let me write a script to make a movie from it. The chances of that happening were obviously slim to none, but if I ever had a shot at making that happen, this was it. I had to make Spielberg think I knew what I was doing. What did a professional screenwriter mask even look like?

They were going to film ET's death scene all week. They dressed us up in hazmat suits, and at the call of "Action!" we surrounded the little alien corpse, doing our thing – pounding on his chest, hooking him up to IV lines, shouting out what drugs to give him, ad-libbing it all, barking the kind of orders we'd issue if someone were actually brought into the ER without a pulse.

This is one of those memories that stand out to me with stark visuals and drama, that look like little movie scenes in my mind. So here's how it reads in a screenplay:

INT. ISOLATION ROOM - DAY

DOCTORS and NURSES close in around the small ALIEN CREATURE lying lifeless on a gurney, under an operating table lamp and surrounded by monitors, wires and tubes.

      KAHN
   An amp of epi, stat!

     DR. LAMPONE
  One bolus of bicarb, IV push!

     DR. MURPHY
  Starting chest compressions!

Murphy begins pushing on ET's chest, as Nurses push meds through the IV tubes.

      KAHN
  Charge up the paddles to 200!

As if epinephrine, or 200 joules of electric shock, could help an extraterrestrial; or pounding on his chest had anything to do with restarting his heart, if he even had one. (Spoiler Alert: He did have one, and it glowed!) But that's what Steven wanted, professionals doing their thing, to give the scene a realistic feel. We weren't exactly wearing masks in that moment; we were doing the thing we'd been trained to do. We were just fish out of water; science nerds on a movie set. Doctors pretending to be actors pretending to be doctors. It was just a bit disorienting.

The following is a template of a test page distributed to me and other docs on set, in which I was asked to replace existing dialogue with actual medical jargon.

```
Magnesium, 50 mgs per ML.
Lithium, 75 mgs per ML.
Zinc, 225 per ML.

            MILITARY DOCTOR
Run the fluid through the Mass Spec.

            MASS SPEC READER (o.c.)
We're finding Beryllium, Chromium,
Niobium.

            MONITOR TECH (o.c.)
His respitory rate has increased.

            BLOOD TESTER (o.c.)
Well, he doesn't use glucose.

            MILITARY DOCTOR
Well, what does he use goddamnit!

            BLOOD TESTER (o.c.)
Fructose.

            SAVE-HIM DOCTOR
Fructose?

            STUDY-HIM DOCTOR
Any enzymes available with that?

            BLOOD TESTER (o.c.)
Yes.  He has phosphorylating enzymes.

            STUDY-HIM DOCTOR
Sounds like Photosynthesis.

            SAVE-HIM DOCTOR
How's the boy doing?
```

My dialogue suggestions on script template of ET: The Extra-Terrestrial *(Universal Studios, 1982). Photo courtesy of the Author.*

But what ended up on the screen for this kind of background was just us docs yelling orders at each other, ad-libbing the way we'd really talk during a cardiac arrest, pretending it was an actual ER case. Of course, the A-Team dialogue was tightly and beautifully scripted by Melissa.

Spielberg was a terrific director. (Duh.) I remember when he directed Henry Thomas, who played Elliott; it was like they were both kids, playing the kind of make-up game I remember playing when I was a kid. This is a clip from that movie running in my mind.

```
INT. SOUNDSTAGE - DAY

Spielberg kneels in front of Henry Thomas,
so they're eye to eye, and speaks to him
like one kid to another.

                    SPIELBERG
          Okay, so this alien has come
          down to earth and chosen
          you as his best friend, and now
          he's dying, and you're
          freaked out, and these govern-
          ment guys are running
          all over, you've just gotta get
          your buddy outta there…

                    HENRY THOMAS
                    (with feeling)
          Yeah…
```

Between takes there was an air of exuberance on the set, especially among the lower echelon players. Lampone and I even took turns giving Drew Barrymore piggyback rides – another brush with greatness! (You're welcome, Drew.)

Spielberg was like a kind of fey college kid himself, and the atmosphere on the set was vaguely frat-like. Frank Marshall and Kathleen Kennedy and Melissa Mathison were all young, and the whole thing felt pretty loose, exuberant, and friendly. In retrospect I suspect they were actually wound tight, they had a lot riding on this movie – but for me it all felt like I'd been adopted by the circus. Which I think brought out the Dancing Bear Syndrome in me, the part of me that loved the crowd to applaud my dance.

Which is how I finally had the unmitigated *chutzpah* to steel my nerves and approach Steven on the second day, and give him a copy of my first sci-fi novel, that Del Rey had just published, *World Enough, and Time* – which he graciously accepted. I asked if he would consider making a movie out of it – like nobody's ever said that to him before – and he kindly said he'd put it on his pile of books to read, and get to it eventually. I thought I knew what that meant, but I was honored just to have him take the thing. Just that much would give me bragging rights. The Dancing Bear took a bow.

Next day on set, during one of those waiting periods when the grips and gaffers run around doing a new set-up, one of the PA's came up to me and said, "Mr. Spielberg wants to see you in his office." I thought, *Oh, shit, what did I do wrong? Look into the camera during one of the last takes?* That's the other half of the Dancing Bear Syndrome – the fear of falling on your face, and earning everyone's ridicule. It meant Spielberg had seen through my mask.

The last takes on camera had actually been my big moments. ET had just gone flatline, alarms were going off, and five of us ran in through the plastic tunnel, into the sealed-off isolation tent. Next time you watch the movie, if you don't blink, you might notice the last doctor running in is holding a clipboard. That's me. Someone always takes notes during a cardiac arrest resuscitation, to analyze afterwards, to see what was done wrong and what was done right; it's called a post-mortem. And then in the next set-up after we ran in, I was at ET's bedside, adjusting the IV line. I shouted out a couple orders, and shortly after that I pumped on the little guy's chest a few times. We all tried to do that, whether on camera or not, just so we could feel like… yeah, I did that.

And I have to say, with all the real gear set up, and all the real doctors and nurses doing what they do, and yelling at each other the way they yell, it all felt pretty real, in a fantastic kind of way. Also kind of like playing in those empty lots when I was a kid. "I got you, you're dead!" "No I'm not, you missed me!" So it turned out ET wasn't dead, either. They missed him, too.

My entrance, stage left, holding a clipboard in the resuscitation scene of ET: The Extra-Terrestrial *(1982). Photo courtesy of Universal Studios.*

Anyway, I went to Spielberg's office after the shot, and here's how it went:

```
INT. SPIELBERG'S OFFICE - DAY

Spielberg goes over his shot list as Kahn
enters and stands off to the side, picking
at his fingernails, waiting to be acknowl-
edged. Spielberg looks up.

                SPIELBERG
        So listen, when I got home last
        night, I took a look at
        your book, and I liked what I
        read. Nice job! I asked
        Frank to read it, and he thought
        it was great too.
```

```
          KAHN
No shit?!! So… you want to make
a movie out of it?

          SPIELBERG
Well… no. But we're kind of
behind the eight ball on the
Poltergeist novelization, the
draft we have isn't working,
and the publisher needs a book
in 30 days. So if you
think you can write it in less
than a month, the gig is yours.
```

I thought damn, I can't complete this task in a month, certainly not this month – I have at least a dozen long shifts in the emergency room I'm already scheduled for. I can't just walk away from that. Those shifts are my responsibility, and I'm a responsible doctor. But wait… surely I can find other doctors to fill my shifts, right? I mean, what if I'd been in a car accident and I couldn't make it to work – wouldn't someone else have to fill my shifts? But this wasn't an accident, this would be a deliberate act. No. I couldn't do it. Or could I? No, no, it wouldn't be right, and besides that, I'm not sure I even know how to write a novelization. I mean, what the hell even is a novelization?

But I also knew I was okay with jumping into unknown challenges, and generally landing on my feet. My first on-call night as an intern, when I was going to be put in charge of three medical services all night, on my own, my Resident – whose job it was to mentor me through this process – gave me his strong advice. And this memory isn't visual so much as literary. I can't recall what the Resident looked like, but I remember his words, and how they made me feel. Maybe I'll write those kinds of memories like a novel.

"There's only one thing you have to remember tonight," the Resident instructed. His voice was soft, but he held my gaze, to give import to his words.

I held my pen poised over my internship notebook. I was excited, but scared. This was my first night running the show, overseeing 50 hospitalized patients. "I'm ready," I told him, masked with super confidence.

"Whatever happens," the Resident said, "don't call me."

Whereupon he left the hospital and went home. I was so stunned, I wanted to cry.

An hour later my beeper went off, and I called back the number from the nearest Nursing Station. It was a nurse from another unit.

"You the on-call Doc tonight?"

I tried to sound cool. "Yeah. What's up?"

"You'd better get up here to Cardiology, the patient in 416 has a bleeding tongue."

I hesitated. But I had this. "He bit it?"

"No, the whole tongue is just oozing. Like flowing blood from everywhere, like an oversoaked sponge, or I don't know what."

Wait… what? "Is that even a thing?"

"Just get up here."

I went to take care of it, and gave the guy a gauze pad to clamp down on, and by golly, the bleeding stopped. It was as if, in that moment, I'd become a doctor. So I knew a thing or two about leaping into situations I knew nothing about.

(Unrelated, but Important Note: This was July 1, the day all internships and residencies in the country start – so every young doctor in the hospital is on their first day of doing things they've never done before. Interns, in particular, were just medical students the day before. So it might not be a coincidence that hospital deaths rise every July, and then settle back to normal over the summer. So probably best to avoid hospitalization in July. Just sayin'.)

Anyway, back to *ET.* After my chaotic inner harangue about being a responsible doctor – which reminded me of Goofy listening to his Angel Goofy on one shoulder and his Devil Goofy on the other – this was my answer to Spielberg.

KAHN

You bet I can finish Poltergeist
in a month!

I'd answered the Call of the Bleeding Tongue, and it had transformed me into a doctor. Now I was answering the Call of the Director, and it would transform me into a Hollywood writer! I simply had to wear a Hollywood Writer's mask! Of course, I still had no idea how I could write an entire novel that fast. It had taken me a year to write the sci-fi novel I just gave him. And as I said, I wasn't even quite sure what a novelization was. I knew it was an adaptation from the screenplay, but I didn't know if it had to be identical to the script, or if the novelist could add new storylines, or what.

I knew, as an "art form," novelizations were looked down upon by novelists – viewed as marketing tools and little else. But I'd also read once that Graham Greene had first written the screenplay for a movie I loved, *The Third Man*, and then wrote the novel afterwards – novelizing his own script – so if it was good enough for Graham Greene, by God, it was good enough for me.

What I didn't realize then was that the 1980's would be the decade of Peak Novelization. There was no streaming of movies in those days, or even DVD's to watch your favorite films over and over. So the only way for fans to experience their most beloved films repeatedly was to read the novelization until the cover fell off. Under the bedsheets at night, hidden inside open algebra textbooks in class, on the beach. Not only that, novelizations were an opportunity to go deeper into the characters, to find out what they were "really" thinking in those visually rich scenes. At least, that's what fans told me years later, when they thought back on that time.

And that time, for me, started now. Did I mention I was scheduled to work in the ER the whole month? A couple other docs had taken our shifts for these 4 days of filming already; I didn't know how I was going to get coverage for an entire month. But I said yes to Steven, and yes means yes. I went home immediately, didn't finish filming any of my other shots on *ET*. And through a combination of pleading and promising blank check untold future favors to a couple other ER docs – thank you, Walter Theis – I got out of all my shifts.

I wrote the Poltergeist novelization in 28 days, and Spielberg loved it – but I'll get into those details presently.

For now, suffice to say, my Hollywood Journey had begun.

Chapter Two
How I Found My Hero's Journey Inside

Though *Poltergeist* jumpstarted my career, the flashiest memories from my years in Hollywood emerge out of my first blockbuster success, writing the novelization of *Return of the Jedi*. That project was the launching pad for all my subsequent jobs in the movie biz, so it stands out not only for all the specific tales it generated, but for the breathless feelings of wonder and adventure that carried me along that whole next phase of my life.

What follows, then, is part memoir, part narrative analysis of my second novelization, *Return of the Jedi*, and part personal Hero's Journey, matching my Hollywood odyssey with a retrospective reframing of my medical years – both quests running aground on the shoals of great expectations and unintended consequences.

So I'll begin that transition from emergency room to sound stage with the screenwriting tropes I mentioned earlier. The Ordinary World, the Inciting Incident, the Call to Adventure, the Refusal of the Call, the Answer of the Call, the Midpoint Crisis, the Collapse of the Hero's Plan (when everything turns to shit), the Ultimate Triumph, and Bringing the Prize Back Home.

The Ordinary World of the Hero's Journey is what's going on day to day when the movie starts. The Inciting Incident is the thing that drops into the hero's Ordinary World and sets off the whole Quest. Simple enough.

Most of us are in a delicate equilibrium in our lives – balancing money flow, workplace frictions, relationship pluses and minuses, dreams, fears, psychological baggage – but it's all kind of working. It's our Ordinary World. You give a little here, take a little there, stand on one leg while juggling a bowling ball and an ice cream cone, too busy or distracted or beat down to even consider the way things might be if you ever really *got* what you wanted. And then a kid on a bicycle races by, knocking you off your pins, and you go flying, and all the things you've been juggling reach their apex and start coming down on you, and you think: Is this the life I wanted? Is it going to be like this forever?

In medicine this concept is called decompensation. Your heart is beating along for years, but cholesterol starts to build up so your heart compensates by pumping harder – which raises your blood pressure – which you *compensate* for by taking BP meds – which cause erectile dysfunction, so you compensate for that with Viagra – which makes your blood pressure plunge too far, tumbling you into shock – and the whole system *decompensates*, and you go into cardiac arrest. So the Viagra was the Inciting Incident in an Ordinary World that was already compensating for myriad balancing acts on the cardiac stage.

For me, in 1981 when I was working the ER at St. John's Hospital, that was my Ordinary World. Runny noses, sprained ankles, lacerations, heart attacks, auto accidents, gunshot wounds, bladder infections, strep throats, ear infections, STD's, psychotic breaks, overdoses, rashes, ulcers, alcohol withdrawal, migraines, gastroenteritis, arthritis, sinusitis, pyelonephritis, bronchitis, depression, panic attacks, scabies, head lice, flu, pneumonia, broken bones, broken hearts, organ recitals ("Oh, doctor, it's my liver, and my kidneys, and oh, my lungs…"), and malingerers. (We were taught in Residency a useful way to determine if someone was malingering was to ask these questions: "Do your teeth itch? Do you get a severe burning between your eyes when urinating? Do your stools glow?" If the patient answered "Yes" to any of these, malingering should be suspected.)

But the day Kathleen Kennedy called and asked for help resuscitating an alien, and Lampone called me in to help – that was my Inciting Incident.

My Call to Adventure was when Spielberg said he had a job for me, if I wanted it – to write the *Poltergeist* novelization in under a month.

But often, heroes don't want to go on the adventure at the outset. Their Ordinary World may not be satisfying in some essential way, but it's *their* world, and they've gotten used to it. Like the devil you know is preferable to the devil you don't know. So it's not uncommon for the hero to Refuse the Call to Adventure, declining to be sucked into a potentially chaotic unknown. The hero says thanks but no thanks, can't do it, and offers up rationales why it just doesn't make sense to upend the way things have always been.

Like in *Star Wars*, when Obi Wan asks Luke to come with him and join the Rebel Alliance, Luke says No Way, not possible, gotta work on the farm, get the crops in, help Uncle Owen and Aunt Beru. Maybe next season, but not now. This is such a common trope in Hero's Journeys – the reluctance of the lead to leave one's Ordinary World, as stultifying or grinding as it might be. Resistance to change. Denial of higher goals, or a higher truth. Refusal to open one's eyes to deep, inner truths.

For me, the Refusal was silent, internal, and lasted about 3 seconds. As I mentioned earlier, I thought shit, I can't complete this task in a month – and moreover, what the hell am I even thinking? I'm not a Hollywood writer, I'm a doctor, and doctors don't do this kind of thing. Doctors are conservative, and measured; they don't skip class. They nod thoughtfully. They play golf. No, I can't do this.

Luke, after telling Obi Wan he can't possibly go off to fight with the Rebellion, realizes his new droids will have led the Imperial Stormtroopers right back to Uncle Owen and Aunt Beru. He races back there to find his uncle and aunt burned to a crisp. Now there's nothing to hold him here. He's not a farmer at heart, and he feels anger about the death of his only family at the hands of the Empire, as well. So he agrees to accompany Obi Wan to Mos Eisley. He answers the call.

And me? After my chaotic inner harangue about being a responsible doctor, my answer to Spielberg was: "You bet I can finish it in a month!" So mine was a brief Refusal.

Thinking back, I believe my decision to go for it was influenced by two very different patient encounters I'd had over the years. The first was as a 2nd Year med student – the first time we're allowed in the hospital, on the patient floors, as we gradually learn how to examine a patient, what tests to order, how to think like a doctor. And because we're interacting with patients, we wear white lab coats, laden with gear – a stethoscope, an ophthalmoscope, a reflex hammer, etc. So we look just like doctors. Not just a mask, but a full costume. Here's the movie in my head, which I relive in excruciating detail every time it screens:

INT. HOSPITAL CORRIDOR - NEAR NURSING STA-
TION - DAY

Nurses and orderlies mill around, filling out forms, carrying trays. Young "DR." KAHN looks over a chart, as a NURSE runs out of a patient's room and shouts to him.

> NURSE
> Doctor, come quick!

Kahn looks around to see who the Nurse is talking to - when he realizes her call was directed to him. He shakes his head No. She grabs him by the sleeve. Pulls him into -

INT. HOSPITAL ROOM - CONTINUOUS

Kahn enters to see a 70-year-old male PATIENT sitting bolt upright in bed, clutching his chest, face pale, teeth clenched, tears in eyes.

Kahn freezes. The Nurse looks at Kahn expectantly and holds her hands up. Kahn takes a deep breath.

Kahn takes a halting step toward the bed, clearly uncertain whether to pass out or throw up. But a glimmer passes across his face, and he mutters to himself.

> KAHN
> Pulse. Must take his pulse.

Kahn puts his fingers to the Patient's wrist. The Patient stares at him with pleading eyes. Kahn furrows his brow and

```
repositions his fingers - as if he couldn't
find a pulse, and desperately wants there
to be a pulse, because if there is no
pulse, he should probably start CPR.

He looks up at the ceiling, as if the
answer might be forthcoming from above. He
shakes his head - then faces the Patient
and speaks hesitantly.

                    KAHN
          Are you… in pain?

The Nurse looks at Kahn as if he were
either completely insane or the biggest
idiot she'd ever seen, and runs out of the
room to find a real doctor. The Patient
GROANS, and slumps, unconscious.

                         FADE TO BLACK
```

Thank God an actual doctor showed up only moments later, to save the day, and the patient, allowing me to slink back out to the hall and promise myself I'd never again put myself in a situation I couldn't handle. So when I wanted to answer a Call, I'd know what to say. So when I put on a mask to make people think I could do something, I actually had the chops to do it.

Cut to ten years later. Here's the flip side. I was now working as a full-fledged, Board Certified Emergency Medicine Physician at a small hospital in the San Fernando Valley, called Rancho Encino. Only 30 beds in the place, and only a handful of doctors admitted patients here. It's what was known to ER docs as a "Sleeper." The emergency room saw so few patients in a day that it was pretty easy to pull a 24 hour shift, from 7 am to 7 am, and still get 4-6 hours of sleep a night.

On this particular night I'd been asleep for several hours, until I was awakened in the on-call room at 6:30 by the nurse on the phone, telling me paramedics were on the way in with a 75-year-old woman in an MVA (Motor Vehicle Accident), unconscious, in shock, and ETA to the ER was 3 minutes.

I got to the Trauma Room just as the ambulance arrived. The patient was unresponsive, bruises over her face and chest, carotid pulse thready, and blood pressure 60/0. So: serious trauma, in shock probably from internal blood loss, heart and breath sounds distant, maybe a collapsed lung. As the nurse and I were starting two big bore IV lines, a couple anesthesiologists wandered by, on their way to the surgery suites. It was heading into change-of-shift now, so other personnel were showing up, some of them sort of interested in what was going on.

One of the anesthesiologists asked me if I wanted him to intubate the patient while I put in a central line, and I said sure, the more help the better. So he tubed her, and then bagged her – squeezed what's called an ambu-bag once a second through the endotracheal tube, to breathe for her.

One of the paramedics said, "I can't get a femoral pulse." That's the big pulse that's easy to find, down in the groin. But I checked, and she still had a carotid pulse, up in her neck. Which meant blood was pumping up to her brain okay, but no blood was getting down to the lower half of her body. That, and all the bruises on her chest, told me she'd likely torn her aorta – sheared off the main artery from her heart, somewhere below her heart – so blood flow was happening everywhere above the chest, but just pouring into the abdomen below the diaphragm.

Just as I was thinking this, I heard one of the anesthesiologists whisper to the other one, in a tone that mixed disdain and disappointment.

"Too bad nobody in this rinky-dink place knows how to crack a chest."

I instantly felt humiliated, insulted, and busted: this guy had seen through my mask, and revealed to the world I wasn't who I was pretending to be.

But here's the weird thing. I *did* know how to crack a chest. In that moment, I felt like an impostor to myself, but at some level I was the real deal. I just didn't feel like it inside. I'd seen ER docs open chests half a dozen times, but I'd only done it myself once before. So I knew I *could* do it. The question was, how certain of himself was the man behind the mask?

Opening up a chest involves sinking a scalpel an inch deep into the chest beside the breastbone, between the 4th and 5th ribs, and dragging the blade all the way down to the back. Then taking a rib-spreader, a tool with two flanges, inserted into the space between the two ribs, and widened along a geared track by turning a crank, so the space between the ribs is opened enough to get a couple hands inside the chest. Of course, this breaks some ribs, but if you're down this road, that's the least of anybody's problems.

Then you deal with the internal catastrophe – whether it's a lacerated heart that needs to be sewn up, or an unbeating heart that needs to be squeezed. Or, in this case, my belief that the aorta had been ripped apart somewhere south of the heart – so the end still attached to the heart had to be clamped off, to stop blood pouring into the abdominal cavity. It's called cross-clamping the aorta, and I knew how to do it.

I was scared. It was a dramatic, commando act, and lots of things could go wrong. But I also knew it had to be done, or this patient was going to die for sure. And besides, it was like the anesthesiologist had thrown down a gauntlet. I had to pick it up, right? That's when the nurse chimed in.

NURSE
I can't get her carotid pulse
anymore.

So that was the final blow, the woman's heart had stopped, she was in full cardiac arrest. That was the Call to Adventure. I knew what had to be done, and beyond that, I'd gone through my entire medical education refusing to repeat that very first encounter with the old man clearly having a heart attack, me saying, like a foolish Dancing Bear, "Are you in pain?" I never again wanted to be not up to the task.

So I Answered the Call, and cracked her chest. Broke her ribs, saw the torn aorta gushing blood, and cross-clamped it with the big, padded forceps used to cut off an artery that big – just as one of the house surgeons walked in with Walter Theis, the ER doc showing up to relieve me for the next shift. When they saw what was happening, the surgeon nodded, said "Nice job," and started handing out orders to get the lady up to surgery stat. Theis broke into a big grin and clapped me on the back, saying, "J Kahn, crackin' chests."

The surgeon, Harvey Kalan, got her wheeled up to the OR with his hand inside her chest, manually squeezing her heart, once a second. He managed to reattach the aorta, but the next week she went into renal failure because her kidneys had been without blood too long, and later she died.

Sad, but not unexpected, for a 75-year-old woman in a car crash that tore her aorta in half. And I did what I had to do – including talking to her family, who showed up in the ER an hour later. Always a difficult talk, for me to give, for them to hear. But I held onto those lessons. When the Call comes, the Call must be answered.

And you have to believe, in your heart, that you've got more than a mask (although you need that too). You've got to have the stuff to get it done.

So when Steven asked me if I could write *Poltergeist* in a month – though the stakes were obviously much, much lower than they were when cracking a chest – I drew from my fears of failure, my fears of looking foolish, and how I prided myself on defeating them by leaping into the breach.

So I leapt. And told Spielberg I could do it. And I did it.

Chapter 3
Writing *Poltergeist*

So my Hollywood Journey began. This part of the Quest – the beginning of ACT 2 in Hollywood movies – is often signaled by a radical change of geography.

In *Star Wars*, it was when Ben took Luke to Mos Eisley, where "You will never find a more wretched hive of scum and villainy." [1] It's far from Luke's family farm – and once in the Cantina, as far from Luke's prior experience as possible, geographically and metaphorically.

And in my journey, it was when I spent the next 28 days holed up in Spielberg's conference room on the MGM lot, writing the novelization of *Poltergeist*. The farthest away I'd ever been from any previous Ordinary World in my life.

I wrote during most of the month of November, 1981, at a conference table in this room surrounded by old school console video games – *Missile Command, Donkey Kong, Centipede, Asteroids.* I didn't use a computer in those days, I wrote longhand in a spiral notebook – so the company also hired a secretary, Cina Motter, who came into the office every couple days and transcribed what I'd written, on an IBM Selectric typewriter.

To guide me as I wrote, I had a copy of the *Poltergeist* script, by Spielberg, Mark Victor and Michael Grais, and a handful of production stills, so I could see what the characters, the house, and the Beast looked like.

I showed up around 9 every morning, and left around 9 each night. There was one window in the room, facing another building across a wide sidewalk. Every few hours I'd get up to stretch my legs and play a video game. Mostly *Missile Command*, at which I got pretty good, but could never beat Spielberg's score.

On Thanksgiving Day, there was only one other car in the parking lot, belonging to the security guard. As I walked past him, he smiled and said, "Oh, you must be one of them whatchamacallits – one of them overachievers." And I guess that's one of the things I was. A Masked Overachieving Dancing Bear.

It was my first Hollywood writing gig, and I was desperate to do it better than anyone expected. I totally immersed myself in the project, writing nonstop, morning to night, seven days a week. I turned in a first draft of the novel after two weeks, but it was short. My first drafts of both novels and scripts tend to be mostly plot skeletons. This happens, then that happens, then something else happens. Then on the next draft I go back and infill with character motivation, backstory, internal monologue, all the things that make the characters three-dimensional and make the read interesting. In addition, those revelations about the characters' interior lives – revelations to myself, as I write them – will necessitate changes in the plotline and relationships. So the whole thing is kind of an evolving, moving target.

After turning in that first draft of *Poltergeist*, I asked producer Frank Marshall if I could flesh it out with things not in the movie – including elements of research on ESP (Extra-Sensory Perception, otherwise known as telepathy) I'd done in medical school. Frank read the first draft, liked it, ran it by Steven, and they said sure, go ahead, we like what you've done so far, write whatever you want, knock yourself out. So I did, adding about twice as much new material in the book as there was in the film.

The research I'd done in med school involved gluing EEG electrodes (Electro-Encephalogram) to the heads of subjects, hypnotizing them and giving them prompts about what to dream, clocking their dreams with the EEG, waking them to tell us their dreams, and seeing if there was any evidence of ESP between subjects during their dreaming. Spoiler Alert – there was evidence in one set of subjects. Details later. But I incorporated a bunch of this material into my second draft of *Poltergeist*.

(This is really tangential, but bringing up this ESP research reminds me that while I was doing it, I got invited, as the junior member of the Sleep Lab at the University of Chicago [where I was being mentored by the renowned sleep researcher, Alan Rechtschaffen, who first identified the stages of sleep] to the

International Symposium of APSS – the Association for the Psychophysiological Study of Sleep. The conference was being held in Bruges, Belgium – where I assaulted Fabiola, the Queen of Belgium.

I was very excited to go to the conference. The first morning, before the talks, I was wandering around Bruges, in awe of its beauty. It was drizzling, so I had a long raincoat on, and as I started wandering up the wide stone steps of the Provincial Palace, I heard a commotion down in the square. I turned to see a crowd rushing the building.

I tensed up, because this was 1970, and I was sure they were protesting the American incursion into Cambodia – there'd been protests all over the world about this escalation in the Viet Nam war, and I thought I was going to be strung up as an object lesson.

Queen Fabiola of Belgium. Photo Free Use Wikimedia Commons, Photographer Lothar Schaak.

But then I saw the mob wasn't rushing the steps in anger – they were cheering the Queen, who was at that moment walking up the steps. Queen Fabiola. She was a chic Queen, in the Jackie Kennedy mold. She wore a pink pillbox hat and a Dior suit, she was carrying a bouquet of flowers in her arms; and I realized she was probably on her way into the palace to welcome the conference.

But when she reached the step I was on, she stopped – smiled – put the flowers in her left hand, and held out her right hand to shake.

But here's the thing. I'd been staying at a Bed and Breakfast, and at breakfast that morning I'd eaten the croissant, but there was an extra roll on the table, so I cut it open and covered it with jelly and put it in my pocket to eat later that morning. But when the crowd mobbed the steps, and I tensed up, my hand reflexively gripped what was in my pocket – and it was the jelly roll. Naturally, when

I pulled my right hand out of my pocket to shake the Queen's hand… I was holding the roll.

We both looked at it like, I don't know, like I wanted to trade the roll for the flowers, or I was performing some odd American custom. Our eyes met in confusion. I shifted the roll to my left hand… just as she put her flowers in her right. We stopped again, perplexed. In my memory this went on for a couple hours, repeatedly putting rolls and flowers in opposing hands, never quite able to connect, while hundreds of mystified Belgians could only stare.

Finally, I saw my moment – both our right hands were free – and I shook her hand. Getting jelly all over it. She said something in Flemish – I think we can all imagine what that might have been – and she walked up into the palace.

I stood there another minute, then followed, and sat in the auditorium. She made a few tactful opening remarks, and the conference began.

That's how I assaulted Fabiola, the Queen of Belgium, and that's the end of my *Poltergeist* ESP tangent.)

Two very Poltergeistian things happened to me during the writing of the novel. The first was on Thanksgiving Day. It had been dry all month, cool and cloudy all day. Around 7 pm I began writing a scene not in the script, a scene I invented. A scene about one of my scariest nightmares and creepiest fears. Spiders.

The scene was inspired by something that had recently happened to me in the emergency room. A patient had come in complaining of ear pain, and when I inserted my otoscope speculum into his ear to look at what I presumed would be a standard infection, a huge, hairy spider lashed one of his legs out at my eye – protected by the magnifying glass in the otoscope, which of course made the arachnid look even bigger.

I jumped back and nearly fell over, and couldn't move for a moment, it jangled my nerves so much. I ended up laying the guy down on his side and pouring baby oil into his ear. The spider suffocated, and I pulled it out with a forceps. So that's the backstory on the spider scene I was about to write.

In the scene, I paralyzed one of the characters in the kitchen, one of the young research assistants (which is what I was in med school). Just standing there, he suddenly couldn't move – as an army of spiders advanced on him across the floor, some slowly, some at speed. Crawled up his legs inside his pants, into his nose and his ears, laying eggs in his mouth. I was really freaking myself out writing this.

And though it hadn't been raining all day, I added a reference to an advancing storm into the swimming pool/corpse scene, soon to follow. There was a storm brewing in the screenplay, too, and I internalized that feeling of nighttime storminess as the scene bounced around my fevered brain. At around 8 or 9 pm I wrote the line, "Lightning and thunder ripped the sky." (*Poltergeist*, Warner Books, 1982).

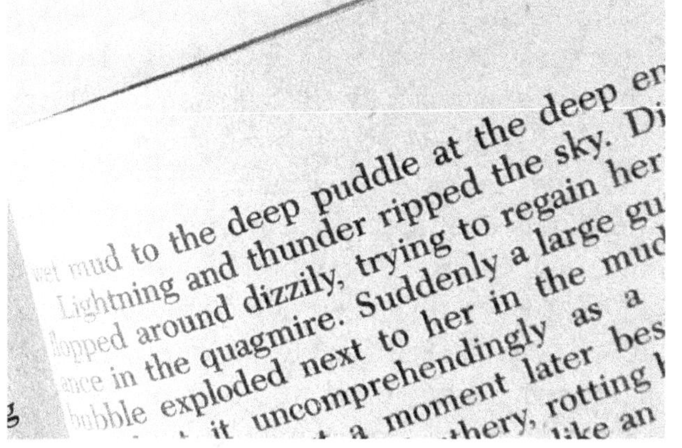

Fateful "Lightning" line from Poltergeist novelization (Warner Books, 1982.) Photo courtesy of the Author.

Page on which "Lightning" line appears in Poltergeist novelization (Warner Books, 1982.) Photo courtesy of the Author.

Within moments, a lightning bolt hit on or near the building I was in, simultaneous with the loudest thunderclap I'd ever heard, and a deluge of pouring rain. All the lights in the building went out. Something crashed into the table next to me. I jumped up. Cina screamed in the other room.

"Aaaahhhh!!!!" Then she ran into my room. "What happened!?!"

Suddenly all the lights in the building went on again – and all the video games began playing themselves. That's when I saw that the crash I'd heard was the metal facing of a wall air conditioner – it had blown off, sailed across the room, and nearly hit me.

Cina and I looked at each other, grabbed our things, and ran out to the parking lot in the pouring rain, in what felt like at least a 10 degree drop in temperature. The rain stopped as soon as I got in my car.

It was like something out of *The Twilight Zone*.

To corroborate that story, let me just say that 40 years later, in preparation for writing this memory, I went back to research Los Angeles weather on that day. I was able to verify, from Weather Channel records for Los Angeles in the month of November, 1981, charts showed it was clear and sunny, with partial clouds, most of the month. Except on that day, on the 26th.

But on Thanksgiving Day, November 26 – after being fair, cloudy and dry all day – from 8:00 pm to 8:16 pm, the wind unpredictably gusted to 22 mph, the temperature dropped precipitously, and 5 mm of precipitation fell all at once. Fifteen minutes later the wind had dropped back down, the rainfall stopped; and by 9:16 pm, the temperature was back up to where it had been all day. The official Weather Channel LA Airport Station temperature recording registers a huge drop during the interval between 8:00 and 8:16 pm. By 9:00 pm the temperature is shown to have returned to previous levels in the 50's-60's.

Here's the actual Weather Underground Channel record for the city of Los Angeles, with the graph illustrating the simultaneous drop in temperature and rise in precipitation and wind from exactly 8:00 pm to 8:16 pm on 11/26/1981, the moment after I wrote that line:

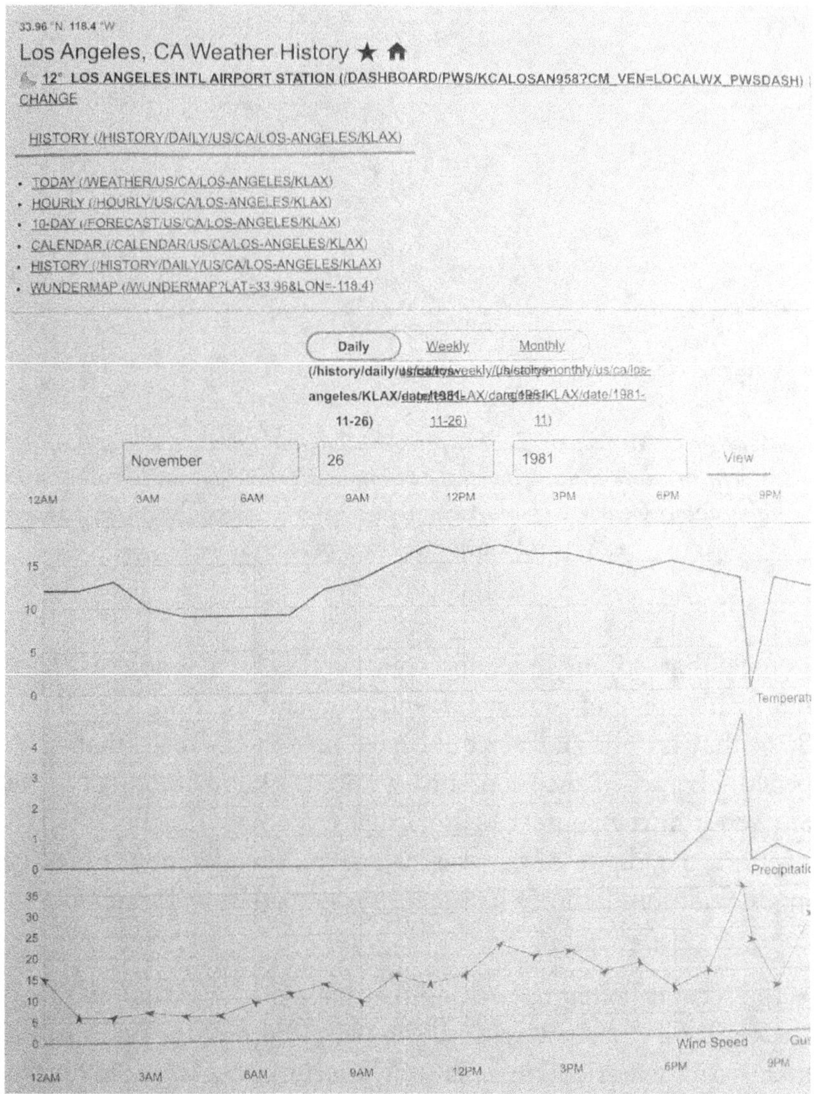

Weather Underground graph of sudden temperature, precipitation, and windspeed shift in Los Angeles, November 26, 1981, 8:00 pm. Graph courtesy of The Weather Company. Photo courtesy of the Author.

The Weather Channel chart below further shows no rain all that day – until a downpour of 4.8 mm inches fell between 8:00 pm and 8:16 pm – along with a concomitant drop in temperature from 13 degrees C to 0 degrees C. And then another brief rainfall at 9:00 pm.

Time	Temperature	Dew Point	Humidity	Wind	Wind Speed	Wind Gust	Pressure	Precip.
12:00 PM	16 °C	7 °C	55 %	SSW	15 km/h	0 km/h	1,006.95 hPa	0.0 mm
1:00 PM	17 °C	8 °C	58 %	SW	22 km/h	0 km/h	1,006.15 hPa	0.0 mm
2:00 PM	16 °C	8 °C	60 %	WSW	19 km/h	0 km/h	1,005.46 hPa	0.0 mm
3:00 PM	16 °C	7 °C	57 %	W	20 km/h	0 km/h	1,005.56 hPa	0.0 mm
4:00 PM	15 °C	8 °C	62 %	SW	15 km/h	0 km/h	1,004.76 hPa	0.0 mm
5:00 PM	14 °C	8 °C	67 %	SSE	17 km/h	0 km/h	1,004.26 hPa	0.0 mm
6:00 PM	15 °C	8 °C	64 %	SSE	11 km/h	0 km/h	1,003.66 hPa	0.0 mm
7:00 PM	14 °C	10 °C	77 %	SSE	15 km/h	0 km/h	1,003.46 hPa	1.0 mm
8:00 PM	13 °C	9 °C	77 %	WNW	35 km/h	0 km/h	1,003.46 hPa	4.8 mm
8:16 PM	0 °C	0 °C	0 %	W	22 km/h	0 km/h	1,003.56 hPa	0.0 mm
9:00 PM	13 °C	9 °C	77 %	W	11 km/h	0 km/h	1,003.46 hPa	0.5 mm

Weather Underground chart of precipitation and windspeed shifts and temperature drop in Los Angeles, November 26, 1981, at 8:00–8:16 pm. Infographics Courtesy of and Copyright by The Weather Company, LLC 1981-2024. Photo courtesy of the Author.

So that striking inflection point on that meteorological chart, that triple spike of rain, wind, and temperature drop from 8:00-8:16, that no one did or could have predicted? Yeah, that happened. Happened the moment I wrote it. I know it doesn't make any sense in the context of my usual cosmology, in the Western scientific paradigm. But… yeah, when you spend a lot of time living in your mind, things like that happen. You're welcome.

The second Poltergeisty thing that happened was the following week, after I'd finished writing. I brought a copy of the typewritten manuscript to a friend in Encino, Mark Ratkovic. I wanted him to read the spider scene, and tell me if it was as scary as I thought, or if that fear was just my own particular neurosis.

I opened the page to the scene in question, and went into the kitchen, as he sat on his couch and began to read.

About five minutes later I heard a shout, and a slam. I ran into the living room as Mark was re-opening the manuscript. Turned out a spider had dropped from the ceiling onto the page he was reading, and he reflexively slammed it shut on the attacking arachnid.

I have kept the squashed, mummified spider intact on that page ever since, as you can see below.

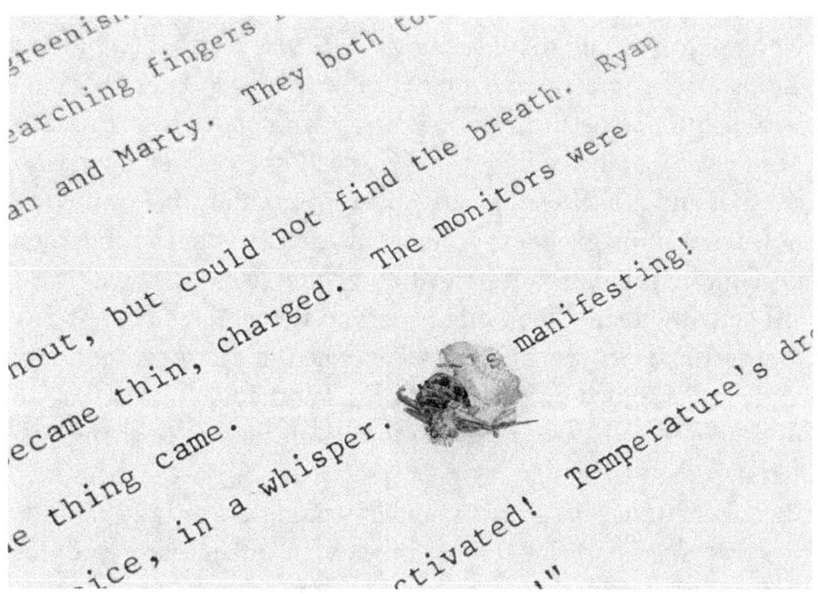

Squashed spider on page after spider attack scene, on original manuscript page of Poltergeist *novelization (Warner Books, 1982.)*

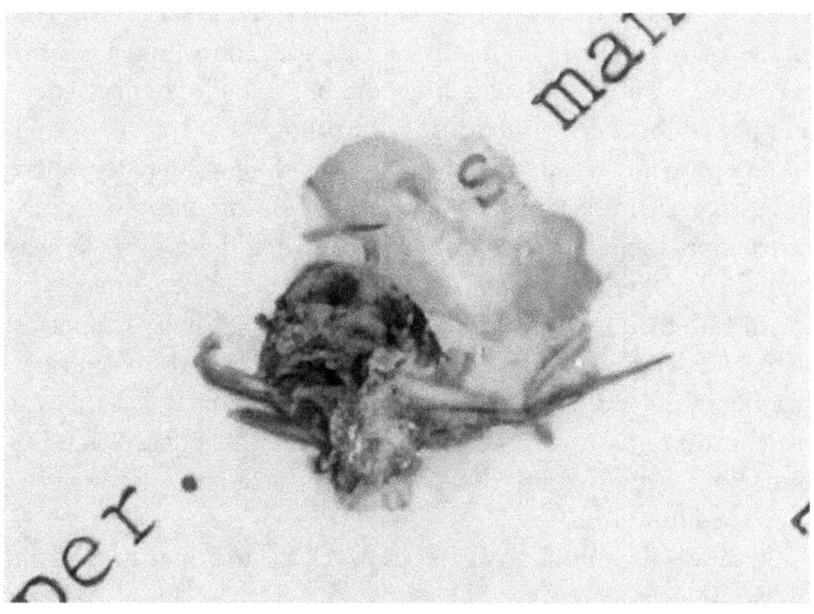

Close-up of same creepy squashed spider. Photos courtesy of the Author.

The *ET* wrap party was later that week. I got to meet Harrison Ford there, a big thrill for me. Indiana Jones in the flesh. Made me very nervous – as if he could see I was a charlatan, I didn't really belong here, with all these celebrities. He was married to Melissa Mathison, the screenwriter of *ET*. A year or two later he called me to ask for some technical medical advice about how to act in a scene he was rehearsing for the movie *Witness*, about a cop who gets shot and is sheltered by an Amish community. He wanted to know what someone goes through who gets shot in the abdomen (as he did in the film) but pulls through and lives.

I'd actually treated lots of gunshots to the abdomen at the LA County ER. Lots of gang fights happened in that neighborhood – in fact one spilled over into the ER itself the first week I was on duty there – so it gave me a wealth of information to share with Harrison.

I explained the trajectory the bullet would have to take, not hitting anything vital. But it would create an inflammatory peritonitis, and the kind of pain that was – how any movement of his body during that phase would cause excruciating ripples of pain outward from his belly. And if it got infected over the course of a couple days, it would just get worse, and he'd get a fever. With luck – or more likely antibiotics – the infection would heal, the peritoneum would heal, and all would be well. He thanked me – and played the scene very realistically, I thought.

I'd been so anxious talking to him at the Hollywood party, where I felt like an impostor; yet completely comfortable giving him instruction about how a gunshot victim should act. And he was grateful for the advice about how to pretend to be someone he wasn't. But then that's what actors do for a living. They wear masks.

The *ET* wrap party was also the first time I'd seen Steven since turning in the *Poltergeist* final draft, and he told me it was the best novelization of any of his movies – which I thought was kind of him, since I didn't think there'd been novelizations of any of his previous films. Still.

There was a contest, at the wrap party, for the final title of the movie. The choices were:

a)   A Boy's Life (That was the working title, during production. Something innocuous, so the press wouldn't be interested in snooping around and give anything away; but also, I think, because Steven saw Elliott's story as his own; he used to fantasize in that suburban housing development he grew up in about some extraterrestrial coming down to earth and befriending him. Kind of like my own suburban growing up fantasies)

b)   ET and Me

c)   Slimehead Goes West

I think it's self-evident which title won – *Slimehead Goes West*, obviously – though I did later resurrect "A Boy's Life" as a chapter title in *Indiana Jones and the Temple of Doom*, for an off-script chapter I wrote about a day in the life of Short Round, Indy's child helper.

Here's the invitation to the wrap party:

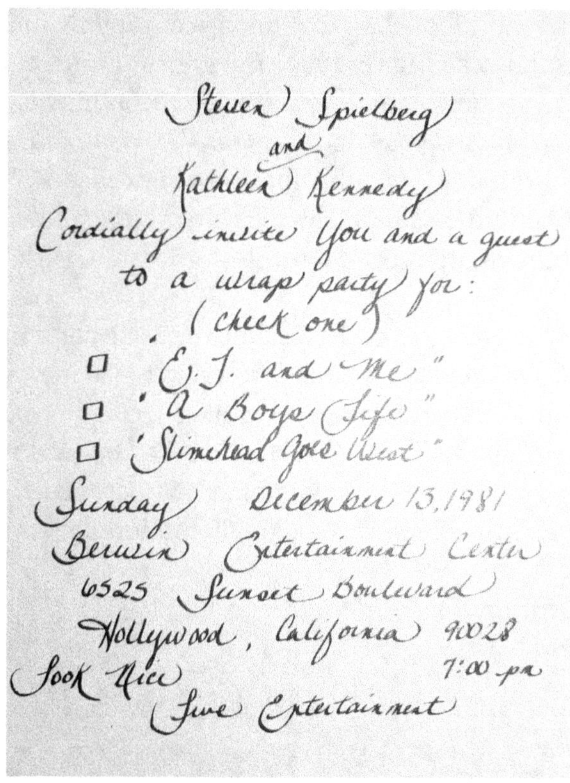

Unpublished Handwritten handbill for ET *wrap party. Photo courtesy of the Author.*

Both the movie and my novelization of *Poltergeist* were released to the public on June 4, 1982.

A few days earlier, on June 1, 1982, I signed a contract with Lucasfilm, Ltd., to write the novelization of *Return of the Jedi*. (More about how that came about in a bit.)

A week after the release of the *Poltergeist* film and novel, *ET: The Extraterrestrial* was released, on June 11 – with my 1 second screen debut as a hazmat-suited doctor carrying a clipboard to record ET's resuscitation.

And, as it turned out, George Lucas was nearing the end of filming *Return of the Jedi*, when he asked his buddy, Steven, if he had any recommendations for who should write the novelization. Could not have been better timing for me. Plus, the *ROTJ* novelization was going to be published by Del Rey – and Judy Lynn Del Rey, whose nose had not bled again since I'd stopped the flow at the Beverly Hills Hotel, heartily supported bringing me on board.

So Lucasfilm asked if I wanted the gig, and once again, I was stunned at my good fortune. I *loved* the *Star Wars* movies. I'd grown up watching *Flash Gordon* and *Captain Video* on Saturday morning TV, and the first *Star Wars* film (not yet called *A New Hope*) gave me exactly the same feeling. Excitement, childlike wonder, total lack of pretention or "depth." Just great fun, with great new visuals.

I said yes, of course – no Refusal of the Call this time – and a few weeks later, they sent me the *Jedi* script. I read it, marked it up, and went up to Skywalker Ranch to have a couple conversations with George Lucas. (BTW, *Raiders of the Lost Ark* was re-released in theaters on July 16 – it was rumored that between *Raiders, ET,* and *Poltergeist,* Spielberg was making a million dollars a day that summer.)

I began writing *Return of the Jedi* on July 19, 1982.

Here's how.

Chapter Four
Return of the Jedi

I'd seen *Star Wars* opening night at Mann's (née Grauman's) Chinese Theater in L.A. on May 25, 1977. But because the crowd was bigger than I'd expected, the only seats left when we got inside were in the first 3 rows. So we got center seats, Row 3. I was looking practically straight up at the screen. When that first Star Destroyer came out of top of frame, cruising away from me, directly over my head… it was practically an out of body experience.

And then *The Empire Strikes Back* kicked it up a notch. It added depth, and drama, and archetypal psychodynamic confrontations – and a cliffhanger ending that made everyone – including me – dying to see how it all turned out in the final installment. And now – unbelievable – I got to see the final installment before anybody else. And more than that – I got to help create it. Holy Moley!

If you were born after that time, it will be hard for you to appreciate the cultural/cinematic earthquake those movies caused on their release. If you want to get all Film School about it, the first *Star Wars* movie explosively ended all the 70's post-Viet Nam depressed, defeated American films that climaxed with the anti-heroes either dying or despondent (*Cool Hand Luke, Chinatown, Five Easy Pieces*, the list is endless). *Star Wars* was pure joy, the Pity Party was over, and it took the country by storm. And then *The Empire Strikes Back* was a better film, as a film. And now everyone had been waiting for two years to see how the whole saga turned out in *Return of the Jedi*. And I was about to help tell it. As if I'd been beamed to Mt. Olympus, to regale everyone with the original Greek myths.

I read the script through several times, and it was incredible, like I'd been given the key to the Dead Sea Scrolls. During my second read-through, I started making margin notes – but now I have to confess, after the adrenaline had settled… there was one little thing that disappointed me just a bit.

The ending – the plot ending, that is, not the character arc ending – was kinda sorta identical to the ending of the first movie. There's a Death Star, the Rebels have to blow it up before it destroys the entire Rebel Base, but the stolen plans reveal a weakness in the structure, so that if a small spacecraft, flying through mazes and trenches and laser defenses, delivers a missile into a tiny target that leads to the reactor core, the whole Death Star will explode.

I mean – if that was how the first Death Star was destroyed, wouldn't Emperor Palpatine guard against that same weakness the second time around? But maybe I was missing something. And I certainly wasn't about to rock the boat out of my dream job. My function, I figured, was to beef up the character elements of the story; the plot elements would just carry the audience along on sheer excitement. Suspension of disbelief.

So I got flown up to Skywalker Ranch for their big 4th of July party (grudge softball match between Model Makers and Lumber Crew), to meet George Lucas, ask questions, get his thoughts and directions, and prepare to do battle with the blank page.

The Skywalker Ranch main building was still under construction, in its later stages, much of the massive structure livable, much not. There was a short video running on a loop in the entryway – a mounted camera had taken one frame/hour of the construction, starting with bare ground, documenting the place being built over two years, in two minutes.

Here's my invitation to the July 4th picnic, and the

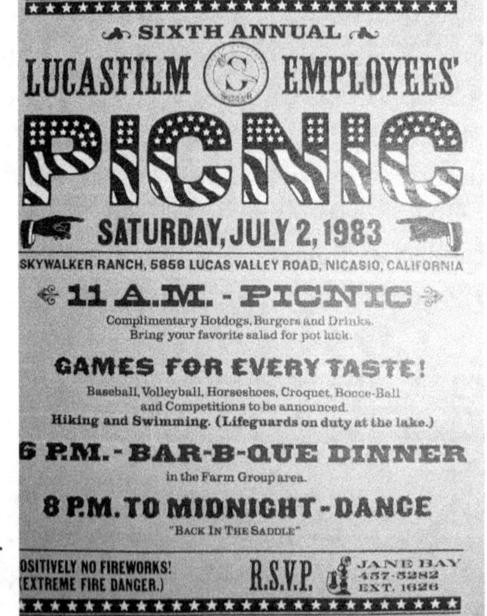

Skywalker July 4 Picnic Invitation, Photo courtesy of the Author.

backside of it with my drawing of the building, and some notes I made about the July 4th party:

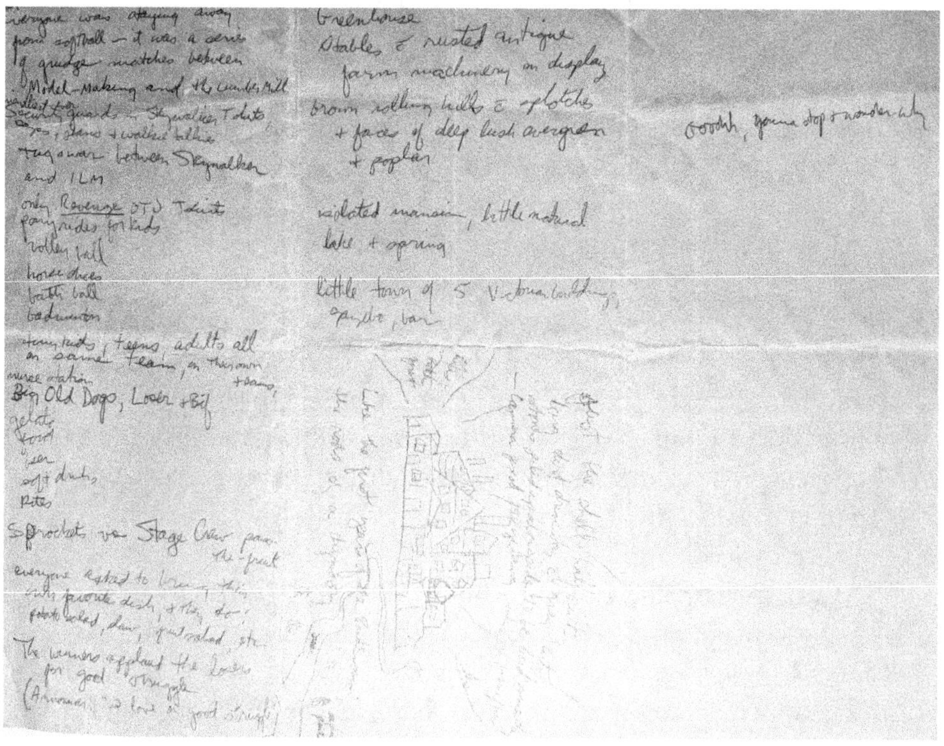

Author's notes and Artistic Rendering on Backside of Skywalker party invitation. Photo courtesy of the Author.

Lucas was a soft-spoken, sweet guy, who seemed a bit overwhelmed by the success that had overtaken him. We talked about the *ROTJ* story, I asked what his overall idea of it was, he said it was basic enduring human archetypes, played out in this space adventure. He looked at me like why did I even have to ask. I asked if I could bring new ideas into the book, as Spielberg had let me do with *Poltergeist.* He said sure, in theory, let's take it on a case by case basis.

He asked if I was certain I could write the whole book in a month, and I assured him I could. After all – remembering the security guard on Thanksgiving Day at MGM – we were all overachievers here, right? He gave me a funny look at that, which made me think maybe he wasn't an overachiever, he was just a small-town guy who'd gotten swept up in this massive cinematic success story that he'd never anticipated. I suppose he had his own mask to bear.

As the meeting drew to a close, I gathered up my courage, and – as I had with Spielberg – I pulled out a copy of my sci-fi novel, *World Enough, and Time*, which I'd jammed into the hip pocket of my jeans, to be unobtrusive, as if, "Oh, I almost forgot and just noticed this in my pants, what a coincidence, it's my book!" But I managed to get something else out.

"So… I wrote this sci-fi novel," I said. "Del Rey published it, kind of fantasy adventure, but like sci-fi based, and I wonder if you'd be willing to read it; I can't even imagine how busy you are, but at some point maybe down the line, if you get a little time between projects, maybe you could read it and consider making another great sci-fi fantasy film out of it? Possibly?"

"Sure," said George. "Follow me."

Wait… what??!!! My God, could this work? Getting George Lucas to make my sci-fi fantasy trilogy? Once again, my wildest dreams come true. Be still, my heart.

He took me into a medium-sized room, maybe 20x20, packed to overflowing. Makeshift shelves lined the walls, stacked with books and scripts. In the middle of the room was a large desk, with teetering piles of screenplays. More towers of books filled chairs and spilled over onto the floor.

He slowly looked around the room, pointing in a different direction with each sentence.

"Let's see," he said thoughtfully, "that pile over there, those are scripts my agent wants me to read. Those over there are the ones he wants me to read urgently. Right next to that is the pile my manager and my lawyer sent me. That shelf is screenplays from all my friends at film school, and those over there are from friends of friends. The ones on that chair are from friends of Marcia, my wife. And that cluster in the corner, I think that one is friends of some of the actors in my films, Harrison, Carrie, Ron Howard… not sure about that pile that fell over. Tell you what – here – why don't you put your book on the top of this pile, and I'll get to it as soon as I can."

He smiled. I smiled. I put my book on the desk, and I left. I don't think he was being mean; just crushed under the weight of his life, and opening a little window on it for me to look through. I felt apologetic even having made the request. As if writing *ROTJ* wasn't my dream job, and now I was asking for more.

I flew back to L.A. and began writing on July 19. From home this time. Cina came over every few days to pick up my notebook, Xerox my latest writings, and take the copies back to her house to type up. Once again, I turned in a skeleton first draft in two weeks.

But I'd added an entirely new section about Princess Leia's life. I felt like she'd gotten short shrift in the script, and wanted to deepen her role. So I wrote about her growing up on Alderaan, some of the influences on her, her inchoate infant memories of her mother, feelings of isolation and separation; how she'd become who she was, forged in the fires of the destruction of the Old Republic. I got the draft back from Lucas with a few notes – and the entire new segment about Leia deleted. Which was neither unanticipated nor unfair, since it didn't comport with the long game story he'd developed for the prequel.

As a little consolation joke to myself, I wrote an imaginary entry in Leia's diary, done in the single-sentence, stream-of-consciousness style of *Portrait of the Artist as a Young Man*, and concluding with a parody of the ending of *Ulysses* – two early 20th century novels by James Joyce, another censored author. If you don't get it, find a copy of *Ulysses*, and read the last couple pages.

Portrait of the Artist as a Young
Jedi

by j kahn

Title Page of Author's Unpublished Leia parody. Photo courtesy of the Author.

```
                    PROLOGUE


   From the Journal of Leia Organa, Princess of Alderaan



     I saw him wander from the mouth of the falcon like one
of the priests who used to give me sacrament on alderaan as if
wasn't there an angel following or a devil or some other god
knows what who would give meaning to my every step but not
haughty like only simple if something simple ever there was
to meaning if you take my meaning or take whatever you may my
darkling solo mio one and only lonely wanderer from well the
deepest well to hell to far corell where banthas jawas flowers
and the devil knows who else from all the ends of the galaxy
know the soloist soloest soloist who ever came to me
if come you can but then you looked at me and then you winked
and all the force was in the wink as if your pulsing solo like
the muscular blind eye of some anemone from endor winkd
and squirted with the force of all your being even would being
scented as you were with sweat and hair and jessamine and spice
like the girls of what vague species near the moorish wall of
sandy dry mon eisley where i saw you first in vision squinting
through the force of which i was such part though little well i
knew it saw you there so first emerging from the falcons mouth
with trailing wookiee as if the tired bird had traveled from far
from priestly errands in a dry and windless temple only to cough
out this meager message just to me this blond and solo coded
secret over lightspeed wavelength for only me to see and hear
i saw you there and asked you with my spirit well as well i
```

Page 1 of Author's Unpublished Leia parody. Photo courtesy of the Author.

```
                                                                     2

asked you as another and my inner eyes beseeched this one and solo

asking him and with my force i asked and knew would force

and then he asked me would i force and in that hyper space

i put my arms around him and drew him down to me so he could

feel my comlink all perfume force and his heart was going

like mad and force i said force i will force.
```

Page 2 of Author's Unpublished Leia parody. Photo courtesy of the Author.

In any case, after I got the rest of the notes from George on my first draft, I filled in all the other character elements and interactions over the next two weeks. I particularly focused on the relationship between Luke and his father, and especially their psychodynamics during the protracted final battle sequence and death scene. That seemed like the meat of the story to me, and I really wanted to make that go deep.

When I finished, I wrestled greatly with the notion of approaching George with an idea I had for changing the ending of the movie – or at least the book. I thought I had a good idea for that, but I didn't want to derail my nascent relationship with Lucas by insulting his story climax. On the other hand, if he went for it, it might be the beginning of a much more solid future of collaboration with him. Big potential downside; but the upside was so tantalizing. I remember the dilemma reminding me of an ER patient I saw in medical school, on the South Side of Chicago, at Billings Hospital – though free-associating to that patient should probably have been more of a caution than a goad.

This naked guy had crawled into the ER with two broken heels and ankles, a burst fracture of the lumbar spine, and a screwdriver stuck to the hilt in his chest. As we were running/wheeling him to the OR on a gurney, he told us how it happened. He'd been *in flagrante delicto* with a young lady in her second floor apartment bedroom, when her husband walked in on them. The aggrieved spouse pulled our soon-to-be patient off the bed, threw him against a wall – then grabbed a screwdriver off the desk and thrust it into the man's chest.

While the husband was momentarily distracted by his wife's screaming, the interloper ran to the open window and jumped out – landing on his feet, causing what's known, in medical parlance, as a *Don Juan* fracture – heel and lower spine compression fractures, not uncommonly seen in people jumping from height and landing on their feet. As Cassanova might have done to escape the wrath of a furious husband.

As luck would have it, the apartment was just one block away from the hospital, so the guy crawled the whole way to the ER. As we were racing him to the Operating Room – me (the med student), a nurse, an aide, the surgical intern, a surgical resident, and the Chief Surgeon – paused at the elevator, and I pushed the Up button. The surgeon, Dr. Block, was a funny, brash, bulldog kind of guy, with great hands (translation: excellent surgeon), but not always politically correct (which wasn't even a term in those days).

As the elevator door opened, he looked at the patient – who still had the screwdriver stuck in his heart (you don't want to pull it out prematurely, or the patient will quickly bleed to death through the hole that's left) – and he spoke sarcastically, to make sure the guy had learned his lesson.

"So, buddy," Dr. Block grinned, "was it worth it?"

And the guy with the screwdriver in his chest thought about it a moment, and smiled back. "Yeah."

And you know what? The guy lived. The Resident cracked his chest, the Intern pulled out the screwdriver, and Dr. Block patched the hole with a pledget before the second gush of blood could be ejected. (That first gush was a geyser, though.) Then he threw in a few monofilament sutures for definitive closure, and it was all over in a minute, except for the Resident closing the chest, and the Intern suturing the skin. The man was discharged a week later. I think he moved to California.

But I took that lesson to heart when deciding whether or not to risk it all with my brazen plan to approach George, to offer my little plot change in the service of his passionate saga. The patient had lived! The potential upside of the dare was worth the risk! So I got up my nerve one last time, and plunged into what I hoped would be an ongoing conversation – I wrote a letter to Lucas suggesting a couple alternate endings that could be accomplished with a couple close-up shots and one line of new dialogue. Of course, it would only be a conversation if he wrote back.

One of my bold notions was that Rebel leadership discovered that if their attack missile went down the wrong exhaust port, it would not only blow up the Death Star, it would start a chain reaction that could spread through the entire galaxy – every star, every planet, all wiped out. I thought this would greatly raise the stakes beyond what they were in *Star Wars*, and the information could be communicated in a couple close-ups, with a little new off-camera dialogue. (Incidentally, my idea wasn't totally conceptually absurd. There were some physicists on the Manhattan Project during World War II who feared that exploding the first atomic bomb would set off a chain reaction in the atmosphere that could destroy the entire planet.)

Here's a handwritten draft of notes for my letter to George, suggesting different possibilities for a new ending:

* fix its funnel beam on the black hole co-ordinates.

Points for letter ~~to George~~

1) Self destruct: blow up entire galaxy by initiating
chain reaction based on the vibrational frequency
of the most elementary particle of the galaxy
(quark, pi meson, whatever) — a chain reaction
converting all the matter in the galaxy into energy
— or — achieving a similar total self-destruction by
funneling an equivalent amount of antimatter through
a black hole whose coordinates are fixed in
the Death Stars computers, from the anti-
galaxy into this galaxy. (and that's what
the Death Star is turning to do at the end)*
So — thematically — the dark side of the
Force ~~is~~ has led to not only local/personal
self-destruction, but, by extension, to the destruction
of everything, to a true armageddon.

2) The Death Star won't be destroyed in
the exploding aura of Endor because
it absorbs all the energy resultant from
anything it destroys and funnels it into
its own all-absorbant storage cells —
thereby becoming more powerful each
time it destroys ~~something~~ — also thematically
appealing. We might ~~suppose~~ see it get more potent
each time it destroys a rebel ship. It might
also blast a couple distant planets during the
final battle, just in order to get more powerful...
and each time that happens, its defensive
powers increase as well, making it that
much harder for ~~the~~ the Rebel ~~ships~~ Fighters
to reach the weak spot. At the last,
the Death Star might just be set
~~spinning~~ by the ~~Emperor~~, with the Death Ray

Author's notes for my letter to George Lucas. Photo courtesy of the Author.

Author's notes for my letter to George Lucas, reverse side. Photo courtesy of the Author.

And for those who can't decipher my cursive handwriting, which is probably most of the people reading this book, here's what the notes for the draft letter to Lucas said about possible new endings:

Points for letter to George

*1) Self destruct blow up entire galaxy by initiating chain reaction based on the vibrational frequency of the most elementary particle of the galaxy (quark, pi meson, whatever) — a chain reaction converting all the matter in the galaxy into energy — or — achieving a similar total self-destruction by funneling an equivalent amount of antimatter through a black hole whose coordinates are fixed in the Death Star's computers, from the anti-galaxy into this galaxy (and that's what the Death Star is turning to do at the end.)**

**fix its funnel beam on the black hole coordinates.*

So — thematically — the dark side of the Force has led to not only local/ personal self-destruction, but, by extension, to the destruction of everything, to a true Armageddon.

2) The Death Star won't be destroyed in the exploding aura of Endor because it absorbs all the energy resultant from anything it destroys and funnels it into its own all-absorbent storage cells — thereby becoming more powerful each time it destroys something — also thematically appealing. We might therefore see it get more potent each time it destroys a rebel ship. It might also blast a couple distant planets <u>during</u> the final battle, just in order to <u>get</u> more powerful… and each time that happens, its defensive powers increase as well, making it that much harder for the Rebel Fighters to reach the weak spot. At the last, the Death Star might just be set spinning by the Emperor, with the Death Ray turned on, to destroy whatever its beam may fall on no matter how near or far — and in <u>that</u> context, the already radiating beam is burning a swath closer and closer to Endor. This would be somewhat more similar to the Star Wars *ending than Alternative 1, but might be different enough thematically, since Endor's imminent demise then becomes a function of something more like random violence (more urban?), due to the death-throe thrashing of the doomed Emperor in his crumbling bunker.*

Either alternative would require a minimum of additional shoot-ing, I think – maybe a brief two-shot between Vader and the Emperor with the requisite explanatory conversation between them. With the Emperor in his throne, looking out the view window, the chair's back to Vader, you wouldn't even need that actor.

You might also (or instead) want a two-shot between Mon Mothma and Ackbar – telling us this info they've received from spies, so the audi-ence knows what the stakes are – but none of the already shot stuff would need to be altered, since Ackbar could decide it would be better to withhold the information (the potential destruction of the entire gal-axy) from the troops, so they don't clutch.

And of course, you'd need some extra special effects scenes, but that wouldn't require much more than what's already underway, I imagine.

I never got a reply, my overture rebuffed. So much for conversa-tion. I'm sure he had way, way too much on his plate at that point to start entertaining major conceptual changes like that; or even read the letter, for that matter. I just had to throw in my 2 cents. Thinking about it now, it seems absurd that I would have thought he had the time or inclination to start revising script/shooting/editing just as filming was nearing its end. I don't know what I was thinking, except I had a better way of telling his story than he did. If anybody at Lucasfilm actually ever did read my letter, I hereby apologize now for taking up their time. At least I didn't end up with a screwdriver in my heart. And I lived to write another day.

I turned in my final draft on Friday, August 13, 1982. Everyone loved it. Of course, in Hollywood they always say that to your face – but I subsequently got offered to write the novelizations of *Indiana Jones and the Temple of Doom, Indy and the Last Crusade,* and *The Goonies* – so they must have at least liked it well enough. In any case I was a no drama kind of guy, which producers always appreciate. And as I was told later, in my television days, I was faster than anyone better, and better than anyone faster.

I actually had to turn down writing *Indiana Jones and the Last Crusade,* because I was head-writing a TV show by then, *Family*

Medical Center (produced by Stu Billet and Jay Feldman), and I just didn't have the time. After that, they stopped asking. I guess they didn't like being turned down any more than anyone else does. Later, when I went to see the movie, I once again thought I had a better idea for the ending. It seemed to me Indy's father – Sean Connery – should have stayed behind to be the eternal guard of the Holy Grail, which would have fulfilled his life's work. Then he could have said a fond good-bye to Indy, with a nice closure on their relationship. Suddenly I wished I <u>had</u> worked on the book early enough to have had a conversation with Spielberg about that – though it certainly would have turned out the same way my letter to Lucas about the *ROTJ* end turned out. Oh, well.

The ROTJ novelization went on to be the best-selling book of 1983, and the only book ever to be #1 on the NYT best-seller list in both hardcover and paperback simultaneously. It stayed #1 for many months, and remains one of the high points in my Hollywood career – which included writing-producing *Star Trek: Voyager* and *Melrose Place*, writing for *Xena: Warrior Princess, Star Trek: The Next Generation, TekWar* and *St. Elsewhere*, and staffing or consulting on a bunch of shows nobody has ever heard of. (*St. Elsewhere* was my first actual assigned television script ever, and showrunner Bruce Paltrow – Gwyneth Paltrow's father – hated it so much he threw the script across the room at the wall. Tom Fontana, his second in command, told me he'd thought it was pretty good. In any case, I didn't get asked back to write a second script.)

But now I think it's time to leave this section behind, and proceed down the bumpy path of exegesis of *Return of the Jedi*, the novelization. All page numbers listed below refer to the standard mass market paperback published by Del Rey.

I go through a chapter-by-chapter plot review and analysis of the entire novelization throughout the memoir – first, in segments, and then reprised at the end, *en bloc*.

Those of you who aren't devoted *Star Wars* nerds like me, may find the level of detail in these italicized analyses tedious. Feel free to skim, you won't miss anything as far as the rest of the memoir is concerned.

For those of you who are total *Star Wars/ROTJ* fans, as I am – these sections may be the main reason you bought this book. I think you'll be well pleased to find a few previously unreported behind-the-pages reveals, as well as insights into my writing process of fleshing out the book, and what was going through my mind when I wrote some of the things I wrote. You're welcome.

We'll start with the prologue.

RETURN OF THE JEDI

ROTJ, PROLOGUE, PAGES 1-5

My handwritten manuscript begins with the iconic line, "A long time ago, in a galaxy far, far away…"[2] – of course, how else could it begin? – followed by the notation of the day of commencement of writing, Monday, July 19, 1982. Two weeks after my meetings with George up at Skywalker Ranch, one week after my unanswered letter about changing the ending. (What hubris I had!)

I wrote the first line, "The very depth of space,"[3] as my emotional reaction to the visual opening of the first film, and how impacted I was by that similar opening of all three films. Deep black space, the stars giving it a depth of field, and just pausing on that for a long chunk of screen time, letting the fact of it sink in, before the first spaceship enters the picture. The very depth of space. It's all I could think of to say, and I wanted the reader to dwell on that conceptually the same way I'd dwelled on it visually and emotionally that first time, in the 3rd row at the Chinese Theater.

(Not long after the book came out, an irate Texas elementary school librarian wrote to me complaining of my use of sentence fragments, setting a bad example for young, impressionable minds. I replied with a kind of smarmy explanation of the difference between creative and expository writing, corrected a typo and some syntax in her letter, and felt quite smug with my cleverness. With the perspective of years, I wish my reply had been kinder, or gentler, or more generous. More Jedi-like. What an asshole I was sometimes, and too clever by half. Or maybe by three eights.)

In the next paragraph on page 1, I refer to the fate of Endor's planet, which had "long since died of unknown cataclysm."[4] Endor was always referred to as a moon, which implied there must have been a planet to which it was attached. But we never see a planet. So I figured it must have had a planet once, and that planet got somehow destroyed by "unknown cataclysm." So that was my reference. I remember thinking at the time that when I was all done with the book, and before I submitted it, I'd come back to this spot, or find a better spot, to go into the specifics of the demise of Endor's planet.

But I forgot. Always seemed like a good idea to make a whole book or movie about that some day, though. The destruction of Endor's planet.

This leads to Vader's opening appearance in ROTJ – on page 2, arriving at the Death Star on an Imperial Star Destroyer. The security shield engulfing both Death Star and Endor goes down as his ship arrives – freaking out the officers on the Death Star, because they realize only one person could have lowered the shield from a spacecraft. Vader. Evil arrives before anyone else. Like since God made the animals before he made people, that snake had to have been waiting in Eden before Adam and Eve even existed. Evil waits.

It's also a foreshadowing of the fact of the security shield, which becomes such an important element at the end of the film.

Right from the start we see Vader's power, and the fear he instills, even in his followers. Establishing the enemy from the outset, seeing how powerful his forces are, tells us exactly what our heroes are going to be up against. Not that we don't already know. But the previous movie had come out two years before, so this is a good reminder.

Mof Jerjerrod, the overseer of Death Star Operations, along with the Imperial Troops, assemble to await Vader's arrival. When his shuttle door opens on the Death Star, I wrote "Only darkness glowed…"[5] because Vader always struck me as a radiant force of darkness, as opposed to a black hole, for example, that only absorbs light.

He tells Jerjerrod that the Death Star's construction is not happening fast enough, the Emperor will not be pleased – and furthermore, the Emperor is on his way. The Emperor, a still darker force than Vader, scares Jerjerrod even more – but on the other hand, his coming arrival heralds the total destruction of the Rebellion, "in a single blow." So way more powerful than Vader.

The specter of this excites Vader so much, the last sentence of the Prologue, on page 5, says, "For the briefest second, Vader's breathing seemed to quicken…" [6]

This was something unimaginable, that his machine respirations could be affected by his emotions. But it was an intentional paradox. It was, in fact, the first tiny clue that there was yet a flicker of humanity in Darth Vader.

And a flicker of humanity in me, as well. As I took another six weeks off from my ER duties to prep and write the novel, I was finding that the more time I spent writing, the more connected I felt to my own human emotions. And the more time I spent in the ER, the more I walled myself off from my feelings, not let them get in the way of the tasks I had to do. Which led to what's called ER burnout.

This was obvious from a vantage point of my life at home, where I wrote, went to bars and restaurants, sang with friends, communed with sunshine, got loving comfort from Jill, and generally got deep rest and joy in the land of the living, a community of friendship.

In the ER, on the other hand, it was increasingly feeling like human life was twisted through a lens of numbers, algorithms, symptom complexes and sleep deprivation, miscommunications, antagonistic confrontations, suffering humanity, slow and sudden death. The ER was life on the Dark Side, and it inexorably made me a dark person. The life of being a sorcerer in the ER was being supplanted by the sorcery of the silver screen.

In the hospital I rarely felt anymore like I was pulling people back from the brink of death. It was, instead, more like having a front row seat on the things people did to themselves and each other; and having to deal with them on a conveyor belt, one patient every ten minutes. It was exhausting, it felt futile, and most of the patients were angry with me from the jump. Angry because they wanted something I couldn't (or wouldn't) give them, or because they didn't want something I thought they needed. Angry for waiting so long, angry for getting so little time with me, angry because they didn't have the money to pay for the visit. We were all being crushed under the weight of the American medical system.

But now I had an escape. I could make up my own stories, where people were triumphing over adversity, solving life's problems; and people were paying me to do it. I still felt like an impostor in a mask; but the mask was beginning to fit. And I liked the way it looked.

The disconnectedness from humanity associated with working ERs was largely a defense mechanism, self-imposed in order to perform various grisly, sometimes pain-inducing procedures. But not only the things I had to do – it was the onslaught of confronting the wide range of horrors people inflict on each other or themselves. It was a world of aggression. Stabbings, shootings, car crashes, overdoses, self-inflicted gunshots, dog attacks, mutilations, domestic abuse, child abuse, sexual abuse, delirium tremens, alcoholism, PTSD, road rage, PCP... oh, yeah, PCP. That reminds me of a story.

The surgical anesthetic PCP, short for phencyclidine phosphate, which later became a street drug known, back in the day, as Angel Dust, was a popular dissociative agent commonly laced into marijuana. Not only did users spin off into a sometimes crazed, psychedelic fantasy world, it made them almost superhumanly strong. The patient that comes to mind was dragged in by five LA County Sheriff's Deputies who could barely contain him. He was barefoot and bare-chested, cuffed behind his back – but struggling so wildly, it took everything those five large, strong men had to hold him. In fact, he took them all down to the floor. On his back I saw the welts of about 20 billy club blows.

They finally got him onto a gurney, on his back. Uncuffed him and recuffed him so that each wrist was restrained to one corner of the steel frame of the gurney, behind his head. At last, he was quiet, he just lay there. We all moved away. The cops said he was beating on his girlfriend – she was in the Trauma Room right now – and he wouldn't stop when they got to the scene. Said they must've hit him 50 times, he just wouldn't go down. Then the lead cop smiled, patted me on the back, and said, "He's all yours, Doc."

That's when the punk swung his legs over the side of the gurney and stood up – twisting the gurney over on top of his back, his wrists still cuffed to the steel bar frame near his shoulders, the wheeled legs of the gurney sticking straight up in the air – and he walked out of the E.R., swinging the bed back and forth on his back so nobody could come near him. He looked like King Kong, or Frankenstein's monster, or some wild, avenging, video game angel fluttering wings of gurney linen over steel pipe. We all just stared in astonishment. It was like a movie moment.

And in the next moment, he cleared the front door, and the cops gave chase. I went to see his girlfriend in the Trauma Room.

That was a freaky, physical confrontation, but I was equally traumatized by having to watch people die, being unable to help, to witness so much suffering and psychosis. So I had to erect psychological and emotional barriers in order to function quickly at a high level. Distancing mechanisms among ER docs included cynicism, inappropriate jocularity, aloofness, and suspicion – it wasn't just me, that was the culture of the ER in those days. And I don't know many ER docs my age who aren't either divorced, post-rehab, or out of that line of work.

I remember watching another Resident sew up the lacerated eyebrow of a mean drunk who kept spitting on him. Finally, the Resident had had enough, and sewed the drunk's ear to the gurney, telling the guy what he was doing – so the drunk knew if he moved, it might tear his ear in half. The guy stopped moving. And I laughed.

I wouldn't laugh anymore – I don't work in the ER anymore.

I displaced some of the violent ambience of the ER by going deep into my fantasy writings, which became a good steam valve both emotionally and creatively. But something had to give in my life. So getting the *Poltergeist* gig was a watershed moment. It was the start of transitioning into a writing career that let me stay away more and more from the ER, the more successful I got in publishing.

And writing *Return of the Jedi* was not only a huge ego boost and creative energy magnifier, it solidified the return of humanity to my soul. From that point on I could dip back into emergency room practice as often as I liked to maintain my skills and get the enjoyment out of it that had drawn me to it initially – saving lives, working within a community of life-savers, challenging myself intellectually and psychologically – and I could work there as little as I liked, to keep a real human connection to both my patients and my family.

I was sensing I was less like Luke Skywalker than I was like Darth Vader – cut off from human feeling by violence and technology; open to salvation only as I was able and willing to be shed of those things.

CHAPTER FIVE
THE QUEST CONTINUES

IT MAY SEEM PARADOXICAL that writing fantasies, even violent ones, opened my heart to be more caring for people than actually… caring for people. But that was my reality. The other interesting crossover between my double lives was that working ERs taught me to be open to endlessly unexpected plot twists in the human condition – a sensibility I brought back to my writing. Here's one of my favorite unexpected ER cases. I've never used this in a script or novel, but I often used the lesson it taught me: to guard against making assumptions about a situation. That is, to write characters in a drama who *do* make assumptions about other characters, to their detriment or jeopardy; and to create situations that lead the audiences to make assumptions, which are then upended.

I was working the LA County ER when three sets of paramedics wheeled in three gurneys, each bearing an unconscious patient – although one of the patients was starting to groggily awaken. As two other docs and I began examining and stabilizing them, this is the story that emerged, from the paramedics and the woman patient who was waking up.

She'd been having breakfast with her 62-year-old husband in their second floor apartment not far from a fire station, when her husband grabbed his chest, groaned, and collapsed, unconscious. She called 911 and did CPR until paramedics, arriving about five minutes later, rang the doorbell.

She ran downstairs to let the paramedics in the front door, and all three ran back upstairs to her lifeless husband. The paramedics went into their routine, kneeling beside the patient on the floor, checking for pulses, putting the paddles on his chest to check his heart rhythm – when one paramedic discovered there were no IV line needles in his kit, so he had to run back down to the rig to get some. The woman accompanied him, so she could hold the front door open, to let him back in immediately.

Meanwhile, the other paramedic, on putting the EKG paddles to the patient's chest, saw the man was in ventricular fibrillation, or V fib. What med students are taught is the "bag of worms heart." The heart has stopped pumping, and the cardiac muscles are all randomly rippling in uncoordinated spasms. This is a cardiac arrest. Sometimes a strong electric current can restimulate the heart to start beating again. So that's what the paramedic did. He pushed the button on the paddles he was holding to the man's chest, sending 200 joules of electricity coursing across his body.

Unfortunately, the paramedic didn't realize his knee was touching the man's arm. So those 200 joules shot through the paramedic's body as well. Knocking him unconscious.

Downstairs, the wife couldn't stand the tension of not knowing what was happening to her husband – so she propped open the front door with a chair from the lobby, and ran back upstairs to her apartment – where she now saw both her husband and the paramedic lifeless on the floor. So she fainted.

The second paramedic got his gear, ran back upstairs, saw three people unconscious on the floor – and instantly deduced there must have been a massive gas leak. He called that in to the Base Station, called for backup paramedics, and began dragging the three victims out of the apartment.

By the time they got the three patients to the ER, the wife was waking up. Not only that, the cardiac arrest patient's heart had been restarted by the electric shock, and he was doing fine; and the paramedic who'd shocked himself had merely knocked himself out with the charge, also no lasting damage.

But meanwhile, the gas company shut off the Main to the entire block and evacuated every building. We spent the next several hours assuring dozens of freaked out walk-ins that the toxic gas symptoms they were experiencing were psychosomatic – there was no gas. Some of them were relieved, some were pissed off that we were dismissing their symptoms.

So don't make assumptions. Or if you're a storyteller, have your characters make assumptions that will surprise both them and the audience when those assumptions are turned upside down. Or let the audience make assumptions that then get upended.

ROTJ, CHAPTER 1, PART ONE, PAGES 6–12

We shift the scene from Death Star to desert. "The sandstorm wailed like a beast in agony, refusing to die." [7] *Giving the desert the characteristics of a writhing beast was setting the stage. This is the Ordinary World of the First Act.*

In a desert hut of nuance and shadow, unknown hands fashion a light saber, and call R2D2 over to get it. We might make the assumption that the mysterious figure is up to some dark deed; or we might assume the figure is Luke, himself now a man of shadow and nuance, burdened by the knowledge of who his father is. Either way, the setting asks us to expect a surprise.

For the first time here, we see Artoo's vocalizations written out. "Vrrrr-dit dweet?" I got a world of shit from fans for trying to write the way Droids and Wookies sound. But that's what a writer does, tries to evoke visual, auditory, olfactory and emotional moments with words on a page. I try my best.

In the next segment, where the winds of Tattooine "seem to come from everywhere at once," [8] *creating a sense of chaos, we get to learn about Jabba the Hut – "the vilest gangster in the galaxy,"* [9] *a creature who both "collected and invented atrocities."* [10] *Every adventure has bad guys, I was just trying to elevate this one to the next level. C3PO and R2D2 are on their way to see him at his palace – a castle of evil at the center of nature's chaos.*

The fussy Threepio does not want to be delivering the message they've been tasked with giving Jabba – but then, "No one worries about Droids," [11] *he complains. Developing Threepio's personality and inner life was an integral part of the book as well as the movie. And he was a fun character to make fun of, but always affectionately, never meanly.*

When they reach the compound, Threepio "musters his resolve" because that's all he could do in this situation – resolve was a "function that had been programmed into him." [12] *I was always trying to reconcile the computer system that he was with the human feelings he exhibited. And felt. Now, in 2025, we're only just beginning to explore these same dichotomies as Chat GPT and other AI programs are being developed into sophisticated "companions." C3PO is the granddaddy of all that.*

When they knock, an Eyeball sticks out of a small opened hatch, and says, "Tee chuta hhat yudd!" Threepio, who has been programmed to understand 6 million languages, responds in Eyeball. And the two Droids are admitted through the iron door, which grinds shut behind them. No escape. Abandon all hope, ye who enter here. (BTW, nobody ever gave me grief about writing out Eyeball dialogue. I guess I was more fluent in Eyeball.)

They're escorted through the corridors by Gamorrean guards, and we learn it is Artoo who's been programmed with a message from Master Luke, to give to Jabba. Threepio is quite nervous, and just wants to get out of there. I'm not sure why anxiety would have been programmed into him. Maybe it just arose out of a self-teaching algorithm. I know I'd learn to be anxious flying around the galaxy in the midst of a rebellion.

They're soon joined by Bib Fortuna, Jabba's major-domo, a humanoid from whose head emerged "two fat, tentacular appendages that exhibited prehensile, sensual, and cognitive functions." [13] Seeing pictures of Bib made me wonder just what those tentacles did, and those three functions seemed likely. After I came up with that, I always wanted to do a book about that race of aliens. Threepio tells Fortuna they have a message for Jabba. Artoo "beeped a postscript," and Threepio translated, telling Fortuna, "And a gift." [14] But this is the first time C3PO has heard about a gift, and it worries him. With good reason.

So much so, that as they approach Jabba's chamber, he whispers to Artoo, "I have a bad feeling about this." [15] This is a recurring joke—Han has said the same thing in other circumstances—so it's a bit of a wink to the audience. Threepio is saying it to Artoo, but really telling the audience, that difficult challenges are coming.

C3PO and R2D2 are brought before Jabba the Hutt, having been instructed by Luke to give Jabba a message and a gift. Threepio is freaked out at being here—and we see why in our first introduction to the Hutt.

He was huge, his eyes were yellow, and his reptilian skin (I surmised) was "covered with a fine layer of grease." [16] Yuck. I was trying to come up with the most disgusting physical attributes I could. Stunted arms, sticky fingers (Great Rolling Stones album!), and no hair—it had "fallen out from a combination of diseases." [17] *I particularly liked that notion, that he had syphilis, ringworm and scleroderma among other things, causing his hair to fall out. (I always enjoy bringing my medical interests into my novels.) His plump tail was like "a tube of yeasty dough," and he "drooled continuously."* [18] *(Again inspired by some of my ER patients.)*

"We're doomed," says Threepio, "wishing for the thousandth time that he could close his eyes." [19] *It occurred to me, looking at one of the production stills of Threepio, that his eyes were always open — and what a horror it would be if I could never close my eyes, never shut out the thing that I didn't want to see. In that moment, I shared C3PO's horror.*

With Jabba, we meet Oola, his dancing girl chained at the neck, soon to meet a sad fate; and Salacious Crumb, a giggling "monkey-like reptile" who fed off the "food and ooze that spilled" [20] *out of Jabba's mouth. I was thinking a little bit of the remora, whose diet is mostly the feces of the shark it's attached itself to.*

As the droids stand before Jabba, Threepio urges Artoo to give him the message, so they can get out of there — and Artoo projects a holographic image of none other than Luke Skywalker.

Luke introduces himself as a Jedi Knight — and this is the first time we learn Luke is now a full-fledged Jedi. He requests an in-person meeting with Jabba to bargain for the life of Han Solo — and the entire court bursts into laughter at the idea. Contemptuous laughter is probably the strongest form of insult and power differential.

But Luke's hologram isn't done making his proposal to Jabba. To sweeten the bargain, and to show good faith, Luke offers these two droids as unconditional gifts. Threepio totally dithers now, at the idea that Jabba will be his new master. Bib Fortuna, Jabba's major-domo, is sycophantishly contemptuous of Luke — telling Jabba that if Luke would rather bargain than fight, he is no Jedi.

Jabba agrees, there will be no bargains: "I have no intention of giving up my favorite decoration." [21] *And with that cue, he indicates the alcove where the carbonized form of Han Solo hangs, "his face and hands emerging out of the cold hard slab, like a statue reaching from a sea of stone."* [22] *A sudden reminder of the thing we've all been waiting to see, but had forgotten about in the moment.*

This is the first time we've seen Solo since his carbonization in the last movie, and it's a stark image – this living bas relief on display for the voyeurism and ridicule of Jabba's entire court. And we are invited to be part of that rogue's gallery, looking on with a kind of morbid fascination.

Jabba's court reminded me a lot of the Hollywood I grew to know as soon as I got the *Jedi* job. Decadent, insular, seekers and sycophants striving for recognition at the pleasure of a few potentates; delighted malice, *schadenfreude*, aggressive sexuality, equal parts wild abandon and secret backstabbing. In fact, there was a joke around town that Hollywood was the place where you knew who your friends were because they were the ones who stabbed you in the *front*.

I was courted by, and connected with, screen agents; then sent out on meetings to pitch ideas to studio executives and what were derogatorily called D-girls – the low to mid-level Development people – often women – at a studio, who listened to your pitch and decided on whether to just say No, or pass it up the food chain to their bosses, with a Recommend, or Recommend With Reservations.

Of course, saying No was always the safest bet. If they said Yes, and then a Higher-Up hated it, the Development Exec's job was on the line. So my job at the pitch was to become the Dancing Bear – to go in and wow them with my idea, my treatment, or my personality. Not easy or natural for the shy kid from Chicago who just wanted to stay beneath the radar. But that was the drill.

And getting stabbed in both the back and the front was just part of the deal. Not to say there weren't good times, too. Great parties, great music, great sushi, and great camaraderie with all the other writers going through the same thing. This was all through the last half of 1982 (I finished writing *ROTJ* in August) and the first half of 1983.

In fact, all of the late '70's and early '80's were kind of like one long weekend in a lot of ways. Jill and I partied a lot, partaking of all those '70's and '80's activities, sensual and pharmaceutical, about which much has been written, and which is probably best left to another memoir. In any case, Jill tired of it before I did, and decided she wanted to start a family, which I wasn't quite ready for yet. She felt our lives had become shallow, and she wanted to go deeper. I was concerned children would be a distraction to my writing, and derail my career. I said I wanted kids, too – just not right then. But she forced the issue, and I could see it from her point of view, her biological clock ticking – from a certain point of view, as Obi Wan would say – so eventually I gave in, Jill stopped taking birth control pills, and we began trying for pregnancy.

My best writing sample/screenplay at that time was a semi-auto-biographical feature film script I'd written called *Code Blues*, based on my experiences working in the LA County Emergency Room. ("*Code Blue*," followed by a room number and announced over the hospital speakers, meant someone had just gone into cardiac arrest in that room, and the call was going out for any doctor in the area to race over there and help resuscitate.) My script showed the gritty realism of the ER, long before the hit series, *E/R*, with George Clooney. When I glanced at it recently, I thought it was okay, but not great, and not well structured. It did garner a lot of kudos at the time for the writing and the storytelling, enough to generate a lot of pitch meetings – but not enough for anybody to buy it. One Exec said, "I like it. It's cynical, but it has heart."

I grew to learn they all said they like everything, nobody ever told you how they really felt about a script. But cynical yet with heart is kind of how I often felt while working in the ER, so at least my script was projecting my reality.

My reality, until I began to lose heart.

It's hard to clock the precise arc of my doctoring unease, so I'll spill it out in segments going forward – in a series of self-contained vignettes that touch on the narrative of a single patient I treated over many months, marking some of the emotional landmarks in my progression. Here's Leo's story, in ten boldface memories.

I

It had been a long day. A homeless man, dead from exposure, brought in stiff as cardboard. A 16-year-old with a bullet hole in his forehead from a gang fight, the exit wound so big that every

time I pumped on his chest to do CPR, pieces of brain squirted out onto the gurney. An old woman who'd died peacefully in bed, but wasn't discovered until six days later, by the smell coming out her window; but without friends to find her any sooner. These patients hammer on your heart, a little bit at a time, and you have to come up with ways to defend yourself against their relentless assault.

At the end of that already long day, a 23-year-old female was brought in by paramedics, unconscious and without a blood pressure, found on her floor beside an empty pill bottle. There were old slash scars on her wrists, and a tracheostomy scar on her neck from a previous respiratory arrest; so this was undoubtedly her last, best effort. A friend showed up to tell us the patient had dropped out of school to work, but had been fired; there was something about boyfriend trouble; her brother had killed himself after returning from Viet Nam.

We did CPR perfectly, by the book; but uninspired, and without event. Never regained a pulse. She was pronounced at 10:17. At the end, she lay alone on the stretcher, naked, fragile, beautiful, shy, quiet, dead. Lovely red fingernail polish. Lately the object of great attentions; now ignored.

Someone filled out her paperwork. Paul and Chuck argued about the '53 Dodgers. Someone walked in one door and out the other, passing through. It was payday, someone remarked, and two people left to get their checks.

Serena went to see another patient. I washed my hands and went to check on Leo, my new renal failure admission. Someone went to tell the girl's mother.

I think that little story actually took up a quarter page in my *Code Blues* script. And that script got me my first screen agent, Stu Robinson (RIP), who went on to get me my first TV jobs. Stu was a great guy and an honest agent. I also once diagnosed his appendicitis while we were having a meeting, and he had surgery that night. When people sometimes asked me how I got into the television business, I said by going to medical school.

And while my first pitch meetings were going on, Jill did, in fact, get pregnant in April of '83, with the baby due the following February, so now I was really feeling the pressure to get a steady job. None of my movie pitches had gone very far (much to my shock, *shock*, I tell you). My agent, Stu, told me the average Hollywood credited writer sold a feature script once every several years, if lucky. And even if somebody bought one of my screenplays or ideas, the average time from sale to getting a film up on the screen – if it even made it that far – was 8 years. So he gave me some sound employment advice: Feature films were a hobby; television was a career.

I relented and started going out to pitch myself as a staff writer to TV shows. And with Stu sending out my *Code Blues* script as a spec writing sample, I scored my first staff job on a Norman Lear sit-com called *E/R* – of all things – with Elliott Gould as a jaded ER doc, and Mary McDonald as the heartfelt doc crossing shifts with him.

It was a CBS show, produced on the Universal lot, and the Executive Producers – known as showrunners in the biz – were Saul Turteltaub and Bernie Orenstein. (Saul was the father of now big time director Jon Turteltaub, who back then was the intern in the office during his summer break from college.) Saul and Bernie were old giants at comedy writing-producing, having done so both in radio and TV for Milton Berle, Danny Kaye, Sid Caesar, Burns and Allen, the whole Borscht Belt of 40's-70's popular mass media. They were a font of knowledge for me about how to write comedy TV in a 3 jokes/page format. Sweet, great mentors for my first job.

And I was so thrilled to be a writer on a real broadcast network TV show. I mean, I'd grown up on TV in the 50's and 60's. One of my favorite sit-coms, *The Dick Van Dyke Show* – about the lives of 3 writers in the Writer's Room of a TV variety show – I think is what lured me into this racket to begin with. And now, here I was, a writer in the Writer's Room of a Norman Lear sit-com, being run by two guys who'd written for Sid Caesar's *Your Show of Shows*, which I'd also loved as a kid. So I was in heaven – and once again, couldn't quite believe my good fortune, after having been tapped to write the final novel in the *Star Wars* franchise, to boot. I was a lucky, lucky guy.

We'd sit, or pace, in the Writer's Room, thinking up storylines, gags, and twists, then go back to our offices to write. The showrunners would give us notes; we'd rewrite, and then they'd do a final "polish" on the script. When it was done, we'd walk across the lot to watch rehearsals on a soundstage. Once, a tram full of tourists on the Universal Tour cruised by, and I heard one of them whisper, "Those are the writers!"

Dude, I was now an attraction on the Universal Tour!

I had to be careful, though – I was beginning to think a little too highly of myself. It was a kind of emergence. Through much of high school I'd been shy, Jewish, bullied, geeky, nervous. Now I was starting to come into my own, starting to own the Dancing Bear in me. Like this identity wasn't solely a mask anymore; I was actually becoming the thing I was pretending to be.

It reminded me a little of one night when I was a third-year medical student, working in the hospital; not much further along than I'd been when the nurse called me "Doctor" into that heart attack patient's room, and the mask fell from my face. But this time, in the middle of the third-year night, I heard the adrenaline-inducing PA announcement: "Code Blue, room 433. Code Blue, 433…"

I ran down the hall to get there – not that I could help with the resuscitation much, I was still just a young student. But as I ran down the hall to the Code Blue, I noticed my reflection in a long stretch of glass doors and panels. White coat flapping behind me like a Superhero's cape, I thought, "Yeah. I am that wizard." The one I'd wanted to be for so long, pulling the dead back to life. Flash forward to the similar feeling I got when I heard, in an awed whisper, "Those are the writers!"

I was becoming the mask. I say that knowing I can sometimes have a tendency to get a little too full of myself – but then, with luck, I bust myself. Or more often, Jill busts me. Brings me back down to earth. Only problem was, with one foot in the movie world, one in the hospital, and one in impending fatherhood, I wasn't quite sure where earth was anymore.

Return of the Jedi had been released one month before I got the *E/R* sit-com job. The book was #1 on the *NYT* best seller list, and would stay there for months. One day Bernie – one of the two showrunners – walked in with his *New York Times* open to the list. He flicked it in baffled dismay at his partner, Saul, and said, "Would you look at this shit? I've been working my ass off 40 years for the biggest names in the business, and this little putz is #1 in the *Times*. How does that happen?" Then he winked at me.

He was truly miffed. But he was also kind of proud of me. And pleased that he'd gotten me on his show.

And I know they were pleased with my apprenticeship because they let me create a new character in one of the episodes – Ace, the Orderly. The character was a 16-year-old wiseass – played by the 20-year-old George Clooney, long before he became the star of another show called *E/R*, the dramatic series in the 90's. Pamela Adlon played opposite him, as Elliott Gould's daughter, though back in those days she was Pam Segall, fresh off *The Facts of Life*.

I remember sitting on a gurney on the set with the two of them, Clooney and Segall, ruminating about the news that day of the actor Jon-Erik Hexum, who, on the set of the series he was filming, had put the barrel of a gun loaded with blanks to his temple and pulled the trigger. The powder blast alone was enough to blow pieces of his skull deep into his brain, and he died. We were all a bit stunned, but I made some kind of callous ER doc joke about it – and then I immediately apologized. I was still working occasional shifts in the ER at that point, and was mixing up those two worlds, still stumbling over how to be a caring human being in the real world. Or how not to deflect those more tender feelings with the cynical disregard of the battle-weary.

Joking about death was the number one way ER docs deflected the pain, and the knowledge that we were all going to die someday. No matter how great we were at doctoring, it wasn't going to save us.

II

It was temporarily quiet in the ER, so I was sleeping in the call room when my phone rang. It was a nurse, asking me to come up to the neurosurgical Intensive Care Unit to pronounce some-

one dead, because all the neurosurgeons were off busy somewhere. The Vegetable Garden, it was called, because the patients were turned and watered every day. It was black humor to avoid the reality, another way to distance ourselves from feeling, so we could efficiently do our jobs. And to avoid thinking any one of us might be a vegetable in the garden one day.

Leo knew all about medical intern humor. His kidneys were shot and he wasn't a candidate for transplant, but he took his joy wherever he could, even if it was morbid jokes about the undiscovered country where he knew he was headed.

I, on the other hand, was angry at being awakened from a jealously-guarded hour's sleep just to pronounce a dead person dead. They were still going to be dead in a few hours, so why couldn't this wait? But when I got up there, I looked over the crop of eight human beings, lying peacefully; untroubled by my presence or absence, all their functions being taken care of by machines or other people, allowing them free reign to meditate, sleep, dream, scheme, discorporate, or whatever; and in that moment I envied them. I walked over to the dead woman, and pronounced her dead, and tried to think of a pronouncement for myself. Dead Man Walking, maybe.

I learned a ton about making TV shows on the set of *E/R*. I learned the Stagehand's Law, for example: Never carry what you can drag, never drag what you can roll, never roll what you can leave. And I learned about acting. One day we were watching rehearsal, and Elliott Gould's character, Dr. Sheinfeld, is at the Receptionist's desk, when the Receptionist tells him his ex-wife is waiting for him in his office. Elliott literally grabbed his chest and crumpled to the floor in a fetal position. I leaned over and whispered to the director, Peter Bonerz, "He's not going to play it that way in front of an audience, is he?"

Peter explained to me that Elliott was into "the physicalization of the subtext." During early rehearsals, he would physically execute an exaggeration of the emotion he was supposed to be feeling in response to what was going on. He'd do that a couple of times. Then when it was time to really play the scene, the physical feeling of that emotion had become internalized, so he could play the feeling on his face, or in his reaction. So the emotion had become subtext.

I've often referred to that idea in the years since then. I see it in films, and in real life, all the time. In *Return of the Jedi*, for example, Luke's missing hand is a physicalization of the emasculation, the weakness – and the absence – he feels in relation to his father, Darth Vader.

In real life, I have recurrent back pain – a physical, occasionally excruciating symptom. But sometimes Jill will remind me of the stresses I'm under during that period – money burdens, aggravation with a colleague, anger at a boss that I'm unable to express. Those emotions are the subtext of what's going on in my life – the back pain is the physicalization of it.

And sometimes, when I can dig deep to figure out what my subconscious, subtextual conflicts are, and understand that the back pain is just the physical manifestation of those stresses… the pain eases, or even goes away. But that's a topic for a different book.

We taped the shows in front of a live studio audience. Before the taping, a stand-up comic would come out and tell jokes and kibbitz with the audience, to get them warmed up and in the mood to laugh. He'd also introduce the writers, where we were standing just off-stage. The first time this happened, I was giddy with pride and embarrassment. The most junior writer on staff, I was the last to be introduced. The comic, Bob Perlow, said, "And finally, ladies and gentlemen, I give you the man who is a Hollywood writer *and* a doctor – the fourth richest man in America – James Kahn!" The audience went wild, and I blushed. (And btw, for reference, junior writers ain't so rich.)

Actually we taped the show in front of two audiences. After the first show, the audience left, and we retreated to a room off the stage, where we frantically rewrote jokes that had fallen flat, or speeches the actors couldn't quite get right. Then we did a quick run-through with the actors, covering the rewritten parts, and a second audience was ushered in, and we taped the whole show again.

Then we'd cut together the best takes from both shows into a single episode for broadcast. The editing process involved "sweetening." The live audience generally laughed where they were supposed to – but if they didn't laugh enough, or if they just chuckled where we wanted a guffaw, we'd "sweeten" their response with prerecorded (canned) laughter of various kinds. Then we could honestly say the show was "filmed before a live studio audience," without mentioning the help we gave with the sweetening.

The show only lasted one season. CBS put it up against another brand new sit-com on NBC, *The Cosby Show.* Cosby was killing us. We begged the network to give us another time slot, maybe against some dramatic shows, for the folks at home who just wanted to laugh at those times. But the network kept us up against Cosby, I think because they were in the midst of a big money dispute with Norman Lear, the creator of our show. Another piece of the Hollywood experience – how money, ego, and power struggles determine what shows get made, and watched.

Of course, Cosby had his own issues, but those didn't come out until much later.

ROTJ, CHAPTER 1, PART TWO, PAGES 13-15

Money and ego have little to do with this section of the novel – it's all about pure power struggles. And a peek into self-identity. After this first glimpse of the carbonized Solo, we change settings to explore torture chamber tropes, as a way to get into the "minds" of our droids – again, presaging Artificial Intelligence issues that have come to the forefront so recently. As our droids are taken to the reassignment room, "Artoo beeped pitifully" [23] *in response to what he saw. So even Artoo has an inner life of feelings and fears. But the psychology we have much more access to is Threepio's.*

C3PO looks for an existential cause of how he could possibly have met this horrible fate – so unfair, so without reason. And what a human emotion that is! More human, paradoxically, than the slight tinge of emotion we saw Vader experience when his breath merely quickened with excitement at the prospect of the Rebellion's total annihilation.

It's also an emotion that traditionally has seen many people turning to religion for the answers to these questions revolving around life's meaning – which becomes an interesting turnaround later in the story, when C3PO is viewed as a god by the Ewoks. Also interesting in light of the recent massive gains in AI technology, which make Threepio's existential ruminations as much science as fiction. Who knows when AI will achieve the same level of introspection we claim to have ourselves?

Once inside the torture chamber, "an agonized electronic scream, like the sound of stripping gears"[24] draws C3PO's attention to EV-9D9, the Grand Inquisitor droid of this chamber of horrors – a droid with "some disturbingly human appetites."[25] So now we're learning the possibility that all droids have feelings, and some of them are kinda psycho. Legs are being pulled off one droid, as "red-hot irons" are applied to another one's feet. There is no functional reason for such inducement of gratuitous pain - Jabba has simply programmed Ninednine to be a sadist. And no reason to have programmed pain into the feet of the torture victim. But the torture 9D9 oversaw being inflicted actually melted the last droid's circuits – whereupon Threepio's wiring "sympathetically crackled with static electricity."[26] More of C3PO's quasi-human inner life.

As Threepio starts elaborating on one of his responses the way he is wont, 9D9 tells him, "a simple yes or no will do." He surmises 9D9 is the kind of droid who has to prove herself "more-droid-than-thou."[27] Threepio has attitude, and we hear it from the viewpoint of his own inner workings – something the book was able to do that the film wasn't.

But when he pridefully tells her he's fluent in over 6 million forms of communication, he quickly realizes his mistake – for now he's to be stationed at Jabba's side, as the official translator. And the last protocol droid doing duty at Jabba's side, he is informed, was disintegrated for displeasing Jabba.

Threepio's anxiety plunges to ever greater depths. As he is taken away to have a restraining bolt installed, R2D2 lets out "a long, plaintive cry" – more of Artoo's childlike character – then he turns to Ninednine and "beeps in outrage."[28] She laughs at his feistiness, and says he'll do well on Jabba's sail barge.

That's a little convenient (for the writer), since Artoo's presence on the barge is essential to Luke's plan for escape. Seems like a big coincidence that 9D9 assigned him there. But I like to think Luke was able to distantly Force-alter one of Ninednine's circuitry pathways just slightly – enough to influence her assignment of Artoo to the sail barge, and Threepio to the throne room.

And "the droid on the torture rack emitted a high-frequency wail"[29] – as if to punctuate the fate of C3PO and R2D2.

"The droid on the torture rack (who) emitted a high-frequency wail,"[30] is, of course, more physicalization of the subtext – the subtext in this case being the presumably horrible fate awaiting Threepio, and his psychological state of calamity. His circuits could be fried any moment. He must have felt like a Dead Droid Walking.

CHAPTER SIX
MEANWHILE, IRL

IN MY OWN LIFE WITH JILL, the physicalization of the subtext of our relationship was that she was now pregnant with our first child, Laura. Jill was excited and nervous, and I was just nervous, trying to look excited. It wasn't real to me yet, this fatherhood thing, though it was in-your-face and in-your-belly real for her.

And so began my next big Journey, into family life. My years with Jill so far had been pretty self-centered, for both of us – filled with movies and music, parties and drugs and wild abandon, a touch of decadence. I actually didn't want kids yet, I liked my life the way it was, and in addition I was afraid having children would be a drag on my Hollywood career, which felt like it was just taking off. But Jill forced the issue and told me to man up. Literally. Turns out it was the best thing I ever did – not just for deep, human reasons, but it ended up making me a better writer. Big surprise.

So Jill was now pregnant. This baby stuff was unknown territory, though, and I felt like I was headed for a big balancing act. A new circle in the Venn Diagram of my life. And in this circle, this mini-Journey, if the pregnancy was part of the matrix of my Ordinary World, then the Inciting Incident was Slim Pickens' funeral.

When Jill was six months pregnant, in October of 1983, I got my first royalty check for *ROTJ*, and it was a beaut. To celebrate, we decided to take a romantic road trip up to the Sierras, where a friend had just bought some land. We set out right after Thanksgiving, driving north, up back roads, first through Mariposa County, and then Tuolumne County, roughly 70 miles west of Yosemite.

This was Gold Rush country, known as the Mother Lode, up Route 49, the 49er Trail, where would-be miners had journeyed from around the world in 1849, to strike it rich after gold was found at Sutter's Mill. It was beautiful geography, full of oak and pine trees, manzanita and toyon bushes, hills, streams, waterfalls, hand-built stone walls, country inns and RV parks, locals and "flatlanders" – what folks like us were known as, city dwellers here to gawk at the natural beauty.

Around December 10 we cruised through a tiny hamlet called Jamestown, which looked like an old west movie set, with old-timey two-story hotels lining the one main street. They'd reportedly been houses of ill repute, closed down by Governor Ronald Reagan in the late 60's, as part of a backlash to the Free Love movement. Even though prostitution is hardly free. In any case, they were all hotels now.

And then a few miles up the road we came to the next, even tinier town, Columbia, population 800. But the weird thing was, the main road was lined with a dozen black stretch limos, and scores of people milling around. It was early afternoon, and we realized we were hungry, so we stopped and began looking for a place to eat.

Some of the men in the mingling crowd looked familiar. They wore cowboy boots, jeans, sports coats and cowboy hats. A couple of them wore hearing aids, and I speculated on some congenital, familial auditory condition. And after we passed one old guy, I whispered to Jill that he looked just like Slim Pickens. Jill said, "Who's that?"

Slim was a longtime cowboy actor, so I guess knowing his name was a guy thing. Here he is in this photo. I don't know if the saddlery he's standing in front of is in Columbia, where all the limos were parked; but that's what Columbia looks like.

Publicity photo of Slim Pickens, Public Domain, photo courtesy of Wikimedia Commons.

The main street was just 2 blocks long, and looked like an old western theme park, with a couple saloons, a Wells Fargo Stage office, a horse-drawn fire engine, a saddlery shoppe, a gold assay office, stables, and a handmade candy store.

We sat down at the first place we saw, the St. Charles Saloon.

Street view, St. Charles Saloon, Columbia, California. Photo courtesy of Dave Thorpe.

Bar in St. Charles Saloon, Columbia, California. Photo courtesy of Dave Thorpe.

Tables in St. Charles Saloon, Columbia, California. Photo courtesy of Dave Thorpe.

It was a tavern with elk heads on the wall, an old distressed bar, and scattered tables. We ordered sandwiches from the waitress who came over, and I asked her what was going on outside, what all the limos were for. She said it was Slim Pickens' funeral. He'd lived here in Columbia for years, and the crowd was a combination of local friends and relatives from around the country, as well as various Hollywood types. He was being buried in the cemetery behind the Church of the Forty-Niners.

I told Jill about my long love of Slim's roles in the movies. He was a great cowboy character actor, going back as far as I could remember. He was also the pilot who rode the atomic bomb down to oblivion in *Dr. Strangelove*.

And his funeral was the Inciting Incident in my next Journey.

The Call to Adventure was sitting on the empty table next to us. It was a real estate brochure advertising land and home sales in the area.

We looked through it as we ate, *oohed* and *aahed* over some of the gorgeous terrain. Jill said, "Do you want to go look at any of these places?" I dismissed the idea: "Nah, just a waste of time." (The Refusal of the Call.) Jill said the whole point of this road trip was to waste time before the next intensely demanding phase of our lives: parenthood. I said, "Okay, you're right. Let's call one of these realtors." (The Answer of the Call.)

So we phoned a guy at a random realty, he asked us what we were looking for, and we said something with a waterfall in the backyard. He said, "You flatlanders always want waterfalls." But he took us to a house up a winding mountain blacktop called Yankee Hill Road, and sure enough, there was a waterfall. We looked over the small house. When we asked the owner what the price was, he gave us a number way lower than we were used to hearing in L.A. – and with the *ROTJ* royalty check burning a hole in my pocket, we talked it over for a minute and said, "We'll buy it."

The owner's wife walked in just then and started crying – her husband hadn't told her he was putting it on the market. We told them to talk it over and call us back, and by the time we got back down to the St. Charles Saloon, they called and agreed, and the house was ours. We planned to use it as a getaway place, for long weekends and occasional weeks away from the pressure of L.A.

A few weeks later I was back in L.A. working ER shifts, and Jill went up to her mom's commune in Carmel Valley for Christmas. I worked Christmas Day in the ER at St. John's, and at the end of my shift was the ER Christmas party at a local watering hole. I drank more than I'd planned to, and smoked a bit as well. Got in my car for the usually 30 minute drive home around 1 am. I knew I was in poor shape to drive, and had the bad judgment to do it anyway. Too macho, or stupid, to call a cab. I stayed off the freeways, though, and stuck to the city streets, rigorously keeping my speed at 30 mph. I didn't get home until almost 2.

I made it in the front door and didn't even have the energy to make it upstairs to the bedroom. So I collapsed on the living room couch, instantly asleep.

Thirty minutes later I was aware of a phone ringing in my dreams, and finally pulled myself awake to understand the phone was actually ringing. I stumbled to the kitchen to answer it (no cell phones then – phones were locked down to specific rooms). It was Jill's mom, telling me Jill's water had broken, and she was in labor 6 weeks early, and what should they do?

I said I'd call back in a minute, hung up, and slid to the floor. Crawled to the refrigerator, drank some orange juice out of the carton, got up and called back. I told them to take her straight to Monterey Hospital – a one hour drive from the remote commune – and I'd meet them there as soon as I could.

I took the first morning flight to Monterrey. When I got there, Jill was doing hard labor. The baby wasn't cooperating, and having decelerations, to boot – her heart rate was slowing with every contraction. The obstetrician asked the nurse to get the forceps out for a forceps delivery – a tricky maneuver in experienced hands, and this doctor did not look experienced. We all kept urging Jill to push! Push harder! At one point she sat straight up, clenching every muscle in her body, the veins on her face looking ready to burst. I heard the nurse next to me whisper in horror, "Oh, my God." Not what you want to hear an obstetrics nurse whisper.

What was I going to do? What would I have done if I'd been the doctor on-call for this emergency birth? No forceps, that's for sure. I didn't know how to use them, and they were fraught with complications even in well-trained hands. Should I refuse to let this doctor use forceps? If not, then what? Nobody in the hospital could do a C-section. Even the nurse next to me was freaked out. I felt more helpless than I'd ever felt in a medical emergency situation. Unmasked fear. Everyone was feeling the same way. Everyone was yelling "Push!"

And then, with one, final, massive push, Laura was born – with the umbilical cord wrapped around her neck four times. Four and a half pounds, she looked so small, and pale, and limp. I could almost hold her entirety in my hand. I was stunned, and overwhelmed, deeply in love, afraid of not being up to the task of caring for her, but committed to trying. She perked up in 20 minutes or so. When we walked out of the hospital a few days later, I held her, and couldn't stop crying.

The next journey had begun. New baby, new career, new getaway house.

And suddenly there were a lot of things going on in my life.

ROTJ, CHAPTER 1, PART THREE, PAGES 15-22

A lot of things are going on at once here.

Threepio is brought to Jabba's vile court to begin his job as official translator. He "hovers warily near the back of Jabba's throne," [31] *trying to stay as low profile as possible. Because Threepio has such human attributes programmed into his "personality," it was hard not to project onto him my own fears and insecurities. I think we all responded to that in him.*

Oola, the dancing girl, refuses Jabba's disgusting sexual advances. I'm definitely getting a Harvey Weinstein vibe here, though I never could have imagined the physical resemblance between Jabba and Harvey back when I wrote this. In response to Oola's rejection, Jabba has a trap door opened in the floor, and Oola falls through it to her death – "a terrible shriek, followed once more by silence." [32] *Similar subtextually, I guess, to what was experienced by actresses who rebuked Weinstein and saw their careers dumped into the abyss. We'll soon come to learn the specifics of Oola's fate, when Luke meets the Rancor in the dungeon below.*

C3PO continues ruminating nonstop, as the bounty hunter, Boushh, brings in the captured Chewbacca, in chains and on a leash. I used the term "leash" specifically to emphasize Chewie's canine aspects, to suggest he was being humiliated, beyond just the fact of his capture.

When Threepio sees the mighty Wookiee warrior in irons, he gives up all hope: "The future was looking very bleak indeed."[33] It was important to keep his speech — even a description of his internal feelings — in the cadence of his formal speech patterns. This bounty hunter, who'd been able to accomplish such a feat as to best the great Chewbacca, "was humanoid, small, and mean," whose helmet had an eye-slit "that gave the impression of being able to see through things."[34]

These were meant to be hints that the bounty hunter was, in fact, Princess Leia — humanoid, small, and possessing special insights due to being strong with the Force. Not that we know that she's strong with the Force yet, but suggesting this bounty hunter has the appearance of "seeing through things" is a subtle clue to what we'll learn later about her.

I think in the film it was more obvious — Boushh looked the size and shape of Leia — but I had to give more subtle suggestions in the novel. Besides which, really — who in the galaxy could possibly subdue the great Wookiee except a close friend?

Boushh speaks in native Ubese — a metallic language — and Jabba calls for Threepio, his new talkdroid, to translate. Jabba asks the mercenary Boushh his price for the Wookiee. Boushh demands 50 thousand, which enrages Jabba, who makes a low counteroffer — until Boushh activates a thermal detonator, discombobulating Threepio and the entire court — and the negotiators settle on a compromise price for Chewbacca.

I wondered, at times, if a chronic anxiety disorder had been programmed into Threepio at his inception, or if that was simply a function of malware and circuitry glitches from his hard knock life.

As Chewie is escorted out to a cell, he spies Lando Calrissian in the crowd, and we come to learn Lando has infiltrated Jabba's court with the intention of helping to try to free Han — for several personal reasons: guilt over getting Solo into this mess, an urge to join the Rebel Alliance and give the Empire some payback, warm feelings for Princess Leia, and a bet with himself that Han could not be rescued.

(NOTE: As Chewie is taken away, "The band started playing, led by a blue, flop-eared jizz-wailer named Max Rebo," [35] and the ongoing party resumes. Except when I wrote the original, I named the jizz-wailer [my name for the music he was playing] RED-BALL JETT. When the final draft was sent to Lucasfilm, they renamed the floppy little musician Max Rebo. Maybe that was his stage name.)

(ANOTHER NOTE: I called the music jizz-wailing because the cantina was supposed to be a den of iniquity. In the first film, Obi Wan had made his iconic pronouncement, "You will never find a more wretched hive of scum and villainy." [1] And jazz music, in our own culture, was more or less invented, or developed in the brothels of San Francisco and New Orleans. Except it was called jizz music back then, referring to a substance much tossed about in those establishments. Jizz later became jazz, but I thought in a haven of depravity such a long time ago in a galaxy far, far away, it would still be called jizz. So that's what I called it.)

(FINAL NOTE: Years later, after Disney had acquired Lucas-Films, a book of short stories was issued, deemed canon, titled From a *Certain Point of View: Return of the Jedi*. And one of the stories in it, "Fancy Man," by Phil Szostak, refers to Max Rebo playing one of his "jatz standards." Not jizz. Jatz. So either jatz is a sub-genre of jizz, the way emo is a sub-genre of punk, or this is simply the Disneyfication of my original work. If so, I can only wonder if it will backfire, the same way fans were outraged when Lucas re-issued *Star Wars* with a re-cut Greedo shooting at Han first, thereby justifying Han blasting him away. But as we all know – Han shot first. And Max played jizz.)

In any case, as the story goes on, Max Rebo starts wailing his jizz-music again, and the ongoing party resumes. Boushh surveys the crowd – and locks gazes with Boba Fett, the bounty hunter who put Han in carbonite and sold him to Jabba – and the two mercenaries size each other up. This is the first appearance of Boba Fett since he captured Solo and embedded him in carbonite – and we definitely get the feeling he's a force to be reckoned with.

The final segment of Chapter 1 begins with Chewbacca being led to his cell and unceremoniously thrown in, the door slammed – whereupon he lets out a long howl that "carried through the entire mountain of iron and sand up to the infinitely patient sky." [36] *The juxtaposition of the sky's patience lends weight to the lack of patience Chewie – and we – feel in this situation. His howl is the physicalization of the subtext of all our inner outrage.*

We move from there to the throne room, now dark and silent, where "shreds of tattered clothing hung from the fixtures, unconscious bodies curled under broken furniture. The party was over." [37] *In 1982, the year I wrote this, a lot of Hollywood parties ended this way. I was just drawing on personal experience.*

The dark figure of Boushh moves among the shadows. We don't know why at first. He goes to the alcove where Han hangs frozen in carbonite. Does he mean to steal Jabba's treasured possession? This is the first clear close-up we have of that iconic image: Han, reaching out from the carbonite in which he's been frozen.

It was unclear to me, when I began writing, how much time had passed since the end of The Empire Strikes Back *– and how long Han had been frozen in Carbonite. I called some of my contacts at LFL, and got someone to relay the question to George, but nobody had a clear idea. And George never responded. I said I thought it must have been at least some months for our team to retreat, go into hiding, and come up with the rescue plan. Nobody could nail it down more specifically than that.*

I decided to say it was 6 months – though I intentionally left some wiggle room, as Han was waking up: "He was, understandably, disoriented, after having been in suspended animation for six of this desert planet's months—a period that was, to him, timeless." [38]

By saying "this desert planet," I left open the question of how long a month actually was on Tatooine. Recent canon has suggested the actual timeline was closer to a year – an interpretation I allowed for with the leniency of my phrasing.

In any case, Boushh now deactivates the force field around the carbonite trophy and lowers it to the ground. Then "after one last, hesitant glance at the living statue before him," [39] *he throws the decarbonization lever. I added the hesitation to reflect the deep feelings Leia has for Han*

– and the fear in this moment that something could go wrong, that the decarbonization might actually kill him.

Referring to Solo as a living statue evoked Pygmalion for me – the sense that the passionate feelings Boushh had for this inert form were so strong, they could bring it to life. Han's upraised hands fell "slackly to his sides." His face eased into a death mask – then a life mask – and then his "eyes suddenly snapped open, and he began to cough." [40] *Prolonging the moment of awakening, starting with a death mask to suggest the possibility that Han might never wake up. (Of course we all know he will, but you try to create tension where you can.) Boushh tries to silence him, so as not to arouse the guards. To keep this moment private – both for purposes of escape, and personal intimacy.*

But Solo was disoriented and blind, after having endured what seemed like an eternity "trying to draw breath." I was trying to imagine the torture of what it would be like to be frozen in carbonite and consciously trying to breathe, feeling you had to breathe, but being unable to. And now suddenly he's overwhelmed with all sensation rushing back, along with every memory – "from his childhood, from his last breakfast, from twenty-seven piracies… Men had gone mad, in these first minutes following carbonization." [41] *But Han just wasn't that kind of guy, is what I'm trying to say.*

He was able to focus down on a few simple questions. Where was he? Where was Lando, who had sold him out? And where was Boba Fett, who had carbonized him?

Boush tries reassurance first. "You're free of the carbonite and have hibernation sickness." [42] *The logical, rational explanation. And btw, let's get the hell out of this place. But Han isn't ready for logic yet. He starts to fight his savior, whose mask he feels with his hands – he doesn't know who this is, and isn't about to jump from a frozen frying pan into an unknown fire. His last view before carbonization was of Boba Fett, and this figure above him wears a similar metal mask. "Who are you, anyway?"* [43] *Solo demands. Not where, or why – but "who" is the most important referent for Han.*

The bounty hunter, removing her helmet, reveals herself to be Princess Leia. "One who loves you,' [44] *she whispered, taking his face tenderly in her still-gloved hands and kissing him long on the lips." And they kiss.*

Ahhhh. Forget all those geographical and analytical explanations. Time to cut to the emotional chase.

End of Chapter One.

But it wasn't quite the end of Chapter One of my Hollywood career. I had three more novelizations to turn out, one each year after *ROTJ. Indiana Jones and the Temple of Doom* was released in 1984, *The Goonies* in 1985, and *Poltergeist II* in 1986.

During this time I was working a lot of ER shifts, as well, partly just to bring in a paycheck. The novelizations paid pretty well for a month of writing, but bills kept coming in all year, and now I had a child to support, too. It was a pretty frenetic existence.

Didn't help that I got appendicitis one night while sleeping in the call room at the hospital. I diagnosed myself pretty quickly, called the lab tech to come to my room and draw the appropriate bloodwork, called in my replacement Doc a couple hours early, called in the surgeon, and went into surgery a few hours later.

I didn't like being a patient.

III

A Code Blue was called over the Telepage for Any Doctor, up on one of the surgical wards. It was four A.M, but I was awake anyway, sitting up with Leo, my end-stage renal failure diabetic patient – I was regulating his Dopamine drip that was maintaining his blood pressure while the peritoneal dialysis depleted his volume to get him out of congestive heart failure. Complicated case. I'd gotten close to Leo during the two weeks he'd been in the hospital, and he was circling the drain, so I was tense and withdrawn, and needed to loosen up, and Leo was stable for the time being; so I wandered upstairs to help out with the Code Blue.

On my way to that emergency, I stopped momentarily, glanced into room 311, and saw a sad old gomer I'd admitted the day before, in full cardiac arrest, vomit on his face, even more lonely now than he'd been in life. An intern was pumping on the old guy's chest, probably to avoid having to put his mouth on the corpse's mouth to force respirations. A nurse in a quandary was opening drawers, looking for some way to breathe the patient.

"I can't find the ambu bag," she said, and ran out of the room to get one.

The intern, biting the bullet, brought his face near the old man's, to blow a breath into his mouth – when suddenly the dying body convulsed once, perhaps as the spirit flew out, and he threw up on the intern's face.

The intern flew back as if punched. I ran on, to the Code Blue on the surgical floor. But who vomits on you is important, I thought. I remembered when Leo threw up on me while I was passing a nasotracheal tube down his throat to get a sputum specimen. He'd apologized profusely, but I really hadn't minded, and in some inexplicable way even felt closer to him for it.

I wished someone felt the same way for the dead gomer in 311.

The week after my appendectomy, I was lying in bed on my back, when one-year-old Laura climbed up and ran across my healing sutures. I screamed in pain and curled into the fetal position, which terrified my little girl, who screamed in fear. I pulled her over and held her close, and we soon both settled down.

Sharing pain and fear is also what brings doctors and patients closer together.

Chapter Seven
But Mostly, The Goonies

If *Jedi* was the best sequel I could ever imagine writing, *Indiana Jones and the Temple of Doom* was the best prequel. *Raiders of the Lost Ark* was an amazing, unexpected, Saturday morning adventure, just like *Star Wars* had been. I'll never forget the opening few minutes of *Raiders*, the raiding party is walking through the jungle, we only glimpse Indy from the back. He pauses at the edge of a river – he hears the hammer of a gun click behind him – he turns his head fractionally to localize the sound – he spins around with his whip, yanks the gun out of the assassin's hand – and steps into the sunlight. Close-up on Harrison Ford. Coolest guy ever.

So getting the *Temple of Doom* novelization assignment was like having a rich feast set down in front of me. Set in 1935, the year before *Raiders*, it opens in a decadent Shanghai nightclub, with Indy in a tux. I set the tone in the first paragraph. First sentences and first paragraphs of my novels have always been pretty much the most important to me – I often can't write any further until I get it just right. That was true of *Jedi* ("The very depth of space."),[3] and it was true of *Indy*. In fact, the first paragraph of this book may be my favorite first paragraph of any of my books. It looked like this on the first draft, and I don't think it changed after that.

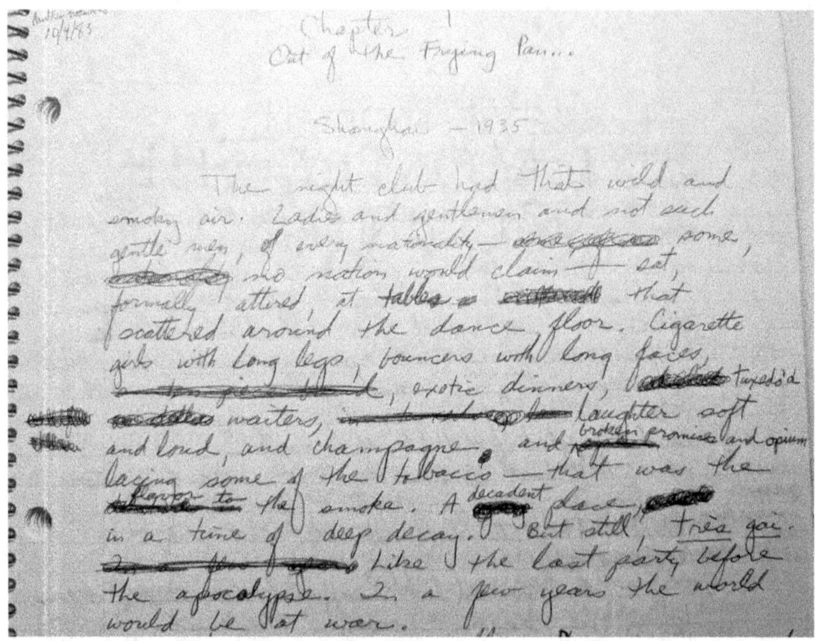

Opening fragment of original handwritten manuscript page of the Indiana Jones and the Temple of Doom *novelization (Ballantine Books, 1984.) Photo courtesy of the Author.*

"The night club had that wild and smoky air." [45] (Like you know what I'm talkin' about.) "Ladies and gentlemen, and not such gentle men (I love wordplay) "of every nationality – some no nation would claim – " [46] So it's a nightclub full of outlaws and expatriates. "Cigarette girls with long legs, bouncers with long faces." [47] I'm playing with epistrophe there, the repetition of words at the end of successive clauses. "Like the last party before the apocalypse. In a few years the world would be at war," [48] are the last two sentences. I was feeling it like *Cabaret*, like the way people spin out of control, each in their own way, on the eve of destruction. In this case leading up to World War II.

I wanted to get across a time of abandon, encapsulated in the Cole Porter song, *Anything Goes* – which we hear Willie (Kate Capshaw) sing in Chinese in the Shanghai nightclub as Indy enters in a tux. "Yi wang si-I wa ye kan dao…" ("In olden days a glimpse of stocking…") She sees him enter immediately, and their eyes meet, and she thinks, "Well, he's pretty, but he looks like trouble." [49] That's what I saw on the actress's face (in my mind). And that's pretty much how their relationship goes from then on.

It was fun to write, but it didn't quite live up to *Raiders* for me. Felt a bit like it was trying to recreate that magic, but didn't quite have it. Like just one crisis after another, and the special sauce was missing. And not for lack of trying – it had all the children in an Indian village abducted and enslaved, sacrificial rites, eating monkey brains, lost jewels – in fact, I tried to write it to resonate with *King Solomon's Mines*, by H. Rider Haggard. But maybe that's why it ended up feeling derivative to me.

Actually, a number of those tropes became controversial at the time. Accusations of insensitivity to Chinese and Indian culture, pandering to the White Savior Syndrome. Indians portrayed as solely helpless or evil? No more than the villagers and bandits in *Seven Samurai*. It felt to me like Indy's tale was more homage to those late 19th century to mid 20th century yarns. The heroine who was always screaming in fear, the hero saving her, the blundering British military Captain Blumbertt, the sinister Oriental priest. Stereotyped? For sure. Resurrecting the old Thugee cult and turning it into a fantasy version of itself? It's a fantasy movie. Does anyone think three people could jump out of a crashing plane on a rubber flotation raft and survive the fall? I'm glad we've moved beyond the exclusivity of the White Savior these days, to give every culture its own heroics and myths. But this was like a Saturday morning cartoon meant to get caught up in without a lot of analysis.

It was criticized for being too violent, too – which led to the creation of a new rung on the movie guide: PG-13, may not be suitable for kids younger than 13.

And Short Round a stereotype? He was an enthusiastic street urchin who loved American baseball, who I just put on the spectrum of Spielberg kid heroes, from *ET*'s Elliott to Goonie Mikey Walsh. Smart, ingenious, ingenuous, vulnerable but bold, and basically good. In fact, Short Round (played by Ke Huy Quan) is arguably the biggest hero in the film, saving Indy from his trance by shoving a flaming torch into his side, cranking Willie out of the lava pit, and even saving the soul of the young Maharaja.

I liked Short Round so much, I asked Spielberg if I could write a chapter about just him, that wasn't in the movie, and Steven told me to go ahead. So I wrote Chapter 2, titled "A Boy's Life." The title itself was kind of a private Easter Egg, since that was also the working title of *ET* while it was in production.

The other thing I enjoyed writing was the Indy/Willie relationship (except for how often she screamed in the movie. That was really annoying.) But I wrote it like all those fast-talking screwball comedies of the '30's, like *It Happened One Night*, or *Twentieth Century*. Rapid repartee, a tough dame who's arguably smarter than the guy, but she's as attracted to him as he is to her – though both are too proud or stubborn to admit it. And I loved matching those bungled romantic moments to the lyrics of *Anything Goes*, throughout the book.

Like on page 104, the beginning of the long, hilarious, fumbled seduction sequence, she thinks the song lyric, "*If Mae West you like, or me undressed you like, nobody will oppose.*"[50] It leads up to a hot kiss, which quickly turns into a farce of miscommunication, ending up with her lounging on her bed, certain he can't stay away, while he's by now ended up fighting some bad guy in the next room.

Anyway, following one harrowing escape after another, many times where all looks lost, Short Round saves Indy and Indy gets rid of the evil Kali worshippers and shepherds the stolen kids back to their village. I think we assume Willie and Short Round both end up in America after the book is over – and as we know, Indy ends up raiding the Lost Ark of the Covenant. (For which, btw, kudos to my buddy and creature fabricator Chris Walas, who was responsible for the melting Nazi face at the climax of that movie.) (As well as the Gremlins in *Gremlins*.)

After *Temple of Doom* came *The Goonies*, published in 1985. If the Indy tale was modeled on *King Solomon's Mines*, *Goonies* was like *Treasure Island* meets *The Adventures of Huckleberry Finn*. *Treasure Island* – by Robert Louis Stevenson, because, obviously, it's about a kid hunting pirate treasure, which is what *Goonies* is all about – but *Treasure Island* is also probably my favorite book of all time, and actually the first book I remember being exposed to, around the age of 4. It was on a record, a shellac 78, narrated and with a few brief scenes acted out, like Jim hiding in the apple barrel and overhearing the pirates plotting to take over the ship. The flip side of the record was Basil Rathbone narrating *Peter and the Wolf*, and I listened to both sides over and over. So *Treasure Island* is dear to my heart, most likely the thing that got me interested in writing to begin with; and I brought that feeling to writing *The Goonies*.

I tried to have some resonance with other 18th and 19th century novels in the chapter titles, as well – those old picaresque adventure tales like *Tom Jones*, or *The Three Musketeers*, which made the titles a series of words and phrases that were going to crop up in the chapter. I think it subliminally situated *Goonies* amidst the narratives of an earlier, simpler time.

But *Huck Finn* is the other model I used. Especially in language and structure. *The Goonies* is Mikey's story, really, so I decided I wanted to write it First Person – really totally from his POV. Which is how it was for Huck, as well as Jim Hawkins in *Treasure Island*. I wanted it to sound like Mikey was telling his story, casually and conversationally – to *you*. Like he was telling it confidentially to each individual reading it. His first sentence is "So my name is Mikey Walsh."[51] Like he's talking to *you*. And he says things like, on page 28, "You know what I'm talkin' about?" Or on page 51: "But don't *you* have dreams?"[52] It makes the tale much more intimate, like he bumped into you in a bar years later, and he's telling you this thing that happened to him when he was a kid, telling you, personally, and in person.

Of course, telling it in First Person created some problems. For example, how did I tell parts of the story that didn't involve Mikey, like the Fratelli escape from prison, or when Chunk got kidnapped by them later on. The first part I solved by describing the escape in newspaper articles at the start of the book – which I then bookended with news articles at the end as a kind of postscript, describing what happened after the events of the movie are over. As for Chunk's side story, I just had Mikey (played by Sean Astin) relate to the reader what Chunk had told him after they got back together again. Worked for me.

Mikey's a likeable kid, as well, which draws the reader in more. He's self-deprecating, insightful, generous even to assholes, funny without meaning to be. And there's a spiritual element running through the story that gives Mikey more depth than a lot of kid-heroes. From the very start, he feels connected to One-Eyed Willy in a way he doesn't understand. Is he genetically related? Is he reincarnated? Kindred spirits? Why does he feel like Willy is somehow calling to him? It's a theme reiterated over the course of the novel, until it becomes, in the end, a metaphor for a boy becoming a man.

But first, a tiny Easter Egg. On page 16, Mikey mentions his mom's arm is broken, in a sling, and he's reminded of when he broke his own arm at a housing development in Cuesta Verde Estates. That, of course, is the housing development where the Freeling family had their *Poltergeist* experience. I was imagining that Mikey's family, the Walshes, were cousins of the Freelings, and visited them down in Cuesta Verde Estates on the way to Disneyland one summer, and while playing with Robbie Freeling in an empty lot, Mikey broke his arm. Maybe that's a stretch to you, but that's how I think.

But breaking an arm playing in an empty lot is a kid activity, and the Goonies are facing the harsh realities of adulthood – specifically, foreclosure. So this adventure they leap into – driven by Mikey – is their last chance to be kids. "This is *our* time," [53] he says on page 88, when they're offered the chance to escape back up to the country club by the bucket in the wishing well – and he convinces them to stay down in the tunnels, to finish their quest for treasure.

And of course, the First Kiss, on page 99 of the paperback, is also one of those archetypal transitions from childhood to adulthood. It ain't just a kiss, either. It's tongue in mouth, hand on breast action. The darkness in the cave gets him off the hook a little, because Andy initially thinks it's Brand she's kissing – but it rocks Mikey's world, and starts building his confidence in a way he hasn't experienced before. I got pages of an edited version from the publisher at some point, with those steamy parts cut out for the YA version of the book. Don't know if they ever did that version though.

I also enjoyed writing a new section that wasn't in the movie, starting around page 130. The Goonies are trapped in a cave filling with water and they jump on a raft that chutes them down the rapids onto a huge, lightless lake, where they become becalmed. I added the scene for two reasons. First, to just pause in the action, to give everyone a breather – both Goonies and readers – to take stock of the situation. But the second reason was to spend a little time going deeper into each of the characters, to get to know them a bit better, to get a richer sense of their inner lives.

First we hear from Data (another role for Ke Huy Quan), who talks about this fantastic underwater city he wants to invent someday. On the sea floor, entirely encased by some kind of "huge, clear, plastic bubble," able to withstand the ocean's pressure, but leaving all the water around them visible, with all the sea creatures and structures lit up by flood lights. The lights and all the power needs of the city would be generated by water turbines driven by ocean currents, a safe, clean, endless energy source. Inside the enormous structure would be different levels, for living, growing and raising food, cooking, playing. And there would be airlocks, so people could go visit the surface if they wanted to. And "life will be devoted to farming and eating and playing and discussing philosophy and working on new inventions."

This was actually a world I first built in my second sci-fi novel, *Time's Dark Laughter* (Del Rey, 1982) – this exact underwater, glass-bubble civilization. In my book, it's an ancient, long abandoned, sea-floor dome that the heroes discover midway through their journey. It's something I've always wanted to see developed, so I put it out in my own novel first, and then recapitulated it here. Hope to see it happen someday.

After Data describes his dream, Steph talks about how much she loves the water, loves swimming and diving and fishing. "It's so quiet and peaceful, no one else around." [54] A very different aspect to the Steph we've come to know, so it deepens her character. She loves the rolling waves, the sense of serenity they bring. It's like her own personal meditation. Away from all the jerky people. It's the dark that scares her – which makes them all look around the blackness of the underground lake they're floating on.

This stimulates Mouth to tell everyone a classic ghost story – the Monkey's Paw. He tells it well, and everyone is entranced – so even though it's scary, it takes everyone's mind off the real trouble they're in on this lake, as the fog starts rolling in. And we really feel for how much Mouth loves to tell a great story. Kinda like me.

And now, since they're all opening up, Brand confesses to his claustrophobia, how he's been scared of small spaces ever since he got stuck in a refrigerator when he was a small boy. Up to now, Brand has been a kind of arrogant, macho jock – but this revelation gives him a vulnerability that elevates him in everyone's estimation.

Andy's fears are more existential. She wonders if there is a heaven, and talks about her fear of hell – and even worse, of limbo, which feels too close to what they're all experiencing now. Damp, cold to the bone, foggy, and without end.

Which takes us to Mikey, who relates their journey to other literary quests, like *The Rime of the Ancient Mariner*, or *Moby Dick*. Then, as the others doze off, the fog clears, a slight breeze picks up, and the raft begins slowly moving again, drifting in the current. And that brings Mikey to mind of Huckleberry Finn – the very kid who inspired the way I decided to write this novel. "Driftin' down the Mississippi, havin' adventures and gettin' into trouble and helpin' his friends and learnin' a thing or two…"[55] And Mikey realizes Huck Finn was one of the first Goonies.

I'd add to that Peter Pan and the Lost Boys on their adventures with pirate Captain Hook.

Then we head back into the finale of the Goonies' adventure – and they discover the pirate ship. "The rigging was all in place, like sheets of giant spider webs – and there were real spiderwebs everywhere, too, which looked a lot like sheets of miniature rigging. For a second, I couldn't tell if I was big or small."[56]

Big or small. So he's right on that cusp now – boyhood and manhood. That's what the theme of the book is all about. This is where his spiritual journey has brought him, where kindred soul Willy has been calling him from the beginning. And when Mikey finally finds One Eyed Willy sitting at the table surrounded by jewels and treasure, they connect. Mikey understands that Willy was here to help him hang on to being a kid for one last long night before the mortgages and foreclosures of adulthood come crashing down. But there's more than that.

Willy – with all his booby traps and contraptions and gags that Mikey has set off and outwitted – was actually the first Goonie. And he can truly rest now that Mikey has given him back the boy inside him; while Mikey can go on to become a man.

Maybe this all sounds too convoluted – and it's certainly unnecessary to having a good time reading the simple adventure tale. But for me, it enlivened the writing and enriched the characters, and made the book more enjoyable even if you weren't aware of why you liked it. I guess if you didn't like it, maybe all this literary overlay is why.

In any case, I had a great time fitting it into the canon of kids' adventures alongside Huck Finn, Jim Hawkins, Peter Pan and the rest. I liked bringing a little of my medical knowledge in from time to time – like on page 93, when Brand is having a claustrophobic anxiety attack, and Steph looks for a paper bag. "We gotta get him to breathe back his own carbon dioxide." [57] I liked making her smart, too. And I loved having Sloth get adopted and Bar Mitzvah'd by Chunk's parents, the Cohens.

As for *Poltergeist II*, I don't have a lot to say. It felt like another way in to the world of The Other Side, where the Beast of the first movie lived. So it was a little deeper exploration of that mythology. It fleshed out the connections between the characters in the two movies, like Tangina and Lesh – and between current day characters and their antecedents, like Kane and his cult. But it felt like a lot of reworking of already trodden ground. Exciting in parts, scary in parts, but not sure if it was worth the effort. Reviews seemed to concur with that view – both for the film and the novelization – and honestly, at this point, it's hard for me to remember much about the plot, or what went into writing it. So forgive me, if I let this one slide by in the memoir. It just wasn't that memoir-able.

It came out in 1986, and was the last novelization I ever did. So it was kind of the end of Chapter One in my Hollywood career. It was also the end of Chapter One (or maybe Act One) of my life in Los Angeles. That was the year we moved.

Chapter Eight
Columbia, California

The end of Chapter One of my life in Hollywood came in 1986, after we'd had our second child, Jordan (a much easier birth than Laura's), and Jill decided she didn't want to raise our kids in Los Angeles any more. I was working random ER shifts while being stumblingly successful writing less than memorable novelizations and random TV shows – but L.A. was feeling weirder and unsafer. There was a kind of panic in the air about child-raising. A mass hysteria about child kidnappings and satanic cult rituals. The McMartin Preschool was shut down when it was alleged by parents to be ritually abusing their children. It all turned out to be false, some of it from well-meaning child psychologists who were actually planting images in the kids' minds through their leading questioning.

And there were panic-inducing urban legends spreading everywhere. One favorite was the toddler who was kidnapped at Disneyland, but the perp was caught exiting the main entrance when the parents recognized their child's red jellies – a popular sparkly plastic shoe. It was all fake news, though.

Anyway, we just didn't want to deal with those anxieties anymore. At least Jill didn't. I still felt more tied to L.A., and my nascent career – but now my family had become a more compelling reason to focus my energies. In the universe of the Three Body Problem, Jill's gravity was pulling most strongly now. Besides, I figured I could work the ER up at Tuolumne General Hospital, write scripts up there, and fax them down to L.A. for my agent to sell. We would move to our waterfall getaway house in the Gold Rush country, and begin the next chapter of our married life.

It sounds pretty cut and dried when I write about it now, yet it was anything but at the time. The reality of leaving all our friends, of dismantling the book-and-art-filled house where we'd been raising our family, the distancing of business connections, the severance of in-person networking and pitch meetings, the sharp transition from urban excitement to relative isolation, the increased friction between me and Jill over whether this was even a good idea – it was a lot to juggle.

It was the next Call to Adventure. A slow, two-truck drive up Route 99 would soon deposit us at the end of Act 1, with a major change in venue to begin Act 2 in Columbia, California.

Columbia was the center of the Gold Rush country, just a few miles up the road at Sutter's Mill, where the Rush started. We'd bought the little house up there as a getaway home a few years earlier, but now we were here full time, to raise our young family. We had a waterfall in the back yard, the Stanislaus National Forest stretching out below us; and a variety of mountain folks scattered through the surrounding hills for neighbors. I'm just going to recount a handful of random memories, to give the feel of the place.

Helen Smothers, our nearest neighbor, was a wonderful, warm spirit, a mountain woman, and the tutor for our homeschooled kids. She'd once won a 100 mile cross-country horse race. Teaching our children in her little cabin beside a stream, she'd once sliced off the head of a hissing rattlesnake with a shovel, and cut it open to show everyone its still-beating heart. And she taught us that wood warms you three times – when you chop it, when you carry it, and when you burn it.

Helen had been good friends with Slim Pickens, and used to go pigeon hunting with him. They'd gone hunting a month before he died, and his boots got so muddy, he left them on her porch, and she said she'd clean them for him. Now, with Slim gone, she had no use for the boots, and when I told her what a fan I was of his, she gave them to me. I wear them on occasion; they're treasured totems, Tony Lama boots, M3232.

Slim Pickens' pigeon hunting Tony Lama boots. Photo courtesy of the Author.

She also gave me one of Slim's favorite, personal, invented recipes, which I gift you here:

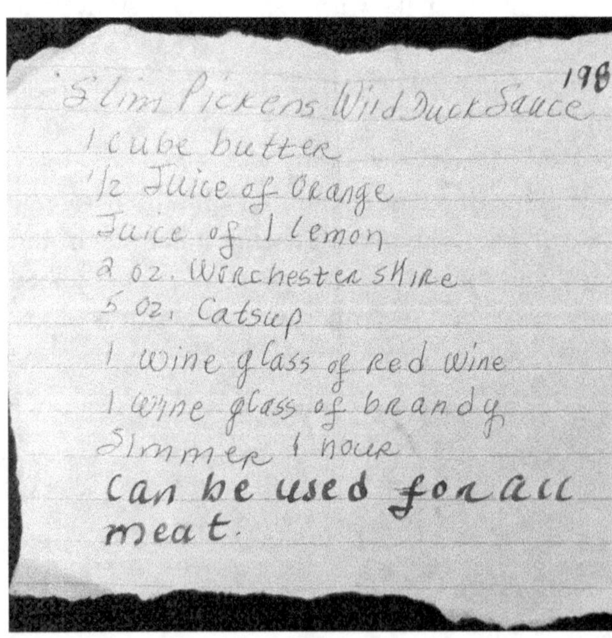

Slim Pickens' Wild Duck Sauce recipe, handwritten by and courtesy of Helen Smothers. Photo courtesy of the Author.

Slim Pickens' Wild Duck Sauce
1 cube butter
½ juice of orange
Juice of 1 lemon
2 oz. Worcester Sauce
5 oz. Catsup
1 wine glass of red wine
1 wine glass of brandy
Simmer 1 hour
Can be used for all meat.

Helen was married to Ray, who drove a cement truck around the county, the sweetest man, big and burly, but shockingly light on his feet when it came to waltzing.

Up the road was old Clayton, a true mountain man, who lived in half a wrecked trailer in the midst of a self-created junkyard in the middle of the woods. There was an old rusted mining steam pump lying around there in the junk heap. I asked if I could buy it, to drag to our yard for the kids to play on. He said Sure, I could have it for $125. I thought that was kind of steep for an old piece of trash, but he said he'd get it working for me if I wanted. I paid him, and we dragged it to my yard by rope behind Ray's pickup truck.

The kids loved it, they called it their "rocket ship," and all was well until Perry walked up the road a few months later. Perry was an honest-to-God gold miner, and about once a month the ground would shake when he blasted in his mine down the hill. When he got to our yard, he looked at the rusty machine sitting in the tall grass, and hailed me over.

"Hey, J, where'd you get that old steam pump?" he asked.

"Oh, Clayton sold it to me."

"Well… I don't know that it was exactly Clayton's to sell."

"What do you mean?"

"Well, it actually belongs to the Patterson boys, and they left it at Clayton's for him to repair. I won't say nothin' about it to them, though; they might just forget the whole thing."

So I was an outsider again, the urban yuppie slow to fit in to this insular world. Trying to fit in, but they all saw through my mask.

There were meth cookers up on our mountain, too, and when I worked in the Tuolumne General Hospital Emergency Room, I saw more meth and alcohol problems than I'd ever seen in Los Angeles ER's. Something like 25% unemployment up there in the hills. Used to be a lot of timber jobs, but most of that was gone, after regulations about clear-cutting and endangered species protection. The habitat of the spotted owl was a big point of contention. I once went into the bathroom outside the St. Charles Saloon, and there was no toilet paper, but some scrawled graffiti read: *No paper – wipe yur ass with a spotted owl.*

I panned for gold in the Tuolumne River, and once I tried to jump a claim that hadn't been worked in a year, but I missed the deadline by one day. I told that to one of our odd-job workers, Jerry Boone, a direct descendant of Daniel, and this is his story about the time a couple fellas tried to jump the Boone family's rose quartz mine claim.

"Everyone knows that rose quartz mine been in the Boone family for generations. So we go up there one day, there's a couple fellas workin' a good quartz vein out the stope, and everyone knows gold runs with quartz. So my pap draws down on 'em, says 'What the hell, you boys know the penalty for claim jumpin'. But my gramp, Tan, he pulls down pap's arm and says, 'Hang on, let's hear their story.'

"So one of 'em pulls a paper out his jacket, and says, 'Ain't nothin' personal, Tan, we's just checking claims down the county, and you ain't filed on this parcel the last coupla years, so we just filed on it ourselves, and now it's ours. No hard feelin's, but that's the law.' And he gives Tan the paperwork on the claim he filed.

"My pap's ready to break heads, but old Tan just nods and gives them boys back their claim, and says, 'Well, the law's the law, I suppose, I guess you fellas just fell into some good luck.' Pap can't believe it, but Tan gets us back in the truck and drives straight to the State BLM office. We go to the maps, and the claims, and we see sure enough, these rascals filed a legitimate claim on the land our family had been filing on for four generations, but missed the last two deadlines out of sheer laziness.

"Didn't bother Tan one bit, though. He filed on the parcel right next to the one we'd always filed on. 'This here new parcel's our actual mine,' he says. Turns out it was a family secret, we'd always been filing on the parcel right next to the one where the mine was, as a trap for claim jumpers. So these boys had actually filed their claim on the land adjacent to the true mine, and now Tan filed on the actual mine parcel.

"Pap was tickled, and wanted to drive right back and tell these boys the bad news. But Tan says no, wait, let's give 'em a couple more days to do the grunt work of getting' all that quartz out the vein, and then we can go pick it up.

"So that's what we did. Two days later we come back and showed 'em what they done, and Tan turned their own words back on 'em, he said, 'No hard feelin's, but that's the law.' Then he pointed out the parcel they'd actually filed on, about an acre further south, and invited them to start diggin' there, if they thought there was any gold or quartz over there, and thanked 'em for minin' all that good rose quartz for us – even had a little run of gold in there – and they left with their tail between their legs. Only too-bad is now we gotta keep filin' on the actual mine, so I guess our secret's out. But it was worth it, to see the look on their faces."

So that's the kind of place Columbia was. I remember stitching up my kids' foreheads on the kitchen table, cutting down my own Christmas tree, chopping firewood, or sometimes trading firewood for giving medical care. I remember drinking beer on the deck watching the sunset, or the stars in the black sky. I remember surprising a big-antlered stag when I opened my back door and both of us jumped a foot in surprise.

I remember staying up all of one long winter night at the bedside of my son, Jordan, when he had the croup, holding a tracheostomy needle in my hand because his breathing was getting so tight, and the winding mountain road back down to the hospital was too icy to drive on, with the snowstorm getting worse by the minute. That was the longest night of my life, improvising a vaporizer tent over Jordan, rehearsing in my mind how to do an emergency tracheostomy – until sunrise, when I walked him outside in my arms, and his breathing eased, and the crisis was over.

IV

I was working Center Booth when she got wheeled in, DOA. She was an anesthesiologist at a West Side hospital, she'd been in an auto accident. The car was crunched, and her neck was pinned to the steering wheel, obstructing her breathing.

She must have been awake and alert until the very last moment. When the paramedics reached her, she was dead – asphyxiated. Clenched in her hand was a pocket knife, Swiss Army, its blade at her throat, an incision already made where she'd begun to do the tracheostomy on herself to open her airway – but hadn't been able to finish. When they rolled her into C Booth, we all examined her attempted incision. She had the right spot, she'd probably done scores of emergency tracheostomies in her career. She just hadn't cut deep enough before she passed out. We all knew how to do trachs too; but could we do one on ourselves, if our lives depended on it?

I palpated my own trachea, feeling for the place. We all did. Even Leo did, when I told him the story.

But I also remember the hammock beside the waterfall.

It was, overall, an idyllic life. Back to the earth, to nature, no artifice, no neon, just our family nestled in the woods. I wasn't getting any work in Hollywood, but I was content in the bosom of my family. Laura grew from three to six, Jordan from one to four. Such great ages, so full of magic in their inner lives, and play on the mountain. I wrote them lullabies and birthday songs, and threw water balloons in the summer and sledded down our front yard in the winter. I grew a beard down to my nipples, I looked like a mountain man, I wanted to see how long it would grow, and I figured it might be easier for my backwoods patients to relate to me.

Jill got deeply into making hand-made paper. I wrote a novel, *Hunter's Moon*, about a gold mining adventure, but nobody bought it. I wrote a couple scripts, but nobody bought them, either. That was painful, all that rejection of my writing, but otherwise life was good, and I figured eventually somebody would spark to some screenplay I sent down to my agent in L.A. And if not… life was pretty sweet here. The mountain folk were accepting me, I started playing and writing more music. Jill got pregnant again, she'd always wanted three kids, and it was a good life.

Meanwhile, I worked in the ER at Tuolumne General Hospital. Saw a lot of the usual ER walk-ins and rush-ins, car crashes, drug OD's, domestic abuse, alcoholism; but saw other cases I hadn't been prepared for in big city hospitals. Once, during a wildfire, we had some firefighters brought in for inhaling poison oak smoke, and they went into respiratory failure; other paramedics came in because they'd walked into a nest of black widow spiders. I treated rattlesnake bites. Chainsaw accidents.

V

Pickup truck screeched to the ER doors, and a couple burly guys dragged in a 60-year-old bloody mess. He'd cut open his femoral artery with a chainsaw, but he was a Christian Scientist, so he wouldn't let us treat him. He wouldn't have come in at all, but his wife and pals dragged him to the ER when he passed out. I put pressure on the wound, but despite all his wife's pleading, and all my trying to convince him we could save his life if he just let us take him to the OR and sew it up, he wouldn't budge. I called the Hospital Administrator, and he brought in the Risk Management crew, and they all shook their heads, but insisted he was *compos mentis*, and he had the right to refuse treatment. So he poured his red life's-blood onto the sheets of the gurney, and died in front of us.

His wife slapped him, and then hugged him, sobbing. His buddies left to get drunk. I couldn't see that I had anything better to offer, but I stopped by Leo's room on the way to the bar later. He told me to leave the guy's chainsaw under his bed.

By this time I wasn't so callous any more about death, or how people faced it, or avoided facing it, or ignored it, or joked about it, or stared it down. It was similar to how Columbia was reconnecting me to the earth – chopping wood, carrying water, planting vegetables, watching the sky, marking the seasons – it was reconnecting me to human feelings again, too. Feelings about life, death, hope, loss, struggle, hunger. I spent hours talking to people just to talk, not to pitch. Exchanging meals with them, sitting on the deck, learning to feel touched by their problems instead of cynical, or snarky, or ironic.

It was a different world from any I'd known before. I learned to laugh with these folks instead of laughing at them. And to ache with them instead of judging them.

VI

A teenage girl showed up in the ER lobby and said, "Somethin' wrong with Grandma. Couple days ago she stopped eatin', then yesterday she stopped talkin'. I got her into the car, though. She out here now."

I walked with her out to the turnaround. "Does she have any specific complaints?" I asked. "Does she seem to be in pain?"

"Just the opposite. All she does is smile."

We got to the car, an ancient Dodge Dart. There was an old woman sitting in the passenger seat. Motionless. No, it was more than motionless. One arm was half-raised, and frozen in place, mid-air. *Rigor mortis*.

And another kind of *rigor*, as well. Her lips were pulled back, baring all her teeth in a freeze-frame death grin, it's called *rigor sardonicus*.

The frozen smile of death. But her granddaughter didn't know Grandma was dead. Or knew, and didn't want to say, because saying it would make it real. I never said it to Leo, either. Why should I? He was still talking. Nothing to see here.

That mountain girl's response to her dead grandma touched me. And it wasn't so different from my own response to my Hollywood career being dead.

Or badly stalled at the very least. But I had a wonderful, loving, interesting, fulfilling, Walden Pond life up in the mountains. For creative outlets I had my music, writing songs for my kids. And I could go back to writing novels, where I'd started, and which I still loved doing – even though nobody had bought *Hunter's Moon*. I figured I'd been writing since I was nine, I wrote for 20 years without thinking about selling anything, just wrote because I loved to write. I could go back to doing that, no problem.

But all that changed in 1988, when I got a call from the producers of *Family Medical Center*, Stu Billett (RIP), Bonnie Bogard (RIP), and Jay Feldman. They'd read the feature script I'd written years before, *Code Blues*, about working in an ER, and they liked it, and wanted to bring me on as head writer on their new show.

I was stunned. I thought I'd put all that behind me, I'd made a new kind of life, happy on the mountain with Jill and Laura and Jordan and the cast of characters who populated our mountain. But as soon as those producers asked me, I was all in. I said yes. And Jill agreed, I had to go for it. She said I'd better shave my mountain rabbi beard before I went to L.A., or they might have second thoughts.

They wanted me to come down right away, but Jill was now 9 months pregnant with Eliot, he was due any day. I told the producers I'd come a few days after he was born. They said okay, but they really needed to start soon – I should bring the whole family, and the company would rent us a condo in Santa Monica.

Another week went by, a week past the due date, and still no Eliot. After much discussion, with Jill and with Hollywood, we decided to pack the kids and all our essentials, and head down to L.A., about a six hour trip. Except that 15 minutes into the drive, Jill began having contractions. We went right in to the Tuolumne General ER. They checked her, said she was hardly dilated, and zero station. They recommended she have a beer on the way down to L.A., and that would likely slow contractions. Mountain medicine is different from city medicine, but we were still in the mountains, so that's what we did.

So after three years up on the mountain, we moved into the Santa Monica condo, Sea Colony, right on the beach. My job started, and Eliot was born one week later – two weeks late – and without any problems. I wrote or co-wrote 167 shows that year, 30 minute episodes, to run in syndication at 11:30, against Johnny Carson.

At one point the producers asked me to write myself into one of the episodes, to play an ER doc. Shouldn't have been too big a stretch, and I'd already had my walk-on in *ET*, but this involved speaking lines, and I pretty much froze on camera. They were able to cut around me, but it wasn't pretty. The Dancing Bear, tripping over his tutu. One mask too far. Still, I should have known I wasn't a stage performer, I was a behind-the-camera, below the radar guy. And that was actually all made clear to me because of something that happened in medical school.

I'd done some research in ESP at the Sleep Lab at the University of Chicago, with some positive results (that I integrated into the storyline of the *Poltergeist* novelization). One day I got called into the lab and was told the Illinois Psychic Research Society had caught wind of our research and wanted someone from the lab to come give a talk to their members. Nobody else in the lab wanted to go, so I was volunteered.

The meeting was in downtown Chicago, in a big grey building on Wabash, in a 3rd floor room about 50 feet on a side, with folding chairs and about 20 people in the audience. The moderator read minutes from the last meeting, something about a haunted house, and then asked for new business, and there were a couple hands raised asking for volunteers to help at an exorcism, or check out a UFO site, and I'm thinking Oh, great, the head of the lab knew what he was sending me into and this was a big joke they'd all have a good laugh about.

But then the moderator was introducing me, and there was polite applause, and I went up and stood at the front and started talking.

I said I was a scientist, and I didn't really believe in the supernatural, and we'd done this study that showed some interesting and suggestive results, but I was sure if there was some real phenomenon going on, it would all be explained scientifically at some point, electromagnetic waves, or pheromones, or I don't know what – but here's what we did.

And as I started talking about the study, I started feeling odd. I felt the hostility of the audience, and I found myself talking slower and slower... and then I heard myself saying "Umm" a lot.

"So we recruited student volunteers for the study, and, *ummm*, we paid them to sleep in the, *umm*, lab, and we glued electrodes, *umm*, to their, *umm*, heads, and, *umm*…"

And then I passed out.

I woke up on the floor with a dozen people surrounding me. One had my shoes off, looking for meridians to push, one was massaging my temple, one was reciting an incantation, two were chanting.

Finally, someone gave me a glass of water and I sat up against a wall, saying "I'm okay, I'm okay," and feeling rather embarrassed.

But then there was a parade of people who came up to me, intimately, like I was holding court – and each one explained to me what had happened.

Man in Tie-Dyed Shirt: "Oh, I am so sorry, and embarrassed about this. I knew some of the folks in the audience were hurling psychic lightning bolts at you, and I could have erected a force shield, but I didn't, I didn't stand up for you, and I am just so, so sorry."

Man with Beard: "I'm not sure if you were aware, but I passed out at the same moment you did. We were on the same astral plane together, and that guy over there, the guy who's smiling, sucked all the oxygen out of the atmosphere on that plane, and we both went down. I had words with him, though, it won't happen again."

Woman in Sari (holding my hand): "You must understand, you weren't saying "Ummm," during your talk, you were saying "Om." You put yourself into a transcendental state, it's not a problem, you must be a very enlightened soul. Bless you."

Woman in Turban (pressing a business card and a 20 dollar bill into my hand): "Call me." Her card said she was a spiritualist.

When I at last felt okay to stand, I got up and a man in a business suit approached me, and pressed his business card into my hand.

Man in Business Suit: "Call me."

His card said he gave lessons in public speaking.

So yes, I needed lessons in public speaking, and acting as well. I decided then and there to stick with writing.

It was a hard year, being back in Los Angeles. Stressful for Jill, she didn't like L.A., and she didn't like never seeing me because I was working so much, even though we lived in the same house. Confusing for the kids, who'd had little experience with curbs and cars, and suddenly had an absentee father. Because the show took all my time: I left early every morning and got home late seven days a week, and I was always tired. Sometimes I wondered why, exactly, I'd left that Edenic existence in the Sierras. But I knew the answer. I was addicted to Hollywood.

Especially since I seemed to have lost it once. I'd had it, and then it slipped through my fingers with the move to Columbia, and now here was my second bite at the apple. I felt addicted to the demand of writing all the time, under pressure; to the romance of the business, the sense I was now part of this magical history of television and film; to the big salary, and the big personalities; to the deference I was given as Head Writer; to the whole, glitzy, melodramatic, stars-in-your-eyes, 20th Century American Entertainment Extravaganza of it. The company even took out a Key Player insurance policy on me, I was so essential to the show. Top o' the world, Ma!

It was a heady addiction, and I didn't want to give it up again.

That was the year I also got offered the gig of novelizing *Indiana Jones and the Last Crusade*, which I reluctantly had to turn down, because I was too busy. And that was the end of my novelizing career – which was okay, since I'd been feeling typecast as a novelizer, trapped in that career world, and this was my escape. I was the Head Writer on an actual television series.

Like all addictions, it was a prison, too, in its own way. But as the Eagles said in *Hotel California*, "We are all just prisoners here of our own device." [58]

Not exactly like being trapped in carbonite, and waiting for the kiss of my true love; but close enough to remind me now of Chapter 2 of the *Return of the Jedi* novelization.

CHAPTER NINE
FLOAT LIKE A JEDI

ROTJ – CHAPTER 2, PART ONE, PAGES 23-27

Han and Leia reconnect as soon as she's released him from the carbonite. He can't see, though, and he wants to know where he is. "She looked at him a long moment… Tears filled her eyes. 'We'll make it,' she whispered." [59] *She knows full well that she's risked everything to save him, including losing time from her duties with the Rebellion – but she just flat out loved the big lug too much to stay away.*

Han, too, "was flooded with emotion all at once." [60] *Which is, of course, so uncharacteristic of Han. Fortunately for the reputation of his gruff exterior, "a repulsive squishing sound" reveals Jabba and all the "most disgusting miscreants of Jabba's court."* [61] *The exact opposite of the love we've just been watching. One of the axioms of screenwriting (and its amplification in novelization) is to begin a scene with one emotion, and leave the scene with its opposite.*

Jabba cackles. His gathering mocks the lovebirds, as Han and Leia both offer Jabba riches to let them go. He scornfully rejects that, though, and has Han taken off to a cell – while he has Leia brought to him.

Lando steps up – disguised as one of Jabba's guards – and takes Leia's arm, as a prisoner. She whispers to him not to worry – even though their plan is going awry.

What I liked about this scene was the way it kept alternating, not just from the opening moment to the exit, but from hope to despair and back again. All looks lost – then the heroes have a plan – the plan goes sideways – but they think on their feet and come up with a new plan. That's what makes them heroes.

Standing defiantly before Jabba, Leia offers carrots and sticks – lots of money to let them go, but if he doesn't, she tells him she has powerful friends. Jabba is unimpressed. He pulls her to him until "her belly [is] pressed to his oily snake skin." [62] *I wanted to drill down on this moment, this image that's so disgusting, even Threepio says, "Oh, no, I can't watch."* [63] *The idea of something so gross it even offends the sensibilities of a droid, takes it to a new level. Until…*

"Jabba poked his fat, dripping tongue out to the princess, and slopped a beastly kiss squarely on her mouth." [64] *Turning it up to eleven. I tried to imagine myself in Leia's position. Gag.*

My hope is that moments like this, coupled with Jabba's ultimate fate at the hands of Leia, instilled in a young, impressionable female audience the notion that, when they grew up, they didn't have to take this crap, #metoo.

After being released from carbonite by Leia, but immediately recaptured by Jabba, Han is taken to a dungeon cell, still blind. As he tries to organize his thoughts in darkness, it all comes rushing back to his disoriented mind that he was saved by Leia, and he has to get out of here. The dungeon walls are solid rock, though, so he can think of nothing he has to bargain with.

And suddenly, as if things could get no worse, he hears a growl — and "the hairs on Solo's arms stood on end." All at once a wild creature bellows and grabs Han "ferociously around the chest… squeezing off his breathing." Once again, all seems lost — but Han knows that voice: "Chewie, is that you?" And "For the second time in an hour, Solo was overcome with happiness." Again, the back and forth emotions — and again, Han is so uncharacteristically overcome with emotion. [65-68]

Chewbacca says, "Arh, arhaghh shpahrgh rahr…" [69]

I was criticized in some quarters for trying to write the sound of Chewie's speech, as I had been criticized for aping Artoo's beeps and whistles. But I loved writing those transliterations, evoking on the page the sounds we all know so well from the films. If someone hadn't seen the movie, these quotes might not have much meaning — but the people complaining about it had seen the film often, so as far as I'm concerned, they have little justification for dismissing my Rosetta Stone attempts. Or if they do feel justified, well, so be it.

And Han understands Chewie perfectly — learning that not only is Leia here with an escape plan, but so is Lando, and so is Luke! And Luke is now a Jedi Knight!

Han scoffs at that, saying, "Come on, I'm out of it for a little while and everybody gets delusions." Chewie protests. Han says, "I'll believe it when I see it." [70]

Whereupon he walked "stoutly into the wall." [71]

Oddly – or maybe inevitably – this passage paralleled a prior event in my life, so I think I was recapitulating my own experience, projecting it onto Han's.

It was at the 4th of July party, 1978, for the faculty and Residents in the brand new, about-to-launch UCLA Emergency Medicine Residency program, which I and three other Residents from the LA County program had helped to create. While still in our first year ER Residency program at USC (LA County Hospital), several faculty members at UCLA had secretly recruited us to take the next year off, help them put together the new Emergency Medicine Residency at UCLA, and then the following year we four would be the first class of second year Residents, helping to teach the first class of first year Residents in the start-up UCLA program. So this July 4th party was celebrating the inauguration of that new program. It was a big deal, and I was nervous.

The party was being held at the home of one of the professors, and I was there with Jill, 40 or 50 doctors and spouses mingling, drinking, smoking, laughing. After being there an hour or so, and accepting several friendly tokes – just to be sociable – I began to feel unsteady. I headed for the kitchen for a glass of water.

In the kitchen, the head of the department offered me a puff of weed, which he described as "some great Oaxacan shit," and which I of course could not turn down. It just seemed like a bad idea to rebuff the department head. So I took a hit and knew immediately I was going to pass out.

I started walking toward the door to the living room. I knew if I could just get through it, I could flop onto the living room couch on the other side. But halfway there, I went blind, a veil dropped over my eyes, everything turned black, I couldn't see – yet I was continuing to walk. I found this fascinating. Walking blind. Maybe there was an adaptive reason for it, maybe I should write this up and send it in as a letter or an anecdote to the Journal of Evolutionary Biology, maybe this meant that evolutionarily it was more important to run than to see. And the moment I had that thought – WHAM – I walked head first into the wall.

Stoutly into the wall. Just like Han, who made a vision joke, "I'll believe it when I see it," and then WHAM, walked into the wall.

I think, just like we are, each of us, every character in our dreams, writers are also all the characters in their novels. And I unconsciously gave Han the same set-up/punchline I'd lived through – including the hubris of smugly concluding something about the nature of sight and then walking into a wall. There's something about Han Solo that's too clever for his own good. A lot like I was. Too clever by three eights, I used to say. (Age has whittled away most of my cleverness, for good and ill. Now I'm too clever by one sixteenth.)

We'll get to what happened to Han after he walked into the wall – but what happened after I walked into the wall is its own story. I knocked myself unconscious, and woke up on my back on the kitchen floor, surrounded by a dozen Emergency Medicine specialists. They were doing what you'd expect. Someone (Harvey) was checking my pupils for dilation; someone else (Chuck) was checking my radial pulse; someone was inspecting my head for lacerations or swelling; someone (Jerry) was saying, "There's one at every party."

I could feel my pulse tapping against Chuck's fingers, and I felt my pulse rate getting slower. No problem, I thought, I was having a vasovagal response to the dehydration, the whiskey, and the marijuana. A slow pulse was just part of the drill. But then I could feel it getting even slower. Forty-six beats per minute. Forty. Thirty-two. And then I realized it was going to stop in a few moments, I was going to have a cardiac arrest, what's called a vagal arrest – also completely understandable pathophysiologically. This was just something that happened to some people, even young healthy ones. But I felt no panic, no fear, no upset of any kind. I felt serene in the knowledge of what was coming. My heart was going to stop.

I knew everyone else was going to freak out. They were going to start pounding on my chest, and calling 911, and getting sober real fast – but I wanted to tell them no worries, it's okay, I'll be fine. And then I felt my heart stop. No more pulse tapping against Chuck's fingers.

Chuck said, "I can't get a pulse."

"There must be a pulse," said Harvey. "Check his carotid."

Marie checked my carotid. "I can't get a pulse either."

"Somebody check a femoral," Jerry said.

Harvey unbuckled my pants, checked for a femoral pulse. Nothing.

Meanwhile, I began to float above my body. No white light, no beckoning hands, no long dead relatives, just floating, up to about eye level with all the docs who were standing around. Jill was at my feet, but she could hardly make out my body through the three-deep crowd surrounding me. Yet I looked into everyone's eyes, watched their faces, and said good-bye, felt calm and curious about what was to come.

And then WHAM! Just like walking into the wall – I was back in my body, and I could feel my pulse beat again, fast and thready 160 beats/minute. Ahh – I thought – I was having what's called a sinus escape, some other sinus node in my atrium was taking over the job that my old sinus node had abandoned, and I was back among the living.

"There, I've got a pulse now," Marie said with huge relief.

"I knew there must be a pulse," Harvey shook his head.

"I told you there's one at every party," said Jerry, the wag.

Nervous relief all around. Except me, I felt a little deflated.

They carried me to the couch I'd been aiming for originally, and I held court for half an hour. And here's the thing. Debriefing my well-wishers, I learned that as far as they could see, I'd been completely unconscious and unresponsive the entire time. But from my perspective, I'd been wide awake for it all. I could see and hear everyone; I thought my eyes were wide open. I told each of them where they were standing, and what they'd been saying.

I felt changed after that – for about a week. Like I'd really been there and back. I'd had a conversation with Death, and maybe he wasn't such a bad guy. Maybe this was a more nuanced journey than I'd been willing to accept for most of my career as a doctor.

VII

Leo used to say that when his body betrayed him, I was his counterspy. At other times, though, he accused me of collusion with the Enemy, sometimes bitterly. When the ulcers on

his foot refused to heal, and the infection began to spread, I wrote an order for a surgery consult, and asked the surgeon to amputate Leo's leg. "What good would I be without a foot?" Leo asked me. "What good are you with a gangrenous leg?" I was being harsh, but I wanted part of him alive; not all of him dead. We were at cross purposes, I saw later. "My body is being eaten away by my diabetes, and gnawed off by my doctors," he said. "I'm being nibbled to death."

We each suspected the other of conspiracy with the Reaper during the Big Battle. Treason most foul. It was, in fact, a war of secret alliances and unexpected betrayals. I was called once when a lady with a bleeding disorder pulled out her intra-arterial catheter. I entered the room to find her sitting in a large pool of her blood, smiling terribly at me out of black, recessed eyes, holding her gushing hand behind her with furtive glee, to keep me from stopping the bleeding.

I thought of that when I accused the old surgeon of malpractice for not amputating Leo's leg in time; accused him of murder with my eyes. But he just replied, "You come back in five years, and we'll talk about it." This shadow of puppet-master death pursued us, every one. Death, pulling the strings.

Leo was just getting bitter at me for prolonging the show.

I wondered, after the 4th of July party, what my brief sojourn on the astral plane meant about the nature of consciousness, or afterlife, or spirit, or the Force… but soon day-to-day life intervened in my metaphysical absorption. I had patients to see, and a car that needed a maintenance check, insurance issues on my house, bills, hospital politics… "the full catastrophe," as Zorba the Greek once said.

But until I was sucked back into all the mundane aspects of life, the experience of floating above my own body did make me feel a little Jedi-like for a while – which brings us to Luke's appearance, in person, for the first time as a Jedi Knight, to the iron doors of Jabba's palace.

ROTJ – CHAPTER 2, PART TWO, PAGES 27-31

Jabba's palace gate scrapes open to reveal, making his unshadowed appearance in this episode, Luke Skywalker – "clad in the robe of a Jedi Knight." [72] I didn't say definitively he was a Jedi – just clad in Jedi robes. Leaving a little room for doubt. In any case he's here to rescue Han, we know not how.

He's older now, and defined by his losses – lost illusions, dependency, friends, sleep, laughter… and the loss of his hand. He's grown more powerful, too, of course. He has a Jedi's patience and perspective, as well as Force control. And there's a darkness to him now, that "gave a depth to his personality where before it had been thin, without dimension – though such a suggestion probably would have come from jaded critics." [73]

I was getting kind of meta here, with a double meaning for the movie critics who'd rolled their eyes at Luke's character in the first Star Wars film, as "thin, without dimension." I was putting those "jaded critics" on notice that this Luke had real depth.

Luke strides into Jabba's lair, Force-chokes two Gamorrean guards, and works his Jedi mind trick on Bib Fortuna: "You will take me to Jabba now." And Bib replies, "I will take you to Jabba now." We hadn't seen that done since Obi Wan told the Stormtrooper on Mos Eisley, "These aren't the droids you're looking for," and the Stormtrooper nodded and echoed him in agreement. [74-76]

When Luke arrives in the throne room, he sees Leia, dressed as a dancing girl, chained at the neck and leashed to Jabba. Luke has to shut out her pain, to focus on the Hutt – and Leia closes her mind as well, so as not to distract Luke from what he must do.

Threepio is thrilled to see Luke, his salvation from this dreadful place. Jabba scolds Bib Fortuna for allowing Luke in. Luke whispers, "I must be allowed to speak," and Fortuna tells Jabba, "He must be allowed to speak." Once again, using Obi Wan's mind trick. But when Luke tries the mind trick on Jabba, to release Han and Chewbacca, Jabba just laughs: "Your mind powers will not work on me, boy." Haughty and dismissive, he is unaffected by Jedi, or even human, thought patterns. [77-79]

Luke speaks plainly, telling Jabba to release Solo or prepare to die. Again Jabba laughs. Threepio tries to warn Luke that he's standing on a… but Luke ignores the droid and Force-takes a guard's gun to point at Jabba.

That's when the grate Luke is standing on drops him into the pit below, where Oola had been dropped earlier. Just what Threepio was trying to warn him about.

So he may be a Jedi, but he still has some things to learn.

ROTJ – CHAPTER 2, PART THREE, PAGES 31-37

When Luke is dropped into the Rancor pit, we see a guard eaten right away, so we understand what Luke is in for. But he's up to the task, meeting the Rancor's brute strength with agility and inventiveness — I particularly liked sticking the long bone in the beast's craw, because I think we all know what it feels like to get even a small fishbone caught in our throat.

Of course, the Rancor's ultimate death is pretty much a foregone conclusion — so my favorite part of the scene is at the end, when the Rancor's keeper weeps. This man and beast had been each other's only friends for so long — and now the poor jailer's life would be an empty shell, devoid of companionship, as after the death of a dearly beloved pet. In the movie, that moment was played for laughs, but I genuinely felt for the guard, and tried to express that.

All of our heroes have been caught, now, and all are brought before Jabba: Luke, in chains, after killing the Rancor; Han, blind from the carbonite freezing; Chewie, led in by Lando impersonating a guard, the only good guy not yet discovered; Leia, tethered to Jabba; and C3PO, his restraining bolt keeping him close to the throne. Yet they remain their cavalier selves, despite Jabba's dire sentence — they'll be taken to the Great Pit of Carkoon, and thrown to the Sarlacc, who will digest them painfully for a thousand years.

Luke just smiles, though, threatening Jabba, "This is the last mistake you'll ever make." Luke, we infer from this, is not only looking forward to freeing his friends, but to killing Jabba, "to free the universe of this gangster slug." This prospect gives Luke a "dark satisfaction." [80-82]

Hmm. "Dark satisfaction" isn't a very Jedi-like emotion. In fact, this installment of the series was originally titled Revenge of the Jedi, but at the last minute, George Lucas decided revenge wasn't a Jedi-like emotion either, so he changed the title word to Return.

(NOTE: Here's my original typewritten manuscript page, now yellowed with age, tagging the fact that it was written decades ago, when that original title first existed.)

Typed, yellowed Title Page of Return of the Jedi *novelization (Del Rey, 1983.) This was the original title of the film and novelization. Photo courtesy of the Author.*

But Luke's dark satisfaction at the anticipation of killing Jabba is no accident. Just as Vader's rapid breathing when he got excited at the end of the Prologue was a hint of a little humanity left in him... Luke's dark satisfaction foreshadows the presence of the Dark Side in him, which will grow as time goes on.

As the prisoners are taken away to their presumed fate, Leia watches them go – noticing Luke's face is fixed in a broad smile. She tries to let his demeanor "expel her doubts," but it feels like she's picking up on a perceived darkness in him.

That's how the section ends in the published book. But in my original manuscript I added one more line, that got cut. Leia: "Luke, old kid, she thought, you're either really brave, or you don't know what's going on."

The Lucasfilm book editor may have felt it was a better button on the scene to end on Leia expelling her doubts. Or possibly the editor didn't care for her flippancy in this grim situation. But for me, my original line kept the focus on Leia's feeling that Luke's smile was inappropriate. She can feel something is up with him, and it ain't good.

So far, Chapters 1 and 2 have been the many-moving-parts set-up comprising ACT I of the whole *ROTJ* narrative. We've put in place Threepio and Artoo, Lando, Leia and Chewbacca, Han, Luke, and Jabba. Like chess pieces on a board, positioning themselves for the endgame.

The conclusion of Chapter 2 comes next, defining the end of ACT I of the film.

ROTJ – CHAPTER 2, PART FOUR, PAGES 37-51

This is the beginning of the first great all-hands-on-deck action sequence in the book/movie, the battle at the Sarlacc Pit. Jabba is on his sail barge, surrounded by his court, attended by Threepio, served by Artoo, and tethered to Princess Leia. Two gunboats accompany the barge, one with the prisoners – Luke, Han, and Chewie – surrounded by their guards: Barada with the long gun, the top-knotted Weequay brothers, and Lando Calrissian, still undercover as a guard.

Han is keeping up a continuous patter of "reckless disregard," to get his guards used to him talking and moving, in case an opportunity for escape presents itself. Reckless disregard is Han's defining characteristic. And Luke uses this time to remain silently introspective – to prepare for the fight ahead, and to remember his youth here on this desert planet.

The place he'd first met Obi Wan Kenobi, who'd first shown Luke the way of the Jedi. The beginning of all he'd gained and all he'd lost.

Lost his uncle and aunt here, lost his way of life, lost his innocence. And Ben had taken him to the pirate city of Mos Eisley, where he'd met Han and Chewbacca, deepened his newfound bonds with the droids, Threepio and Artoo, and gone on to save Leia, and lose Obi Wan, and… it all comes rushing back to him now, floating above the sands of Tatooine. "I grew up here," he says simply to Han. Grew up in so many ways. It's a poignant moment, in such a few words that say so much. "And now we're going to die here," Solo replied. Always the cynic. [83-84]

Luke is confident, though. "Just stay close to Chewie and Lando. We'll take care of everything." [85] *Han knows this kind of bravado – in fact, it's the kind of thing he might well have said himself in other circumstances. But it gives him a sinking feeling, here, if everything depends on a kid who thinks he's a Jedi who can wield a Force Han doesn't even believe in. "A fast ship and a good blaster"* [86] *are all Han believes in, and he wishes he had them now.*

But it won't be long before he gets his wish.

(NOTE: Lando, by the way, while waiting for Luke to make his play, is thinking about a scam he once ran on the planet Pesmenben IV. Just an inside joke – my grandfather's name was Ben Pesmen, and I think all my artistic genes come from that side of the family.)

"Blood lust and belligerence were testing new levels" [87] *on Jabba's Sail Barge, as the party grows more out of control before the execution of the prisoners. It brought to mind, for me, what were called "Celebration Lynchings" in the South, in the '20's and '30's – grand, often drunken picnic events, where innocent Black men were hung before a crowd of thousands. Those death parties were also "a long time ago," but not long enough, and bloodlust in the world doesn't seem to get much tamer as time goes on.*

Threepio is being forced to translate an argument between Ephant Mon and Ree-Yees, with Salacious Crumb kibbitzing. It ends in a fistfight that Threepio uses as an excuse to fade into the crowd – where he bumps into Artoo, who's serving drinks. Threepio is surprised to see

Artoo here, but Artoo seems confident, even nonchalant. Which annoys C3PO, who's quite upset at the prospect of Master Luke's imminent execution.

Jabba, further excited to see the fistfight unfolding before him, tugs on the leash that holds Leia by the neck. Pulls her close to him, and forces her to drink from his glass. It's disgusting, but Leia closes her eyes and tries to appear obedient – waiting for her moment. She consoles herself that there are worse things than touching this creep.

This leads her to think about some of those worse things. Like the night Lord Vader had her injected with chemicals by his pain-droids, and tortured her to get information about the location of the Rebel base. She'd almost broken, but she'd endured those agonies and degradations – just as she can endure Jabba.

At this point, I wrote a whole page that got cut in the final novel, describing Leia's specific memories of Vader's torture of her. Cut, I assume, because the additional creep-factor was just too much, once we come to realize Vader is her father.

But moments like these were an opportunity to get inside Leia's head, to give her some depth that the movie was unable to develop. I especially liked getting us all to feel revulsion at Jabba – knowing the satisfaction we'll feel when he finally gets his due.

Here are my handwritten pages of Leia's internal monologue, and my typewritten cut-and-paste version, as well. Cut-and-paste was real, back in the day. No computers. The horizontal lines you see are typewritten sections from another sheet of paper, cut and pasted down on the main body of the manuscript. The yellowing of the page is real, too.

This omitted passage would have gone on page 41 of the paperback – filling in the space from the line, "with a natural, inner strength," to the line, "She slid a few feet away from Jabba." In my handwritten manuscript below, there are almost two pages of Leia's memories of her torture by Vader, followed by the single typewritten page.

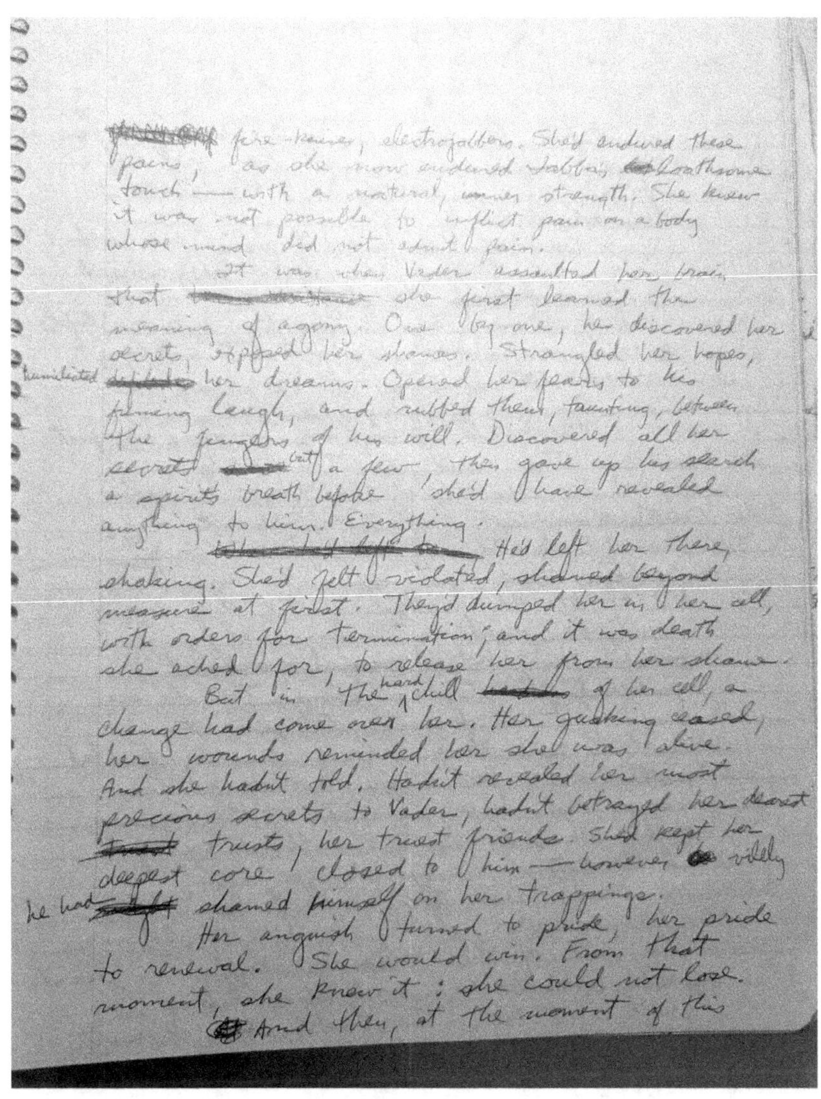

Handwritten original manuscript first page of Leia's memory of her torture by Vader. Photo courtesy of the Author.

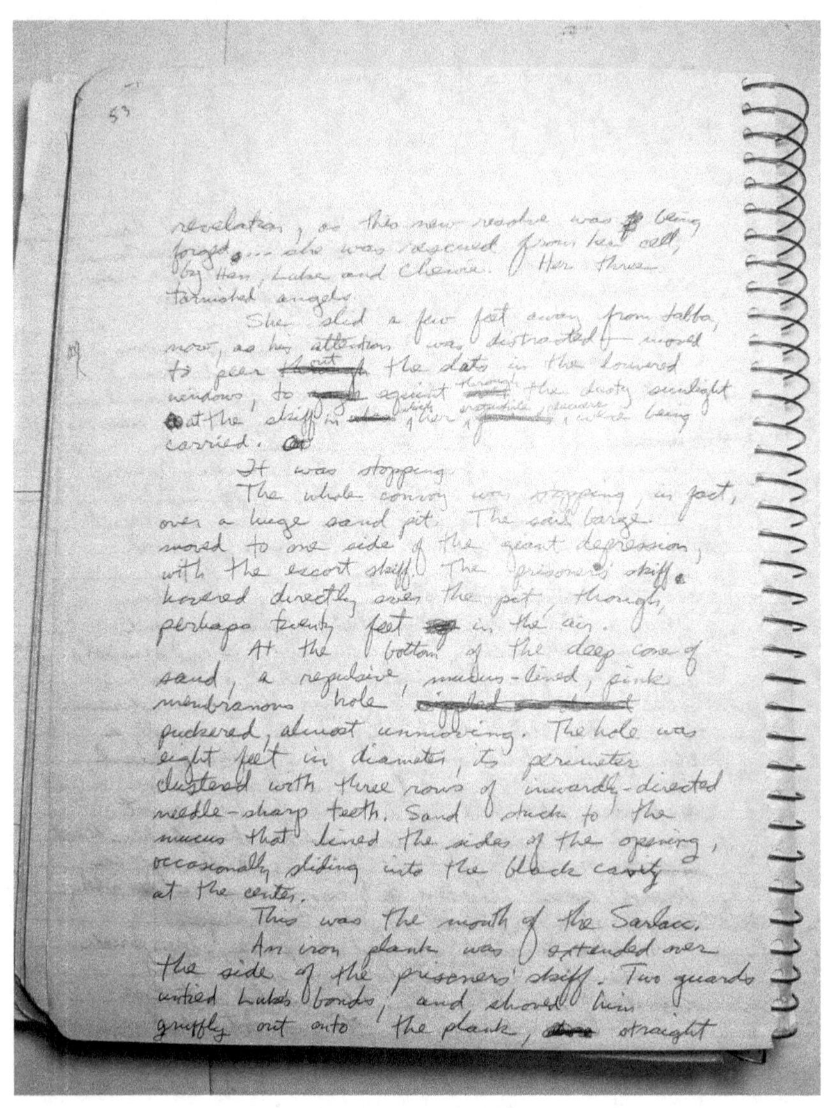

Handwritten original manuscript second page of Leia's memory of her torture by Vader. Photo courtesy of the Author.

46.

with a natural, inner strength. She knew it was not possible
to inflict pain on a body whose mind did not admit pain.

It was when Vader assaulted her brain that she first learned
the meaning of agony. One by one, he discovered her secrets,
exposed her shames. Strangled her hopes, humiliated her dreams.
Opened her fears to his fuming laugh, and rubbed them, taunting,
between the fingers of his will. Discovered all her secrets
but a few, then gave up his search a spirit's breath before
she'd have revealed anything to him. Everything.

He'd left her there, shaking. She'd felt violated, shamed
beyond measure at first. They'd dumped her in her cell, with
orders for termination; and it was death she ached for, to
release her from her shame.

But in the hard chill of her cell, a change had come over
her. Her quaking ceased, her wounds reminded her she was alive.
And she hadn't told. Hadn't revealed her most precious secrets
to Vader, hadn't betrayed her dearest trusts, her truest friends.
She'd kept her deepest core closed to him -- however vilely he
had shamed himself on her trappings.

Her anguish turned to pride, her pride to renewal. She
would win. From that moment, she knew it: she could not lose.

And then, at the moment of this revelation, as this new
resolve was being forged...she was rescued from her cell,
by Han, Luke, and Chewie. Her three tarnished angels.

She slid a few feet away from Jabba, now, as his attention
was distracted -- moved to peer out the slats in the louvered

Original typewritten manuscript page describing Leia's memory of her torture by Vader. Photo courtesy of the Author.

You can see evidence of the old cut-and-paste in that last type-written page.

After that redacted, tortured memory and interlude, the published novel resumes…

Leia senses the Sail Barge stop, and looks out the slatted window to see the convoy paused over a giant sand pit – at the bottom of which is "a repulsive, mucus-lined, pink, membranous hole" surrounded by "rows of inwardly-directed, needle-sharp teeth," with a "black cavity at the center." [88]

"This was the mouth of the Sarlacc." [89]

And this is where our heroes are about to be thrown. All I had to work from was a black and white photograph of the Sarlacc pit, but I imbued it on the page with the most graphic, physical, colorful, horrific prose I could come up with.

I have so much fun writing creepy creatures.

"An iron plank was extended over the side of the prisoners' skiff." [90] *Thus begins the first move in this battleground game of chess. Walking the plank, of course, is the hallmark of the pirate adventure, putting this chapter of Star Wars firmly in the continuum of great buccaneer tales. In this case the guards untie Luke's hands, the reasons for which are obscure to me. Maybe Jabba wanted to see him flailing? Certainly, he needs his hands for what comes next – so maybe Luke mind-tricked the guards into releasing his bonds. In my mind, that's what happened.*

He takes a moment to let the desert "warm his soul" – for, as mentioned earlier, this would always be his home. He winks at Leia on the Barge, and she winks back – they must be Jedi-mind connected by this point – and Jabba has Threepio make a speech, hoping Luke will die honorably. This statement coming out of Threepio's mouth doesn't scan well for him, it's against all his programming to speak happily of his master's death.

Jabba informs them he will entertain pleas for mercy, and Han shows his characteristic bravado. But Luke is calm. "Jabba, this is your last chance… Free us or die." [91] *It seems like a hopeless threat, given the circumstances. But as earlier, it seems like an un-Jedi-like sentiment, again suggesting Luke hasn't realized his full Jedi potential. Jabba's court laughs — but Artoo secretly rolls up to the top deck of the Barge. Something is afoot.*

Jabba gives a thumbs down. Luke gives Artoo a signal, and Artoo ejects an object in a high arc toward Luke. Luke jumps off the plank — catches it on the way down — lets the rebounding plank spring him high in the air — where he catches what Artoo has thrown. Luke's lightsaber. Game on. And now it's full ahead war.

This is Luke's own lightsaber, that he made himself in Obi Wan's old hut on the other side of Tatooine — and which we realize now is what we saw him inserting into Artoo at the very beginning of this story. And he wields it "as if it were fused to his hand." [92]

As in any war, once the first shot is fired, all plans are moot. A lot of things are happening at once. As Lando grapples with a guard, the helmsman falls over the side into the Sarlacc's mouth — with a horrific scream. Another guard falls to the side of the sand pit — and an oozy tentacle darts out of the Sarlacc's mouth, pulling the soldier to his thousand years of digestive doom. Showing us physically exactly what the stakes are.

As Jabba shouts orders to his minions, Leia sees her chance. She jumps behind him, grabs the chain that tethers her to him, wraps it around his many-chinned throat from behind, and pulls with all her strength. "The small metal rings buried themselves in the loose folds of the Hutt's neck, like a garrote." [93] *I wanted to give Leia a little help with the strangulation, and help the reader feel Jabba's death struggle.*

He almost breaks her grip, with his huge mass. Yet Leia ignores her pain, and focuses "all her life-force… into squeezing the breath from the horrid creature." Jabba's "reptilian eyes began to bulge from their sockets… his oily tongue flopped from his mouth… until he finally lay still — deadweight." [94-95] *I really wanted to make this a testament to Leia's strength of will.*

Leia will soon sever the chain, but in this moment, she's freed herself from this despicable monster. As I mentioned earlier, it's my deepest hope that thousands of young girls who read this in the book, internalized it, and grew up with the strength of knowing they didn't have to take the kind of sleazy, power-mad depredations men like Jabba dole out.

As Luke grabs his laser sword to ignite the battle at the Sarlacc Pit, Boba Fett quickly goes into action. We haven't seen the famous bounty hunter fight before, we've only heard about his exploits, and watched him load the carbonited Han onto his ship in the last episode. We see him now, but it's so chaotic on the skiff, it's hard to keep track of all the things going on.

Boba Fett flies down to Luke's skiff from Jabba's Barge, and aims his gun at Luke – but Luke cuts it in half with his light saber. Fett wraps Luke in a cable, but Luke cuts it free and knocks Fett unconscious. So maybe Fett wasn't such a formidable foe after all.

Meanwhile, a cannon blast from the Barge throws Lando overboard into the sand pit, where he slides slowly toward the Sarlacc's mouth.

The other skiff attacks the prison boat, and Luke jumps into the midst of a dozen guards, taking a page from Boba Fett's opening maneuver, and following a Jedi rule-of-thumb: "When outnumbered, attack."

Han, still blind, grabs a spear to hold down to Lando, to pull him back up on board. But now Boba Fett is back up, taking aim at Luke, who's decimating the guards on the other skiff. Chewie barks at Solo to swing his spear at Fett, but Han swings it the wrong way. Chewie yells again, Han course-corrects – and hits Boba Fett in the back, igniting his rocket pack.

The jet shoots Boba Fett over the skiffs, ricocheting him into the side of the sand pit – and straight into the mouth of the Sarlacc. Chewie tells Han what happened, and Han wishes he could have seen it. It surely was a satisfying moment, to see the bounty hunter who froze Han in carbonite meet his just desserts.

Of course, Boba Fett will return in another book, another movie, and ultimately his own TV series – so he did manage to escape from the Sarlacc's belly. But for now, it's just another passing moment in the fog of war.

More chaos in the battle at the Sarlacc Pit. A deck gun on the Barge hits the prisoners' skiff, knocking it on its side and sending Han over the edge, where he dangles from the rail by his foot. Chewie is tangled up in debris elsewhere. Luke wipes out the guards on the second skiff, then begins hand over hand climbing up the wall of the main Barge, to dismantle the deck gun that's doing so much damage.

Leia is assisted by Artoo's cutting tool, to sever the chain tying her to the dead Jabba. They run out together, but pause when they see Threepio *lying on the floor, his eyeball getting pulled out by Salacious Crumb, the reptile-monkey. Artoo gives the monkey a zap, as Leia helps Threepio up, and the three of them run out the door.*

The barge deck gun hits the tilting skiff again, knocking it even more sideways. Chewie is jolted loose, but he manages to hang on with one hand, while he grabs Han's leg with the other — as Han tries to reach Lando, who slides a little further down the sand pit every time he tries to move.

The tricky part in all this is maintaining a sense of comedy in the midst of thrilling battle. It's a little easier because we know the characters, and we love to see them laughing in the face of long odds — and as Han always says, "Don't ever tell me the odds." [96]

Luke reaches the deck gun just as the gunner is about to let off the coup de grace on the dangling chain of Chewie to Han to Lando. One of the gunners shoots the light saber from Luke's hand, though — exposing his artificial hand that replaced the one Vader had cut off. It gives him pause — again to reflect, even momentarily, on all he's lost.

The main gunner shoots at the prison skiff again — tipping it further down. Far enough that Han is able to actually grab Lando's outstretched wrist. Solo yells at Chewbacca to pull them back up — but at that moment one of the Sarlacc's tentacles slithers out of its mouth and grabs Lando around the ankle.

Again, the situation has gotten even worse — but we can somehow create a comic element out of it, because it's so <u>much</u> worse. Wounded comrades, tipping skiff, hanging on for dear life, slipping down a sand pit, deck cannons shooting at them… and now a Sarlacc tentacle? It's deadly… but laughable.

The deck gunners line up their sights for the final kill shot — but Leia has commandeered the deck gun at the other end of the Barge — and she wipes out the main deck gun with a single blast. Leia rocks! And it's nice to see her save the others for a change.

Which brings us to the end of the battle at the Sarlacc Pit. Using one of the big deck guns, Leia blasts the other big gun that's about to destroy the skiff where Chewie and Han are trying to pull Lando from the clutches of the Sarlacc's tentacle. As she does that, Luke Force-grabs his light saber from the deck and decimates the guards surrounding him. He shouts at Leia to point her gun down toward the deck.

Artoo knows what this means. I think Luke must have pre-programmed him for this moment. Artoo beeps instructions to Threepio, who refuses the order. But Artoo just bumps him off the Sail Barge, down to the sand, and jumps down after him.

Meanwhile, the Sarlacc tentacle is pulling on Lando's leg, while Han still holds on to him. Chewbacca grabs a laser pistol to shoot the tentacle, but it's too far for accuracy. So Han tells Chewie to give him the gun. Lando protests: "I thought you were blind!" Solo reassures him: "I'm better." Cracking jokes in the face of death. [97-98]

Somehow this doesn't reassure Lando, but he doesn't have a lot of say in the matter. Han gets the gun from Chewie, squints, pulls the trigger, and hits the tentacle — which lets go of Lando and slithers back into the Sarlacc's mouth. The mighty Chewbacca pulls Han back onto the skiff — along with Lando, who Han is still holding on to.

Back on the great Barge, Luke gathers Leia up in one arm, and grabs a rope dangling from the rigging. This is a wink to the audience — a callback to the same maneuver in the first movie, when Luke threw a grappling hook to the rafters, grabbed Leia, and swung them to safety by rope. It's a classic pirate movie trope - which connects it to the earlier moment at the start of this battle, when Luke was made to walk the plank.

As Luke leaps off the Barge, he kicks the deck gun trigger — and the blast goes straight down through the deck, where Leia had aimed it. The Barge starts massively exploding, while Luke and Leia swing on the rope to the skiff where their friends await them — and Chewie, Han and Lando help them aboard.

They sail the skiff over to where C3P0 and R2D2 are half buried in the sand, and haul them out with a giant electromagnet. And as Jabba's Barge continues to explode and burn, our heroes have "a great, long moment of hugging, laughing, crying, and beeping." [99] The catharsis after the crisis.

As the Sail Barge erupts in conflagration, they sail off into "the scorching afternoon light of Tatooine's twin suns." [100] Like they've been in hell, and now they're leaving.

That's the end of Chapter 2 in the book, and the end of ACT I of this adventure in the movie, as well. Our team has re-met, sacrificed, fought, overcome a mighty enemy – and they're all closer for it. Recharged, and ready to take on the even mightier enemy they know awaits them.

We can expect ACT 2 to involve a change of venue, increasing obstacles, and a rededication to the original Call to Adventure – to destroy the Death Star.

CHAPTER TEN
STRUGGLES WITH THE BLANK PAGE

WHEN TAKING ON my own mighty enemies, I've always had a tendency to either leap into the breach, come-what-may, or over-prepare. For *Poltergeist*, I leapt. Approaching the blank page of the *Jedi* novelization, I made a list of questions.

The following is a page of notes I made for myself, and for George Lucas, and then crossed out each list item as it was addressed. It's difficult to read, I know, due to the cross-outs, but I'll decipher it in the pages following the scribbles.

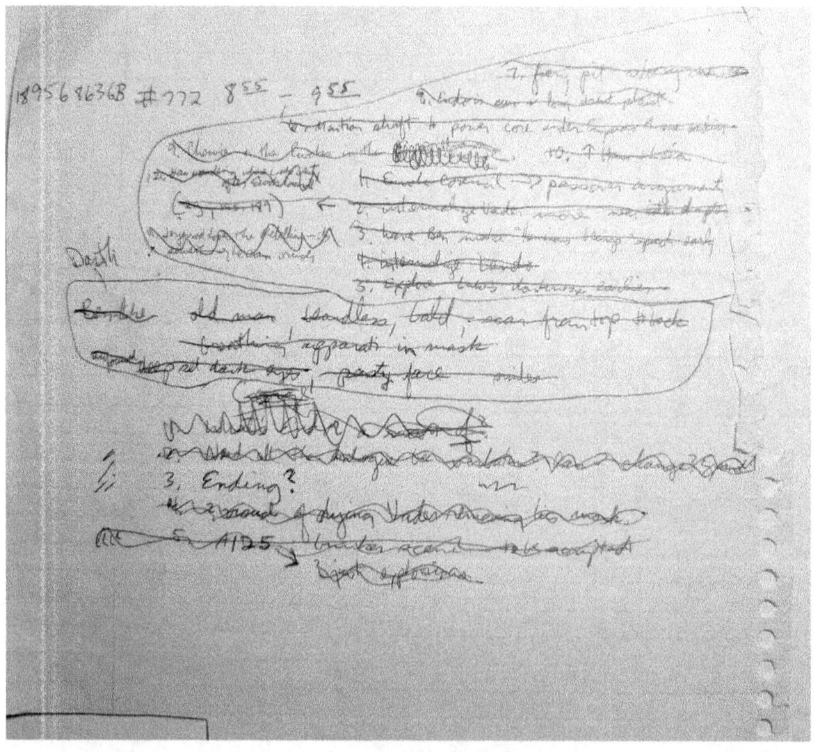

Notes scribbled to myself to ask George Lucas before starting writing on the novelization.

First, the numbers in the upper left – 189568636B. I have no idea what those refer to.

This is followed by #772, which was the airline flight number I took from LAX to SFO, to go talk to George with my questions. 8:55-9:55 is the ETD and ETA. I was flying either PSA or Southwest, but can't remember which. It was the regional airline whose flight attendants used comedy material during their pre-flight instructions. "When we land, be careful opening up the overhead compartments, because, as you know, shift happens."

These light numbers are followed by a boxed-in section of 12 numbered out-of-order items. Out of order because I ran out of space after item 5, and began listing other notes wherever I had the space. Not really thinking ahead. I'll take them in the order they're listed.

7. fiery pit story with Vader and Ben (the c with a line over it is the medical notation meaning "with.") This note refers to the laser swordfight between the two young men at the lava pools of Mustafar, where Anakin, beaten by the young Obi Wan, loses his legs, slides partway into the lava, and begins his transformation to Vader. This scene wasn't in the *ROTJ* script, and wasn't seen until the conclusion of *Revenge of the Sith*, the 3rd prequel. I asked George what that final duel was, what their falling-out was about. He outlined it, vaguely and briefly, so I got to refer to it in broad terms when Force-Obi Wan talks to Luke.

8. Endor's sun & long absent planet This was just a note to include something about this element that was never mentioned in the script. I asked George about it and he just shrugged. I didn't end up contributing much more than that in the novel; just a passing reference on Page 1 of the Prologue: "At the feathered edge of the galaxy, the Death Star floated in stationary orbit above the green moon Endor – a moon whose mother planet had long since died of unknown cataclysm and disappeared into unknown realms." [101] I wanted to go back and elaborate on that history, but never got around to it.

6. Mention shaft to power core under Emperor's throne earlier This was to establish the location of the shaft where the Emperor would ultimately get thrown to his doom, so that piece of geography didn't come out of nowhere at the end of the story.

9. Chewie & the Ewoks in the Ewok village I had in mind making a bigger connection between the Wookiee and Ewok species, because they looked so similar, but I don't think I ever went anywhere with it. Not sure why I crossed out the last words here so vigorously.

10. ^ Han & Leia I thought their relationship needed beefing up, so I deepened it where there were opportunities – like going into their feelings in the moments around Leia releasing Han from carbonite. "She looked at him a long moment, her blinded love," and, "He too was flooded with emotion…"[102-103] You know, all that mushy stuff.

12. Han wondering where Luke went after Ewok Council After the Council, Luke tells Leia they are both children of Vader, and they hug – the embrace seen by Han. Luke leaves to confront Vader, and Han goes down to talk to Leia – misreading her relationship with Luke, and trying to suppress his jealousy. My note here had to do with that, and Han wondering if Luke's absence had something to do with Leia.

1. Ewok Council > Passover arguments I was working on things our heroes could say that would convince the Ewoks to join the Rebel fight against the Emperor. There were obvious moral reasons, like good vs. evil, and pragmatic reasons like the Death Star would likely destroy Endor by sapping all its energy. But I was looking for the kind of interesting, philosophical issues that get raised at Passover Seders. Like "Treat the stranger as you would be treated, for we were once strangers in a strange land." That is, ask the Ewoks to treat the underdog refugee Rebels as part of their own family. Or analogizing God to the Force, how there is a piece of that Oneness in all of us. The argument that finally sways them is Leia's: "Do it for the trees."[104] Comparing us all to the *leaves* on the trees, facing a great forest fire. Kind of a pantheistic argument, with hints of climate change to come.

2. Internalize Vader more near later chapters < eg, ms. 189
This is pretty self-explanatory. When I look at my manuscript page 189, I see it's during the final 3-way confrontation between Vader, Luke, and the Emperor. Vader is secretly contemplating how he will overthrow the Emperor and assume the throne with his son, Luke, at his side. Vader senses fear in the Emperor, and intends to capitalize on it – as the Emperor notifies Luke he's about to have the Death Star destroy the entire Rebel fleet.

3. Have Ben make "luminous beings" speech early This is to foreshadow the Force-images of Obi Wan, Yoda, and Vader appearing at the very end of the story. To reinforce that even Vader is a "luminous being."

11. Jerjerrod loves the Rebellion – it's something he can crush Just a small insight into what makes this relatively minor character (at this point in the canon) tick.

4. Internalize Lando Lando got kind of short shrift in the first draft, so I went back and did several pages of inserts to describe what he was thinking and feeling at various junctures. As I've mentioned before, this is a common process of mine, to make the first draft more of a skeleton plot story, and then go back to infill with internal monologue, memories, motivations, etc, on subsequent drafts. This is also where I inserted his memory of Pesmenben IV, in homage to my grandfather.

5. Explore Luke's darkness earlier I went back and gave hints about how like Vader Luke actually was in some ways. They both lacked patience. They both felt satisfaction defeating a foe. When Luke warns Jabba if he doesn't let them go, Jabba will die, "Luke was unable to suppress the satisfaction in his voice." [105] So Luke, too, can enjoy killing an enemy. And there are moments pausing on the physicalization of the subtext – that is, on physical embodiments of what lurks beneath. Like when Luke takes a moment to look at his mechanical, damaged hand – like his damaged soul – that connects him so deeply to the man who cut it off.

These numbered notes are next followed by a second, boxed-in area, indicated by the word **Darth**. These are characteristics I wanted to give Vader when his mask came off at the end of the book. These attributes are:

Ben-like   old man,   beardless,   bald,   scar from top to back
Breathing apparati in mask
Unfocused deep set dark eyes,   pasty face   smiles

I was trying to make the first visual we have of his naked face show the first manifest inklings of his humanity. A Ben-like gentleness, an old man, bald, scarred, unfocused, and smiling. I also wanted to make it clear that without the internal breathing apparatus, he would soon die – which gave him a vulnerability that hadn't been obvious before.

And finally, these notes to self are followed by the scratched-out heading **George** above a list of questions I had for him.

1. What's Endor a moon <u>of</u>? Discussed above.

2. Need all the dialogue be verbatim? Can I change? Expand? The answer to this was yes, up to a point. Some of the dialogue felt stilted or wrong to me, and he said I could modify whatever I needed to, as long as it didn't change the story. I did expand quite a bit, in various scenes – though the one big addition I made, a whole section about Leia's backstory, he cut entirely, since it contradicted the backstory he already had in mind for the prequels.

3. Ending? This is about the note I wrote him, already discussed, about how he might change the ending. As referenced earlier, I thought the current ending was too similar to the end of *Star Wars Episode IV*, and I had a way of changing it slightly and raising the stakes, a change that would require only one extra pickup shot. He didn't go for it. I was extremely ambivalent about bringing this challenging idea up in person to George – and ultimately didn't, sending him a letter instead.

4. ? visual of dying Vader removing his mask I never got sent a photo of what he actually looked like under the mask, so I had to imagine it from George's description.

5. A/25 bunker scene – to be scripted > ? just explosion This refers to a late addition script page that I didn't get sent, and didn't have access to. So I just made it up in the novel.

If *Poltergeist* was the first act of my Hollywood career, *Jedi* was my Act II – and that was how I prepared for it.

Our heroes, meanwhile, have just escaped Jabba and the Sarlacc Pit – now it was time for them to launch themselves into their own Act II… with Chapter 3 of the novel.

ROTJ – CHAPTER 3, PAGES 52-67

So begins ACT 2, moving to different locations, and refocusing on the ultimate challenge – blowing up the Death Star.

With Jabba and his court dead at the Sarlacc Pit, our companions walk through a Tatooine sandstorm to get to the Millennium Falcon and Luke's X-Wing. Han's vision is returning as the carbonite sickness wears off, and he finds himself deeply grateful that his friends would risk so much to save him. He's usually such a sarcastic cynic, this feeling is new for him, and it makes him a little uncomfortable, and a little confused.

But it also makes him humbled in a way he's never been. Always before, he was the loner, the cowboy, the rogue. But now: "Once, he was alone; now he was a part." [106] *A part of something bigger than himself.*

(NOTE: I'd rewrite it slightly differently if I were working on this draft today. As a matter of wordplay, I might say: "Once, he was apart; now he was a part." It also makes me think of a line in a song I wrote many years later, *Waterline* – if it were sung by someone like Han, having a similar insight: "Thought I was a loner/I was just alone.")

The others all see the change in Han as well. It's a gentle moment for everyone – the recognition of a friend who is evolving.

Then it's all business, and they're anxious to get to the Rebel Base – except for Luke, who tells them, "I have a promise I have to keep first… to an old friend." [107] *He doesn't say who that is, but we all know he means Yoda.*

So the group splits up – Han, Leia, Chewie, Lando, and Threepio in the Millennium Falcon, to get back into the rebellion; and Luke in the

X-Wing with Artoo, where he pauses to look at his damaged hand: the exposed wires and titanium bones replacing the hand Vader cut off. It's a reminder of what the stakes are, and also of the deeper meaning this conflict has for Luke than for the others. On the one hand (pun intended) he sees the beginnings of his terrible transformation to becoming his father, sliding into the Dark Side. On the other hand, this is about bringing down his father.

He pulls a glove over the damage – he doesn't want to think about all those implications right now – "And for the second time in his life, he rocketed off his home planet, into the stars." [108] *Like the beginning of his Act Two.*

Luke is enormously ambivalent about his father – he knows he must destroy him, but destruction isn't a good Jedi trait, and besides, killing your own father is hardly an easy lift. All of this is, of course, worse than my ambivalence about approaching George in person with a suggestion that his ending wasn't great, and I had a way to make it better – but I used that feeling to help inform what Luke was going through.

My first encounter with serious ambivalence was as a 4th year medical student, when I did a psych rotation, up on the locked ward. Three of us had a conference with the attending psychiatrist before we entered the ward, so he could prepare us.

He told us the definition of schizophrenia according to Bleuler (Swiss contemporary of Freud) was characterized by the Four A's: Alogia (the weakening of logical thought), Autism (the predominance of inner life, distant from external reality), Ambivalence, and Affect disorder. Young Med 4 James Kahn raised his hand and said, "Why is ambivalence in there? We all have lots of ambivalence about a lot of things."

The psychiatrist nodded, and said, "When you see schizophrenic ambivalence, you'll appreciate the difference." That sounded suspiciously like the legal punt, "I can't tell you what pornography is, but I know it when I see it," but he was leading us up to the locked ward now, so I let it go.

And when the door opened to admit us, the first thing I saw was a naked patient sitting on the floor, screaming, "Yes! No! Yes! No!"

I guess, like Luke Skywalker, he was rocketing off into the stars. And I had a better understanding of schizophrenic ambivalence.

ROTJ – CHAPTER 3, continued

At this point we return to Vader, the object of Luke's ambivalent ruminations. Always good to touch bases with the main antagonist, to see what our heroes are up against, to keep reiterating just how evil this foe is. Vader is on the Death Star, awaiting the arrival of his master, the Emperor, now approaching on a shuttle from a recently arrived Destroyer. Once more I brought in inklings of Vader's still-human emotions – his excitement at Palpatine's visit. "A feeling of fullness, of power, of dark and demon mastery – of secret lusts, unrestrained passion, wild submission." [109] There's an almost sexual component to the power dynamic, as if Vader is in the thrall of his first desperate love affair. An intrinsically human emotion.

Yet physically, the Emperor was "shriveled with age and evil." [110] A master Svengali, yet with something of gentle regard for his acolyte, Vader. So when Vader kneels before him, he says, "Rise, my friend. I would talk with you." [111] Trying to draw a paradox between Palpatine's evil and camaraderie. Trying to make him a little more complex, like we all are.

And as they walk, we reveal that Vader isn't quite such a naïve flower after all. His secret plan is to learn all he can from Palpatine, hone all his mastery of the Dark Side – then usurp the Emperor's throne, destroy him, and rule the universe with his son at his side; his son in whom he'd already sown the seeds of darkness, his son whom he would shepherd fully to the Dark Side, to rule the universe together. His son, Luke.

The Emperor knows nothing of the specifics of Vader's plan – but he, too, wants to corrupt Luke to the Dark Side, and he senses Vader is eager to make that happen himself. He cautions Vader to have patience. It's a challenge Vader and Luke share. But it's a trait Vader must clutch, if he's to complete his ultimate betrayal of Palpatine.

ROTJ – CHAPTER 3, continued

Meanwhile, we find Luke on Dagobah, Yoda's home planet. Luke has mixed feelings about being here – there's that ambivalence again – for though this is the home of his mentor, the place also holds a dark piece of

Luke's soul. This is where Luke once had a vision of his own Dark Side – a vision of decapitating Vader, only to find out it was his own head he'd cut off. In dreamspeak, he was telling himself that he and Vader were one.

He finds Yoda waiting for him in his small hut – and Yoda is frail, now, his voice weakened. At 900 years old, his life force is fading. He tells Luke there's only one more thing Luke must do in order to become a full-fledged Jedi – he must confront Vader.

Luke wants to know if Vader is truly his father, and Yoda confirms it – though he's upset by the fact that Luke has already rushed to confront the Sith Lord before his own Jedi training was complete.

"Beware of anger, fear, and aggression," Yoda tells him. [112] (This tenet is so central to the Jedi philosophy, it's what caused George Lucas to change the original title of the movie from Revenge of the Jedi to Return of the Jedi. Revenge is so not a Jedi-like emotion. And this is Yoda's core truth.)

As Yoda lies on his deathbed, he tells Luke that when he is gone, Luke will be the last Jedi. But he urges Luke to pass on his knowledge. "There… is… another… sky…" [113] And then he dies. Disappears. His dying words foreshadow the next revelation, though it's couched in the poetic phrasing of "another sky." Maybe he was just talking about Jedi Heaven; but then Luke's last name is Skywalker, after all.

So Yoda is gone. Luke is grief-stricken and hopeless, with no one to turn to for guidance – until, of course, the shimmering image of Force-Ben shows up.

Force-Ben tells Luke his father, Anakin, betrayed his Jedi training and was seduced by the Dark Side of the Force, becoming Darth Vader – and Obi Wan takes the blame of that transformation on himself. He feels that his pride at the belief that he could train Anakin was what allowed Anakin to be seduced.

Luke is stunned by this story, and his first response is to think there must still be some good in Vader – that small kernel that was once Anakin. Obi Wan doesn't believe it, though. To him, Vader has become the epitome of evil. But Luke is horrified by the implications: "I can't kill my own father," he says. [114] This is Luke's bottom line, and for everyone paying attention, this isn't just foreshadowing – he's telling us how this is going to end. Or at least how it's not going to end.

Obi Wan describes his own plight at first trying to lure Anakin away from the Dark Side, until they had to battle over the molten fire pits on Mustafar (though that specific locale had not yet been named by George Lucas – he only described to me the broad outline of the light saber fight, and Anakin falling into a lava pit, his legs destroyed.) "He is more machine, now, than man,"[115] Ben tells Luke – Luke, whose own hand is now a machine. But just as Luke is now part machine, Obi Wan is telling us Vader is still part human, somewhere deep inside.

But Obi Wan also tells Luke that though Vader defeated him once, he hopes Luke has learned the lesson of patience, and that will serve him when he has to confront Vader for the final time. Luke reiterates that he can't fight his father. Obi Wan says, "You were our only hope."[116] Really putting a lot of weight on Luke's shoulders.

"But Yoda said I could train another,"[117] Luke protests. He's looking for any way out of this mess.

And now Obi Wan reveals the last secret he's always kept so close: "That other is your twin sister."[118]

Wait… what? This is the big revelation. Luke and Leia are siblings! They were separated at birth to protect them from the Emperor, who feared their double Jedi power. But it's a secret Luke must never reveal, or Leia will be in terrible danger.

Obi Wan goes on to explain to Luke that when Anakin left for the final time, he didn't know his wife, Amidala (not yet given a name in this trilogy,) was pregnant. (This storyline changed as the prequels emerged, but for now, this is the story I was given from George.) So the twins were separated and hidden to protect them.

Leia was taken to Alderaan, to be brought up as the daughter of Senator Organa. And Luke was taken by Obi Wan to Tatooine, to be raised by Obi Wan's brother, Owen.

(NOTE: The notion that Ben and Owen were brothers was an idea I made up. It felt to me, watching *Episode IV*, that they had a conflicted fraternal relationship. Owen warned Luke to "stay away from that crazy old man," though Ben's attitude toward Owen felt more tender. In my mind, they grew up on their father's farm, but Ben was restless, and wanted to become a Jedi Knight. There were family fights about it – their father wanted them both to take over the farm after he died, and he especially wanted Ben, the oldest, to take charge – but Ben listened to his own Call to Adventure and left. Shortly after that, their father died. Owen has always held Ben responsible for their father's death, and told him never to come back.

But one day Ben did come back to the family farm – with the infant Luke – and asked Owen to take him in. Owen refused at first – "I told you never to come back here!" – but his wife, Beru, insisted they keep the boy – they couldn't have children of their own. Owen finally relented – but made Ben promise never to return. Ben agreed – but remained living in the desert, a recluse, so he could watch over Luke from a distance at least.)

On Alderaan – Obie Wan continues his story to Luke – when Leia became part of the Rebel Alliance, she'd always been told by her adoptive parents that if she were ever in mortal danger, to contact Obi Wan on Tatooine. And that was the beginning of reuniting the twins. And though she's not a Jedi, the Force is strong in her, as it is in Luke. Obi Wan tells Luke it is Leia's destiny now to grow into her power – but it is Luke's destiny to face Darth Vader. A destiny he cannot escape.

And it's always been my destiny to be a storyteller.

Chapter Eleven
More Adventures in Hollywood

I was, in fact, a writer on a short-lived show called *The Storyteller*. Short-lived meaning it never aired. This wasn't until 1990, so now I'm making a memoir-jump into non-linear storytelling. *The Storyteller* was a show within a show. A Norman Lear production, the actual title of the series was *Jody Gordon and the News*. Thirty minute episodes, the premise was that Jody, a young news director at a local TV channel, gets home late every night and talks to her mother on the phone, telling her about her day. That goes on for 15 minutes – we just watch Jody on the phone – and then she ends the call, saying she has to go watch her favorite show, *The Storyteller*. She turns on the TV, and there she finds a man – played by David Strathairn – standing in his library. And he tells a 12 minute story, to camera. Strathairn's tale was the story that I (and three other writers) wrote.

It was really more of a radio show than a TV show, but it was fun writing a story for a raconteur, and watching him tell it. We wrote a dozen episodes, but the series got canceled before it aired, reputedly over contractual conflicts between Lear and the network. The idea of the show made a big imprint on me, though, and I've done it for myself in recent years – told short stories directly to camera on my YouTube channel. Because that was, you know, my destiny, I guess. There's still a bit of the Dancing Bear syndrome attached to it, but somehow it's less painful when I'm separated by a video screen.

That show never aired, but it quickly got me my next two writing jobs, for shows that did make it onscreen. The first was *Beyond Reality* – a kind of pre-*X Files* series about two academics who investigate supernatural phenomena, and get in trouble. Shari Belafonte was the professor of parapsychology, and she was the nicest person ever, though I couldn't quite wrap my head around her being a professor of parapsychology. The premise was that people would come into our professors' office with some personal paranormal problem – a haunted house, a poltergeist, a reincarnation, a telekinetic event – and our duo would investigate. The idea for the show I think came from the executive producer, Shukri, who had a family story he swore was true. So he wanted our show to be based on real people's personal stories, and then fictionalize them. And he wanted every show to start with a card that said True Stories.

We (the writers/producers) didn't feel we could make an assertion like that. So Shukri settled for Based on True Stories. One of our producers, Ricky Manning – who didn't believe in any of that paranormal lore – felt that was even a stretch. His suggestion was to start each episode with a card that said Truly Based on Stories.

The other show was *TekWar*, a future-cops action sci-fi series based on novels written by William Shatner, ghostwritten by Ron Goulart. In the 22nd century, people can have chips (called Tek) inserted into their brains that let them go into a meta-world of their dreams. (It ain't gonna take another century to get there, btw.) Tek is an addictive experience, though, so it comes with all the usual baggage of an addictive drug, including crime lords, prostitution, corruption, and greed – with the added wrinkles of identity crises and the nature of reality that come with brain-implanted computer chips.

Drop into this mix Jake Cardigan, a classic noir ex-cop who lost his badge, now working as a private investigator for a security firm run by – in the TV series – William Shatner himself. It was a fun show to write, and ran a couple years on USA Cable network. I got to know Shatner a bit when I went up to Toronto to be on the set of one of the episodes I'd written that he was directing. He was complimentary about my script, and we got along, but I felt uncomfortable with the sometimes demeaning way he treated some of the crew when he got angry. A lot of directors behave that way at times, it's a tense job, with lots of money on the line, all crammed into a tight shooting schedule, so I don't mean to single Shatner out for that kind of bad behavior; but I also wouldn't say we were pals in any way. The closest we ever got was maybe physically, bumping into each other at the bathroom door on the set.

Which reminds me of all the stars I've peed next to over the years.

The first time happened when I was pitching a story to some executive in the Producer's Building at Paramount. Not a memorable meeting, and when it was done, I went to the public bathroom down the hall. There were two urinals, separated by a shoulder-high divider, and as I was peeing in the one on the left, Sylvester Stallone walked in, and took the urinal to my right. He unzipped, turned his head to look me in the eye, and said, "Yo."

I was so intimidated, I dried up. Stopped peeing, couldn't finish. I smiled, nodded, zipped up, and left. Had to go downstairs to finish.

Next time was at the Egyptian Theater on Hollywood Boulevard. I was going to see a restored version of *The Vikings*, starring Kirk Douglas, Tony Curtis, and Janet Leigh. Douglas was going to be there to do a Q & A at the end of the film, and it was a film I loved, so I was excited to be there. Just before the movie was about to start, and everyone was seated, I decided to go to the bathroom. So I jumped out of my seat, ran down a long corridor – and when I got to the bathroom, there was a guard standing in front of it. "Can I go in there?" I asked. He nodded, so I entered.

There was a long line of urinals, all empty except for the one nearest the door, where Kirk Douglas was peeing. I walked all the way to the other end of the line, so as not to disturb him, and started peeing in the last one. A moment later a third guy entered, and there was something up with him. His arms were waving slowly but uncontrollably, and he had difficulty walking. Looked like choreoathetosis, or maybe cerebral palsy, or maybe just some kind of drug reaction. He was looking wildly all around, almost as if he were possessed. He went to a urinal halfway between me and Kirk.

After a moment, Kirk and I both leaned back while still peeing, and gave each other a look behind this guy's back – like "what's up with that?" – then we shrugged, and went back to peeing. I left first.

My last star-urinal encounter was at the Friar's Club, on Little Santa Monica Boulevard, in Beverly Hills. It was at Milton Berle's Memorial Roast shortly after he died in 2002. All the great, old Hollywood comedians of my youth were there, mostly making jokes about the size of Berle's reputedly enormous genitalia. Alan King, Don Rickles, Sid Caesar, Carl Reiner, Mel Brooks. At some point, I had to go to the bathroom. Caesar and Reiner were just walking out, and as I was doing my business at the urinal, I realized it was Red Buttons standing by the sink, telling a story to someone. Of course, I listened.

It was a long, involved tale about an argument he was having with his wife, which he walked out on, to go pick up his dry cleaning. Then there was a long detour about the dry cleaning story, and by that time I was done peeing, and couldn't stand there much longer, though I wanted to hear the end of the story. So I went to the sink and washed my hands as fastidiously as I reasonably could, while he was going on about a missing pair of pants. Finally, I had to stop washing, and proceeded to dry my hands.

Now Red got to the part of his story where he pulled into his driveway, went to the front door with the dry cleaning over his shoulder, opened the door… "And waddaya think I saw?"

I'm standing there watching him, still drying my hands, and he turns to me and says, "Do you mind? I'm telling a story here!"

I excused myself and left, before the punchline. When I got back to my table, though, I told the guy next to me what I'd just heard. He shook his head with a smile, and said, "Red never tires of telling that story. He came inside to find his wife having sex with the maid."

Illicit sex, of course, reminds me of *Melrose Place*, on which I wrote for five years, eventually becoming Co-Executive Producer. Which reminds me, I got the *Melrose Place* gig based on a script I'd written for a previous series that had only run one year – *Medicine Ball*. Kind of an early iteration of *Grey's Anatomy*, about interns and residents at a teaching hospital. My script was titled "Sex, Lies, and Adhesive Tape." Which may have been what attracted the *Melrose Place* producers.

Melrose Place was great fun, though I began on shaky ground. I'd never written a soap opera before, so I was unsure how to perform in the Writer's Room. Consequently, I spent the first week or so being rather quiet, just listening and absorbing. The format, I learned, was to do what's called a "Cold Open," with the show opening on some interaction between two of the 10 stars, the scene ending on some dramatic twist or outburst – then cutting to the show's credits, and on to the first commercials, before returning to the show.

But a week into my new job, the other writers were discussing an opening scene, then cutting to a *second* opening scene between two other characters, before cutting to credits and commercials. I raised my hand, perplexed, and said, "So we're doing a bipartite opening?" There was a long silence, and then Chuck Pratt, one of the producers, said, "He speaks! And it's gibberish!"

Everyone laughed, and it broke the ice on my entry into this new world. But it made me reflect on how that was kind of my whole story. My interior fantasy life has always been rich. Full of adventure, aliens, monsters, heroes, deceptions, clues, wounds, collapses, revelations, and triumphs. Yet when I speak – or write, which is my preferred method of speech – it can sometimes come out gibberish in public. Untranslatable, baffling, inconsequential, confusing.

Although I'd written for other shows before, Melrose Place was my proving ground in television. Being in the Writer's Room, trading ideas and stories and jokes and personal lives with other writers on a daily basis was just the best thing ever. Writers, I discovered, were generally smarter than the shows they wrote, I think even on the really smart shows.

We'd come up with stories and organize them into "beats," and then treatments, and then scripts, and then rewrites over and over – 32 episodes a year. Every six weeks we'd spend a couple days creating a 6-10 page document projecting the story arcs for the next six weeks of shows, for every character. Like in the first episode of this arc, Amanda and Peter might get married, and in the sixth episode they'd get divorced, and along the way Peter would invest in a bad stock, and Amanda might have an affair with Michael.

Then all the writers and producers would march up to the top floor of the Spelling Building on Wilshire, and one of us – usually Frank South, the showrunner – would spearhead pitching the whole thing to Aaron, a gnome-like guy who was alternately sweet and cranky. Spelling's producing partner, Duke Vincent, was rarely there. Rumor was he'd bankrolled Spelling at the beginning of Aaron's producing career. Vincent was an ex-Navy jet pilot, one of the Blue Angels, so where he got Hollywood-level money to produce is anyone's guess, and there was a lot of speculation.

The writers' contingent in those meetings was led by Frank – a generous, kind, meticulous playwright – joined by Chuck Pratt, a big guy with a big presence and a joke for every occasion.

Spelling gave us all our notes on the six-week arcs, as well as on every script; notes that were generally unpredictable and often odd. For example, on the cover of one of my scripts, he wrote, "Great script! But you have Kimberly renting an apartment for $900 in a neighborhood I know very well, and you can't get anything there for less than $1400! Change it!" Well… okay, sure.

Sometimes in a six-week arc we'd insert a really goofy story point (Amanda's evil twin comes to town!) knowing he'd say to cut it – so he wouldn't be so focused on another beat we really wanted to keep but were afraid he might not like. We did that more often with network executives who – despite their inability to know how to tell a story – would sometimes try to exert control over the writing process. As long as Spelling had our backs, though, the network couldn't say too much, because Melrose was so popular.

We did some cool stuff too. One of our producers linked up with University of Georgia faculty artist Mel Chin to stage a kind of subliminal art show over a number of episodes from 1995 to 1997. Multiple artists from the University of Georgia and California Institute of the Arts created art pieces that were used subversively in various shows. For instance, in one episode, a pregnant Alison (Courtney Thorne-Smith) was draped with a quilt on which the chemical structure of the then illegal birth control pill RU-486 was stitched. Then at the end of that season, all the art was exhibited at the Museum of Contemporary Art in Los Angeles – and in an audaciously meta coup, two of the characters in the TV series

(Amanda and Kyle, played by Heather Locklear and Rob Estes) toured the art exhibition in one of their scenes together, making the exhibition itself part of the dramatic arc of the episode. Eventually the whole lot was auctioned off for various charities.

Producing a television series was a fascinating craft, combining high pressure, creative juices, unique skillsets, complicated interpersonal politics, and buckets of fun. It started in the Writer's Room, where seven of us would gather, spend a little time whining or crowing about our lives and the state of the world, and then get down to trying out story ideas. Often the writer who was up in the rotation to write the next script would bring in an idea, and then we'd spend a couple days wrestling it into a show. One of us would be up at the white board writing ideas and beats as they came up from the group – how the cold open would start, how the episode would end, what the first act climax might be, and so on. Someone was writing it all down on a computer, too. Then the writer of the moment would take the laptop notes, turn them into a beat sheet, a treatment of the story, turn that in to the group, get notes from the showrunner, and finally go off to write the script.

That writer had a week to write the first draft. Then all the writers would mark up that script with notes, the showrunner or other executive producer would compile them, and finally give them to the writer in a note session, alone in the office. The job of the writer in those sessions was to not be defensive, and to try to take every note. When I was the producer, I gave young writers one piece of advice about managing the taking of notes. If I said some particular scene wasn't working, the writer should say, "This is what I was trying to do. Is the scene not working because I shouldn't have tried to do that, or because I should have tried doing that but I did it poorly?"

Then the writer had around three days to turn in a second draft, on which one of the producers then did a final polish, and that final draft couldn't be more than 55 pages. (Rule of thumb was one page per minute of screen time.) Then that draft went into the production machine, where it got turned over to the actors, the director, and the heads of all the departments – camera, lighting, hair, makeup, wardrobe, props, casting, music, etc. It was a process of well-oiled, controlled chaos.

The writer and a couple producers and the casting director held casting sessions, in which actors were brought in to read for various guest roles. The music supervisor would come by our offices with suggestions for music placement. The producers would hold a Tone meeting with the director of the week. We had a stable of three or four directors, and then the occasional guest director.

The Tone meeting, held several days before the episode was shot, was where the director met with the showrunner, another producer, and the writer of the episode. The purpose of the meeting was for the writer-producers to tell the director the tone of the episode, what individual scenes were important, what emotional notes to hit, which scenes to direct with humor, or irony, or tension. The writer-producers also had strong ideas about some suggested shots, and how to keep "the look" of the show consistent with all the shows that came before. The director would talk about his own ideas (there were no women directors back then) concerning how to shoot the episode, camera set-ups, thoughts about relationships to emphasize, and so on. But it's the writers who run the Tone meetings.

Production meetings were always energizing. Led by the showrunner, the writer and the heads of all the departments sat around a big conference table and went through the script page by page, each department head talking about the issues on that page relevant to their department – what props were needed in this scene, how should the actor's hair look in this act, what mood should the lighting reflect in this interplay, what clothes should these two actors wear? It brought me right back to being a kid, playing all these make-believe games with my friends, telling each other what to do and how to do it.

Meanwhile, the actors were rehearsing with the director. And every day the writer got notes from the set, and from the departments, that necessitated more rewrites for individual scenes, leading to "revision pages" which were then reissued to everyone involved and inserted into the script, replacing what had come before. Each set of revision pages was a different color and date, to make sure everyone knew they were operating on the same, latest draft. Blue, pink, yellow, green, goldenrod. (The writers' bowling team name one year was The Goldenrods.)

Finally, after several days of rehearsals on the set, the show was taped (seven pages a day on a 50-55 page script), and then edited. The editor did the first cut, and then a couple more cuts with the producers sitting beside him, giving notes, changing sequences, deciding on dissolves versus cuts, sometimes losing or rearranging entire scenes – until the final product came in at 49 minutes, which made room for 11 minutes of commercials in a one-hour show.

When the final cut was done, it went to "music spotting," where the producers watched it with Eddie Arkin, the guy in charge of scoring the episode, and mutual decisions were reached about when to bring music into a scene, what it's tone should be, what instruments might be used.

Then at last there was "sweetening." We sat in a dark room in front of a theater-sized screen and went over the whole episode in fine detail, adjusting sound, adding foley (sound effects like footfalls, or a garbage can crashing in the street), doing fine-tuning edit tweaks. And finally, that episode was ready to air – while three or four other episodes were in various stages of the whole process. I found it demanding and exciting, and I think I brought my emergency room multi-tasking abilities directly to bear.

But it certainly wasn't all fun and games. There were disagreements, both personal and creative. There were power struggles, petty behavior, even some back-stabbings. Towards the end of the run, when it was clear we weren't going to get renewed past a seventh season, showrunner Frank, the nicest guy ever, was treated very badly by the powers-that-be.

One of my starkest, snarkiest memories had to do with Jack Wagner, who played Peter on the series. One of the male leads (though he would have likely called himself the star), Jack was a guy's guy – affable and genial, but he could be wound pretty tight inside. He always knew his lines cold, but before the taping phase he could be really demanding of the writers – demanding that his lines be changed, that is. These exchanges rarely got heated, but sometimes tense, there was a lot of back and forth, and sometimes, on camera, he'd say the line he wanted to say instead of the one that had been written for him.

He'd been pushing to direct an episode for a couple years, and finally Frank gave him a directing assignment. Alas, it was for one of my scripts. It's always a little nerve-wracking to see one of your scripts tackled by a first-time director. You want them to succeed, but they're learning the craft on the fly, with the clever, emotional, taut, intricately plotted masterpiece you just turned in. And the new director, in turn – since it is his first test drive – wants to do it all artistic and shit. Which brings us to the Tone meeting.

So in this Tone meeting, Jack said he had a great idea about how to shoot the scene in the clinic lounge between Peter and Michael (Jack Wagner himself, and Thomas Calabro). "Okay, we'll start in tight on a bagel getting buttered by a hand, we don't know whose, and the camera follows the bagel in close-up as it moves off the counter, and across the room, while the dialogue is going on off-camera, I'll do it all in a oner…"

"Whoa, stop, halt," said showrunner Frank. "First of all, we don't do oners."

A oner (pronounced "wunner") is a one-shot, a single tracking shot with no cutaways. The problem with oners is, there's nothing to cut to if a problem arises in a scene. If we want to lose a little dialogue in the middle of the oner, the picture on the screen would go from a moving bagel on the counter, to the same bagel suddenly traveling in midair five feet away. Instead, we need individual shots of the actors speaking their lines, so we have cutting options, different ways to edit, sometimes to accommodate bad line readings, or unsatisfying camera angles.

"Second of all," said Frank, "this isn't a scene about a bagel. This is about two cads vying for the same woman, and we want to see their faces, and their reactions to what the other guy is saying."

"No, no," said Jack, "it'll be great, because we think it's Peter buttering the bagel, but actually…"

But no. All three of us, Frank, Chuck and I, all ixnayed the agel-bay.

Except when the dailies came in – the taping of the scene in question – Jack had done the bagel oner. This led to some angry fights, recriminations, the elimination of the beginning of that scene, with the loss of that dialogue; and I, in particular, was left with a three-day stomach ache at the mutilation of my script.

Cut to the annual Spelling Christmas party at the Beverly Hilton Hotel on Wilshire Boulevard. Very fancy dress, all the celebs out in force. Parties like that always made me kind of uncomfortable. I never schmoozed well, I never knew quite what to say, I felt out of place among all the Hollywood royalty – but I was in the business, so I had to at least make an appearance. I went with my wife, Jill, of course, though she always hated those things even more than I did. At least I knew my co-workers; she knew no one. She said it also seemed to her like all the actresses were cupping their hands under their boobs and lifting them up and out, parading them around in front of themselves, like a gift, their breasts preceding them into every room, like a bedazzlement announcing every encounter; leading with bosom. Of course this was a slight exaggeration.

So we were standing in the midst of all the glamor, with a very loud band raising the ambient decibel level. We were pretending to be anthropologists studying a strange, newly discovered tribe, when I saw Jack Wagner and his beautiful soap opera (General Hospital) star wife, Kristina, talking to each other, all by themselves. I thought, "Okay, it's a Christmas Party, it's been a hard year, Jack's been a pretty reliable actor for the most part. It's time to bury the hatchet."

So I took Jill by the hand, walked up to the beautiful couple, made introductions, and made my peace. "Jack, I know we've had our differences, and maybe all of it didn't turn out as we'd hoped, but I just wanted to say I thought that scene you directed in the bar between yourself and Michael, that was really beautiful, wonderfully staged, great performances, great lighting, great camera work. Really nice job." And I meant it.

But then there was a pause; a pause that grew more awkward as it lengthened. I was feeling stranded, out on a limb. Finally, Jack's wife, Kristina, trying to lighten things up, nudged him gently in the ribs with a smile and a stage whisper, saying, "Jack, this is the part where you're supposed to compliment *him*."

Jack nodded; considered; looked at my chest, tipping his head slightly. "Nice tie," he said.

After *Melrose Place* wrapped, I did a one-off script for *Xena: Warrior Princess*, which was pretty cool. The episode was titled *The Abyss*. Got a lot of cred from my kids for that one. Then I got a gig as Supervising Producer on the last season of *Star Trek: Voyager*. I was so excited. I was assigned to work in Gene Roddenberry's old office on the Paramount lot. But there were a lot more politics in that room than I'd experienced before; it was toxic at times, about which the less said the less remembered. The bloom was starting to come off the rose. It just wasn't as much fun as it used to be. I do remember Raf Green as a great, young junior writer; and Bryan Fuller, who went on to run lots of great shows, knew more about the detailed lore of every *Star Trek* series than anyone I'd ever met.

After *Voyager* wrapped, I had a two-season run on a syndicated show called *Doc*, kind of a sweet series about a family practice doctor played by Billy Ray Cyrus (Miley's dad) and his friends in the clinic. We had good relationships in the Writer's Room, though the leadership could get toxic sometimes. It just goes that way on a lot of shows, I think, that the personalities who push their ways to the top get there with a kind of trigger-finger aggressiveness that I suppose is the reason they got into that position. Not always true, but it is a recurring theme.

In any case, after that my Hollywood jobs dried up. I couldn't get work. I made a couple bad choices (fired a great agent I shouldn't have, out of frustration), and I ran into some bad luck.

When I was writing for the show *Medicine Ball* (my episode "Sex, Lies, and Adhesive Tape"), the series was sued by a young doctor, a Resident at UCLA, who maintained his ideas had been stolen. I testified in deposition that his ideas were common stories in medical culture, told by many, and accessible to anybody.

Years later, when I couldn't get work for two years, I learned that the executive in charge of the network thought that *I* was the doctor who had sued them – so she blackballed my name, all their shows were told not to hire me, I was trouble. When I found out, I arranged a meeting with her, explained the mix-up, and she apologized profusely. But the damage was done. Once a writer hasn't worked in two years, people wonder why, and become reluctant to take meetings. I felt like I exuded what's called "flop sweat," an invisible aura of failure.

It was starting to feel like my career was being hobbled by a web of lies, misunderstandings, and vendettas – all of which swirl around the next segment of *Return of the Jedi*, along with smuggled plans, regrets, second thoughts, and heightened stakes.

ROTJ – CHAPTER 4, PAGES 68-82

Chapter 4 resets all the characters, everyone poised to plunge into the next element of the dramatic arc. Luke. Han, Leia, Chewy, Lando. The Rebel Alliance. Vader and Palpatine.

We open with Vader talking to Palpatine at his throne on the Death Star. In the second paragraph I go into some detail about the "black chasm" that channeled down to the core of the battle station, to the power unit that "reeked of ozone."[119] This is, of course, the abyss into which the Emperor is thrown at the end of the story, and I wanted to bring it up here so it didn't just feel like a convenient manhole at that final climax.

There's some backstory about Senator Palpatine's political maneuvering that catapulted him to the position of Emperor, using all the Dark forces at his disposal. So "his soul was the black center of the Empire."[120] The bad guy can be complex, even nuanced, but in the end he's gotta be the really big bad guy. Content in this position, Palpatine now tells Vader they will soon destroy the Rebel Alliance, and bring Luke over to the Dark Side.

Meanwhile, the entire Rebel fleet is gathered at the edge of the galaxy, led by Mon Mothma, herself once a Senator of the Republic, even as she was secretly organizing Rebel cells to resist the emergence of the Empire. Now the upper echelon of the Rebels – including, of course, Han, Leia, Chewie and Lando – get their marching orders from Mon Mothma about the attack on the Death Star. The smuggled plans have revealed a weakness – and furthermore, intelligence suggests the Emperor is on the battle station now. So destroying it could bring an end to the Empire.

Smuggled plans demonstrating a weakness in the Death Star's defenses that will allow it to be destroyed by lobbing a missile into its core is the same story that led to the destruction of the first Death Star in Episode IV. The element that raises the stakes in this narrative is that the Emperor is on the battle station, so he'll be destroyed as well, and with that, it is hoped, the Empire itself will collapse.

The Death Star is protected by an energy shield generated from the moon, Endor. The shield must be deactivated, and then the Death Star main reactor must be obliterated by a small attack force, to be led by Lando. The commando team going to Endor to take down the generator includes Han, Leia, Chewie, and, just for giggles, C3PO.

That's when Luke shows up, back from Dagobah, to say he'll join the commando team going to Endor. Leia hugs him, relieved at his safe return — but she senses something is up with him. And he's not ready to tell her yet that she's his sister. A lie of omission.

So off they all go, to their appointed assignments. As the stolen Imperial shuttle approaches Endor and requests clearance from the Death Star to lower the shield so they can land, tensions are high among Han, Chewie, Leia and Luke. They're not sure the stolen clearance code still works, and they're nervous about all the Star Destroyers and TIE fighters flying around. In typical Han fashion, he tells Chewie to "fly casual."[121] That was just a brilliant scripted line, embodying the entirety of Han's character in those two words. So thank you, Lawrence Kasdan (or George Lucas, if that was you).

The code works, the shield goes down, and the shuttle makes its way toward Endor. But Luke realizes that his Force-connection to Vader is a huge liability: Vader knows he's here, and Luke's presence could endanger the entire mission. "I shouldn't have come,"[122] he says. It's the beginning of his realization that his destiny is diverging from that of his comrades. They have to destroy the shield generator. He has to destroy Vader.

And he's not wrong. Because Vader, on his Star Destroyer, does sense a presence — and sets off to fly back to the Death Star, to tell the Emperor Luke is here. It's time to bring him over to the Dark Side.

These two beats — Luke's realization that Vader is here, and he has to face him; and the mirror of that, with Vader realizing that Luke is here, and he has to tell the Emperor so they can bring Luke over to the Dark

Side – constitute the mid-ACT 2 turning point, the midpoint crisis, the point of no return. The stakes are raised, and the goal no longer quite the same. Luke is no longer here just for the Death Star. Now it's personal.

I was once told by my agent, Ted Chervin, not to make it personal. "Don't go looking for love in all the wrong places," he said, quoting the line from the 1980 country song by Johnny Lee. Meaning I should stop pestering the producer who'd once shown an interest in me but now wasn't answering my calls. Meaning know when to quit. (Johnny Lee, incidentally, sang a song I wrote, *Love Handles*, in an episode on the Norman Lear sit-com, *E/R*. Alas, when I later called him to see if he'd sing any other songs I wrote, on any of his albums, he never answered. That's life in Hollywood. And that's looking for love in all the wrong places.)

My most poignant story about misplaced love was in the LA County ER. A 52-year-old lady kept coming in, twice a week, because of eye pain. I offered to examine her, but she refused. She wanted to be seen by Dr. Ellis, the ophthalmology resident who'd seen her before. He was the only one who could help. I beeped him, but he was in surgery, he wouldn't be out for two hours. The patient said that's all right, she could wait.

Two hours went by. I offered to see her again, she refused again. Another hour passed, finally Ellis showed up. She told him the pain was deep in her eye, like the last time – he'd have to use the big ophthalmoscope in the Eye Room to check it. The Slit Lamp.

They went in the Eye Room. No windows there, so the room got black when the lights were out and the door closed. So the patient's pupil could dilate as much as possible, so the lighted prism on the big mounted ophthalmoscope was able to peer past the enlarged pupil, deep into the eye, through the aqueous humor, through the patient's lens, all the way back to the retina.

I went about my other duties. Ten minutes later I got a call from surgery, they needed to ask Dr. Ellis a question. I opened the door to the Eye Room, paused to let my eyes accustom to the dark, to tell him he was needed elsewhere. I saw their two forms, sitting opposite each other, her chin on the chin rest, peering into the small, bright light; his face just inches away from hers, peering through his microscope into her eye. And I heard her whispering.

"You can see all the way into me, can't you... past the back of my eye, even... into my soul... no one has ever looked that deep..."

"I'm just looking into your eye," said Dr. Ellis, trying to sound professional, far more distanced than he physically was. "I can't find any reason for your pain..."

"You take my pain away..." she whispered. And she began to moan.

He stood up, turned on the ceiling light. "Okay, we're done here."

But she let out a huge, cathartic, orgasmic moan, and I could see her hand was up her dress. She pushed back from the scope on the table, extended her legs out in front of her, and really let go now, gasping, weeping tears of ecstasy.

Ellis and I looked at each other. "I think she loves you," I said.

He raised his hands. "I never touched her." He exited. I looked at the woman slumped in the hospital chair; and I could see, she was briefly pain free.

So maybe there is no wrong place to go looking for love. Looking for deep contact with another human being.

I think, in fact, separation from human contact may the greatest torture of the soul anyone can be subjected to. It's why solitary confinement in prisons around the world is the harshest punishment of all.

VIII

She was young, twenty-seven or so, with malignant lymphoma, histiocytic type. Her white blood cell count was actually zero at one point, but in any case, chronically so low during chemotherapy that she was always kept in reverse isolation. Which meant she had to stay in her room, door closed, window shut. Everyone who entered her room had to wear mask, cap, gown and gloves. This was all for her protection – she no longer had any white blood cells with which to fight infection, so she had to be kept in an environment which prevented exposure to any bacteria or viruses.

Which meant she rarely saw anyone. It was such a hassle to suit up in sterile paper gowns that her doctors saw her only on morning rounds, when they had to. Her condition was so depressing the staff avoided being around her anyway. Family and friends were afraid of "catching something," even though it was explained the isolation was for *her* protection, not theirs. She must have felt like she was being punished for having the disease, or maybe her hair falling out made her so ugly no one wanted to be near her.

Leo had been in strict isolation for a time, when he had the staph pneumonia; and except for my company, he had no visitors during that period. He was already blind from his diabetes, had lost all feeling in his hands and feet, and an auditory neuropathy was dampening all sound. But he said all that sensory deprivation was nothing compared to the social isolation.

The young woman's white count never did rise. In fact, she became aplastic and lost all her blood cells. She oozed blood from every orifice for a couple days, until a nurse went in to change the sheets one afternoon and found her dead, most likely bled into her brain.

Scores of people came to her funeral, I heard. So much easier to offer sympathy after the fact, than stare the fact in the face, in the moment, in the hospital.

But all human lives must come to an end, and so must all stories. And our Jedi tale is getting close.

CHAPTER TWELVE
THE STAKES ARE RAISED

ROTJ – CHAPTER 5, PAGES 83-103

As the second half of ACT 2 kicks in, the obstacles become greater, as battalions of Stormtroopers show up in increasingly greater numbers to thwart our mission.

We see Endor for the first time. Lush, verdant, rippling ferns – the exact opposite of the emptiness of space, the deserts of Tatooine, the high tech corridors of the Empire, and the gritty, dented hardware of the Rebel Alliance. In this bucolic Eden, our commando squad hides their stolen Imperial shuttle under a canopy of mulch and dead branches. Leia, Chewie, Han, Luke, Threepio, R2D2, and a handful of nameless supernumeraries. I referred to these Rebel commandos as "elite ground-fighters," though most of the fan world knows their kind as Redshirts. The group's mission is to destroy the Imperial field generator at its bunker some miles away, so the Rebel fleet can mount its Hail Mary attack on the Death Star. Someone's going to have to die, and these thankless souls have targets on their backs.

(NOTE: Not always totally thankless. In _Episode IV_, we were told a lot of brave Rebels died to get us the specs of the Death Star that showed us its weakness – and then in the film prequel, _Rogue One_, we got to see those brave Rebel deaths after getting to know some of the "Redshirts" personally.)

Before our heroes can even start out, though, they spot two Imperial scouts in a glen. Impetuously, Han runs out to take them down, with Chewie not far behind. Han is just so happy to be back in the fight, he's unrestrainable. Unfortunately, after a brief combat, two more Imperial scouts appear, and take off on their speeder bikes to warn the garrison. Leia grabs the bike of one of the two fallen scouts, and sets out in pursuit – with Luke hopping up behind her.

This is another great Star Wars chase scene, high speed at ground level, weaving between trees, roots and vines, under low bridges, and over branches. The descendant of the American movie car chase scene, and nobody does it better. As they catch up with one of the scouts, Leia pulls alongside him and Luke jumps off her bike and onto the scout's bike, knocking him off, to his death. Imperial Redshirts have an even shorter life expectancy than Rebel Redshirts.

Two more scouts on bikes show up in pursuit. Luke tells Leia to stay on the tail of the one in front, and he'll take the two behind them. Alas, Leia gets in trouble with her quarry, but manages to jump clear of her bike just before it crashes and explodes. Leaving her unconscious, and the scout thinking she must be dead.

Luke dispatches his two scouts, in skilled and clever ways more fun to watch than to talk about. Still, it was fun to write (and, hopefully, to read.) His bike got wrecked, though, so he was left to walk back to his commando unit.

And while Vader goes to tell the Emperor his "sense" of who he thinks was on that stolen shuttle on Endor, the Rebel commando unit awaits Luke and Leia's return. When Luke finally does make it back, they're all concerned that Leia didn't. It's decided that Luke, Han, Chewie, and the two droids will go search for Leia, while the rest of the unit proceeds to the field generator to hide, awaiting further instructions.

Around this time, Leia wakes up under a fern. Groggy but seemingly okay. She looks around to get her bearings, and sees for the first time – as do we – an Ewok. Wicket. He looks like a furry little teddy bear – but he has a knife, and she's unclear about his intentions. To me he looked like a small Wookiee, and I wondered about making a connection between their two species. But George said they weren't related, and after my flights of fancy about Leia's backstory that had gotten cut, I didn't want to push my fantasy agenda about Ewoks any further.

Wicket threatens Leia with a spear, but she's not having any of it. This little guy doesn't scare her in the least. And when she scratches him between the ears, he purrs like a kitten. Unfortunately, her guard was down when a laser bolt hits nearby, scaring Wicket into the underbrush. An Imperial scout appears and trains his gun on Leia. But Wicket stabs him in the leg, Leia grabs her gun, kills the scout – and now she and Wicket are best friends.

The Ewoks are a whole new set of Threshold Guardians – characters who may turn out to be friends or enemies, it's not always clear which – but who hold the key to the next level of our quest.

This encounter felt like it was about Leia bringing her best feminine energy to the initial encounter, being kind to Wicket, which enlisted his help when it was most needed. Had Han been in the same position, you gotta think he'd have just bopped Wicket on the head as soon as the spear came out.

As Wicket escorts Leia off to safety, she submits to a sense of awe and oneness with the magnificent splendor of this natural realm – the giant trees, lush foliage, sweet furry creatures – she feels somehow part of it all. Almost as if she were connected to it by a living… Force. She felt as if she were a part of this forest, these trees, a "part of them across time, and space, connected by the vital, vibrant force, of which…" [123] Which, we will come to learn, is strong in her. Foreshadowings like this are sometimes better expressed in print than on the screen, where elements like pacing prevent such introspection or insight.

Meanwhile Vader has his audience with Palpatine, and tells him a Rebel force has penetrated the force shield and is on Endor. The Emperor just nods and says he knows. Vader goes on to say his son is with the Rebels. Palpatine is curious about that revelation, and surprised he was unable to sense the boy's presence. He orders Vader to go down to the moon, and is certain Luke will come to him, "Of his own free will… His compassion for you will be his undoing." [124]

This trope shares a lot with numerous mythologies Lucas is drawing from. Vampires, for example, in the Bram Stoker version, can only enter your premises if you invite them in, of your own free will. A strong soul cannot be coerced, only seduced – and the Emperor is intent on seducing Luke to the Dark Side.

Down on Endor, the search party finds Leia's wrecked speeder bike and a torn piece of her jacket – but no Leia – which is of concern, though both Luke and Han are trying to act too macho to reveal just how worried they are.

Chewie, on the other hand, is distracted by a wonderful smell – fresh meat. He sniffs out the raw food, and grabs at it before the others can race over to stop him – and they're all hoisted up in the net that the meat was baiting. After a lot of grumbling and blame throwing, they cut their way out, crashing back down to the ground – only to be surrounded by a hostile party of Ewoks brandishing spears.

Han is about to shoot his way out with his blaster, but Luke stops him – he has a feeling about these furry little guys. The Ewoks gather our heroes' weapons, and tie them up, chattering away as they do – until they get a closer look at Threepio. They prostrate themselves before the droid, and begin chanting. When Luke asks Threepio – who is, of course, fluent in over 6 million languages – what they're saying, he explains that he thinks the Ewoks believe he – C3PO – is a god. Chewie and Artoo think that's hilarious, and Han demands that Threepio use his "divine influence" to get them out of this. But Threepio says he can't – it's against his programming to impersonate a deity.

This has resonance with the scene in Chapter One when C3PO is taken into Jabba's torture den. So unfair, so without reason, he felt in that moment. A moment in which he searched for his life's meaning, as do all who turn to religion for that answer. And now he's being regarded by the Ewoks as their god – the entity who gives meaning to their lives. All very puzzling for the protocol droid.

So the captive entourage proceeds to the Ewok village – Han, Luke, Chewie, and Artoo hanging upside down on poles – and Threepio borne on a litter, like a royal potentate. The lowly Threepio can only savor this moment of elevation above his owners, who so often treat him so dismissively. It's a feeling we can all relate to. Viewing the majesty of the approaching village, content for the moment to bask in his new role, he simply thinks, as any god might, "And it was good." A biblical thought, for a newly biblical entity.

Doctors frequently tend to think of themselves as God-like – though not consciously. It's just an attitude they – we – bring to the table. We know more about the patients' bodies than they do, we're expected to tell them what to do, what pills to take, what surgeries to undergo, we feel at ease in that position of authority – and when we take on that mantle, we believe ourselves to be the ones Who Know Best.

There's also an aspect of being our patient's champion. In the mortal struggle against death, we are there to do battle in our patient's name. We're their knights in white-coated armor. This is all heady stuff, and it's easy to see how Threepio was relishing his newfound pedestal.

Of course, the flipside is when you fail. When Death wins, or disease claims a victim's limb, or spleen. It's a steep fall for a doctor to lose those contests. Whenever it happened to me, it left me feeling empty, guilty, ashamed, and angry, no matter how good a job I'd done "doctoring." Death had just done a better job "deathing."

IX

They wheeled the old man in quickly, and he had The Look. It's scary, at first, to watch someone get The Look. You know they see something you can't, or something you won't. "I'm going to die," the old man said. He saw it clearly.

Reminded me of Leo. Leo's wife, Amy, told me that the day he came into the hospital, before they left the house he'd stood in each room of their home, looking at every wall and corner, taking it all in, certain he'd never see any of it again. I told her not to worry, we'd get him back home without fail.

And now this man today had The Look. He sat straight up as they wheeled him in, and his teeth were chattering. "You're not going to die," I told him. But my voice was like wind in his ears.

And now our stalwart heroes take a pause in their grand adventure, preparing to face their final confrontation, and what may well mean death for some of them.

ROTJ – CHAPTER 6, PAGES 104-124

We pick up at our intrepid adventurers' arrival in the Ewok village – unceremonious to them, though they are soon to be at the center of an Ewok ceremony. And in contradistinction to all the back and forth action scenes in the previous material, nearly this entire chapter is set right here, in the village. After so much hubbub and criss-crossing narratives, we need a pause, to take a breath, to get our bearings, restate the story and the stakes, and get ready to launch into the next series of battles.

The village of "diminutive monkey-bears" [125] – which is what they reminded me of – is a labyrinth of trees, vines, rope bridges, scaffolding, webbing and tunnels. Our heroes are tied to poles, carried upside down to the largest hut, where Han is put on a spit and suspended over a small fire, while the tribe decides their fate. With characteristic understatement, Han says he doesn't like the look of this. Han has a way of telling the audience how to feel.

The situation deteriorates when Chewbacca roars at an Ewok, and Artoo zaps another one. Luke tells Threepio, who knows their language, to calm things down – but Threepio apologetically explains Solo is going to be the main course for dinner tonight. As their deity, Threepio is obligated to preside over the ceremony. That's when Chief Chirpa enters with the village's new guest – Leia! She'd been brought here by her new little Ewok companion.

Leia demands her friends be freed, but the Ewoks have other ideas. Leia, worried, asks Luke what he can do. This is the first moment that Han is nettled by Leia's seeming closeness to Luke – a feeling that will be amplified later on.

Luke orders Threepio to tell the Ewoks that if his friends aren't freed, he'll become an angry god, and use his magic on them. Threepio protests, reluctant to violate the Ewoks' religious beliefs – but Luke closes his eyes and uses the Force to levitate Threepio. Threepio is surprised he has such power – but the demonstration works, and the Rebels are freed.

That night, Threepio tells the Ewok Elders the story of the Rebellion, in order to enlist their aid in the struggle against the Empire. They're fascinated – but their response is that the Empire is not their problem. Endorian isolationists.

Next, Han makes his pitch for their help, in his own inimitable fashion; and then Luke follows, pleading on behalf of the galaxy – which is just too abstract an argument for the Ewoks.

Finally, Leia tells them, "Do it for the trees." [126] Wicket nods, and expands on her philosophy, telling his tribe they are all leaves on the great tree of life, all connected, and all must work together. It was basically an early eco-argument, set within the context of the Force as a counterpoint to Imperial colonialist exploitation.

Between Leia's strong-woman takedown of misogynist Jabba, and this rousing call for protecting the interconnectedness of all of nature, this is a pretty forward-looking space opera.

Our heroes are freed, amidst great celebrating and goodwill – though Luke stands apart, with an unexpected darkness in his heart – he senses Vader's presence not far off. When he wanders away from the bonfires and gaiety, Leia sees him and follows, and asks him what's wrong. She doesn't know yet why she feels so connected to him.

He tells her he senses Vader's presence on Endor, and he has to leave his friends before he endangers their mission. And he has to face Vader. Leia wants to know why. Isn't it more important just to destroy the deflector field generator?

First Luke stuns her by confessing Vader is his father – and as if that weren't enough, he tells her Vader is Leia's father, too. So Luke is her brother.

Whoa! Before Leia can even digest this news, Luke tells her he can sense there's still good in their father, and he has to face Vader so he can save him. Luke and Leia embrace, and Luke goes off to face his destiny.

But Han has witnessed their embrace, and full of jealousy he storms up to her, wanting to know what that was about. She can't tell him now; she's had no time to assimilate all this news. All she can do is cry, and ask Han to hold her – which he does, now totally confused, the big lug.

The next morning, as Vader stands near the Imperial landing platform in a cleared space on the forest moon, overseeing the arrival of his stormtroopers, armored walkers, and weapons being deployed to protect the field generator, Luke is brought to him by a squad of guards to whom Luke has surrendered. The head guard gives Vader Luke's lightsaber.

Vader dismisses them and faces his son; and they both know this is the beginning of the final battle.

ROTJ – CHAPTER 7, PAGES 125-146

Luke tells Vader he knows there is still good in the Dark Lord. That's why Vader couldn't kill him earlier. And we've certainly seen evidence of this, from the climaxes of the first two movies. It always seemed like Vader should have been able to kill Luke when he was on his tail flying to destroy the Death Star in Episode IV; and then again when Vader cut off Luke's hand – that was a laser swordfight Vader ought to have won outright. So Luke's accusation of good in Vader now rings true – to us and to Vader, though he denies it.

In fact, it seems to anger Vader to be accused of still having any good within him. His self-identity is so wrapped up in being Palpatine's evil apprentice, anything that could diminish that just rankles him. This is known as Empty Unit Narcissism by some psychologists – a patient's belief he's not just a terrible person, he's the worst person ever, nobody is worse than he is. A kind of narcissistic pride in his own malevolence. So to have that belief challenged – it just steels Vader's resolve to kill his son if Luke won't be turned to the Dark Side.

Meanwhile, the Rebel fleet is planning its imminent lightspeed attack on the Death Star – its success dependent on the commando team taking out the field generator on Endor – followed by the attack squadron led by Lando, flying the Millennium Falcon, to destroy the Death Star at its core.

And we're into the back and forth now. Han and the commandos have made their way to the shield generator. Paploo the Ewok steals a guard's bike to draw the other guards away, and the commandos make it into the bunker with a stolen code, as…

Vader brings Luke to the Emperor on the Death Star. Luke is so full of rage, searching for a way to kill the Emperor – especially when Palpatine, like a benevolent master, has Luke uncuffed. The Emperor quizzes Luke about who continued his Jedi training after Obi Wan failed – and he sees in Luke's heart that it was Yoda, and Yoda is now dead.

Luke is furious he allowed the Emperor to read his thoughts this way, it feels like such a violation – but he gives himself up to the mental assaults, lets himself be buffeted, as Yoda had taught him: let your opponent waste his strength in his attacks, until he expends himself, allowing you to deal the victory blow.

(NOTE: This is how, by the way, Muhammed Ali defeated George Foreman for the boxing World Championship in Zaire in 1974, with his "Rope-a-Dope" strategy, letting Foreman pummel him on the ropes, round after round, until Foreman was so exhausted that Ali could come back and wallop him in the last round.)

But Luke also sees fear in the Emperor. And that lets him know he can win.

Palpatine takes Luke's lightsaber from Vader, and points out the moon Endor through the window. He tells Luke the Rebel attack is doomed to fail. Even now, his friends are walking into a trap in the bunker on Endor. And when the Rebel fleet gets here, they'll discover they've flown into a trap, as well; and Luke will get to watch them destroyed.

This feels like the end of ACT 2, the Collapse of the Hero's Plan. Luke has come so far, and it's all come to naught. Everything they've been struggling to achieve was engineered by Palpatine, who lured them here, and is now set to crush the Rebellion. With Luke forced to sit here and watch.

Luke is so distraught he almost Force-grabs his lightsaber — but stops himself. He must not succumb to anger, and to the Dark Side — as...

Han and Leia and the commandos make it past the first level of guards inside the field generator bunker, and move on to the inner core, as...

The Rebel fleet bursts out of hyperspace, going into attack mode on the Death Star — only to realize the deflector shield isn't down yet — it only looks down because the signal is jammed. And as Rebel fighters crash and burn against the shield, and Imperial Star Destroyers and TIE fighters appear, Lando and the Rebel Generals realize this was, indeed, a trap.

So the battle is joined, as...

Chapter Thirteen
Racing for the Logo

Racing for the logo is what one of my producers used to call the moment in the script nearing the climax, when the momentum of the action carries everything forward at increasingly breakneck speed, without much pause for contemplation. Here we go.

Han and the commandos make it into the control room of the bunker, and start placing charges to blow up the field deflector generator – when they find themselves surrounded by dozens of stormtroopers, weapons aimed at them, and ordering them to surrender. The commandos are hopelessly outnumbered. They give up. As…

On the flagship Super Star Destroyer, an underling asks Admiral Piett for the order to start the all-out attack on the Rebel Fleet. But Piett says no – his orders from the Emperor are merely to keep the Rebels from escaping. Palpatine has something more sinister in mind for destroying them – as…

Palpatine, Luke and Vader watch the aerial dogfights from the throne room. Like a silent fireworks display. But now the Emperor reveals to Luke that the Death Star's weapon system is fully operational. He radios his control room and tells them to fire at will. And Luke can only watch in horror as the beam from the Death Star shoots out at a huge Rebel Star Cruiser – and in the next moment, vaporizes it.

Luke's despair and anger overwhelm him. He sees his lightsaber lying on the throne. "And in this bleak and livid moment, the dark side was much with him."[127] Embodied in the light saber. Luke is succumbing to the Dark Side of the Force.

Now that the Hero's Plan has collapsed, Luke can't see a way to win without succumbing to the very thing he's been fighting against. His own Dark Side.

ROTJ – CHAPTER 8, PAGES 147-163

General Ackbar and the high command of the Rebel fleet are stunned to see the Death Star operational, and vaporizing their Star Cruisers. He orders a retreat. But Lando convinces him they won't get a second bite at this apple. They have to press on with the battle, until the deflector shield comes down. Ackbar acquiesces – but he looks hopeless.

Back in the throne room, Palpatine points out the carnage to Luke, explaining the entire Rebel fleet will soon be destroyed, along with Luke's friends on Endor. Luke, angry beyond control now, Force-grabs his lightsaber from where it sits on the throne, and in a single motion, brings it down on Palpatine's skull. Luke is beyond Dark Side/Light Side philosophies. He's just in the moment now. And he wants Palpatine dead.

But Vader is right there, to block the blow with his own lightsaber. Father and son face off for the ultimate lightsaber duel, as Palpatine looks on with a smile, watching Luke's descent into dark anger.

On Endor, Han, Leia and the others are now prisoners in the clearing before the bunker, surrounded by hundreds of Imperial stormtroopers. With the end seemingly imminent, Han and Leia hold hands, allowing themselves to experience their love in these last moments. Maybe their warrior skills can no longer save them – but they can exit this life in the solace of their love.

Suddenly Threepio and Artoo enter the clearing – stop when they see the situation they've walked into – and turn around to run back into the woods. Stormtroopers chase them. But as they're about to be captured, 15 Ewoks drop out of the trees and take down the stormtroopers. Teebo blasts a loud note from a ram's horn – and that's the call to action to the whole Ewok nation. The Battle for Endor has commenced.

Hundreds of Ewoks descend on the battalion of stormtroopers, countering laser blasters with rocks and arrows. Chewie jumps into the bushes as Han and Leia shelter under the arches of the bunker. Han tries to open the bunker doors with the stolen code, but this time it doesn't work, the door lock has been reprogrammed. They need Artoo to hack it. Han contacts Artoo over the commlink, and tells him to get over here.

The battle rages all around them, high tech vs. low. Classic David and Goliath stuff. The Ewoks are getting laser-blasted while they use their primitive weapons. Sometimes several Ewoks mob a stormtrooper to bring him down. And Chewie is right in the midst of the fray, protecting his little genetic cousins, as they protect him. (Even though George said Wookiees and Ewoks weren't related, I have to believe they shared some distant antecedent that even George didn't know about.)

Artoo makes it over to the bunker door, with Han and Leia giving him cover fire. He plugs into the lock – but a laser blast fries him, and he falls over, smoking. Han goes back to trying to hotwire the lock, as the fighting intensifies, the Ewoks hurling boulders with catapults at Imperial walkers, and dive-bombing stormtroopers from animal skin hang-gliders.

Meanwhile, up in the sky, the dogfights are escalating, and Lando devises a new, desperate strategy – having the Rebel Star Cruisers go head to head at close range with the Imperial Star Destroyers. "Like tanks at twenty paces." [128] That was the visual I was trying to evoke from the production stills I had of the space fight. The Rebels aren't likely to win those confrontations, but better that than systematic annihilation by the Death Star.

And in the throne room, the lightsaber duel between Vader and Luke gets more intense. Vader is actually pleased to see Luke's skill level. He's already thinking that after Luke comes under Vader's wing, for further tutelage, they'll more easily be able to destroy Palpatine and rule the galaxy themselves, father and son, side by side.

But with a flurry of attacks, Luke actually drives Vader to his knees and stands above him, poised for the killshot. In that moment he even has the thought that he could kill Vader and take the Sith Lord's place at the Emperor's side. Momentarily, it makes him feverish with power.

Vader is stunned by his son's unexpected strength, and for the first time realizes Luke might kill him. Fury and revenge fill his soul.

But the Emperor, seeing all this, is filled with glee, watching the Dark Side energize both combatants. He shouts out joyfully, "Let the hate flow through you! Become one with it! Let it nourish you!" [129] Like a manager of a bare knuckle boxer in the ring, caught up in the screams of cheering spectators.

And that wakes Luke up from his fugue-state plunge into hatred. What am I doing? What am I becoming? He lowers his sword. "I will not fight you, father." [130] *He remembers who he is, and what he's promised himself.*

Luke is wrestling so hard with the core of his own very being – must it always take violence and hatred to triumph?

Vader sneers that Luke is unwise to lower his defenses. But when Luke Force-connects his mind with Vader's, it makes him think of the times Vader could have killed him, but didn't – in the dogfight at the first Death Star, in the lightsaber duel on Bespin. And the time Vader could have killed Leia when she was first captured – but didn't. Luke says, "Your thoughts betray you, father. I feel the good in you." [131] *Luke says it partly to get under his father's skin – and who among us, as a rebellious teenager, hasn't wanted to do that? And that really pisses Vader off.*

The Dark Lord throws his saber at a girder supporting Luke, sending Luke tumbling into the darkness, as Vader's lightsaber flies back into his hand. And now Vader must stalk Luke into the shadows. But Luke has pushed the notion of patricide from his heart, and rolls his lightsaber across the floor to Vader. Vader takes it, again exhorting Luke to come over to the Dark Side. He knows Luke's feelings are strong for his friends, but...

Suddenly Vader can see into Luke's heart, to his true feelings, to his concern for... his sister! Luke's feelings have betrayed him, and now Vader learns for the first time that Luke's sister – Vader's daughter – is alive. Vader smiles at Luke. "If you will not turn to the Dark Side, perhaps she will." [132] *Tables turned – Vader knows how to get under his son's skin, too.*

And that's just too much for Luke. The last straw. "Never!" he screams, Force-grabs his lightsaber back into his hand, and redoubles his attack in a frenzy, blow after blow, finally forcing Vader to his knees – and cutting off Vader's right hand!

Just as Vader had done to Luke. The son overcoming the father, poised to kill him – until he looks at Vader's severed hand, the same as his own, and realizes once again how much like his father he's become, how he's become the very thing he hated.

And once again, in that moment, the Emperor is so overcome with excitement at all this hatred, he can't restrain himself. "Good! Kill him!" he shouts to Luke. "Your hatred has made you powerful!" [133] *Palpatine is speaking to himself with those words, as well as to Luke.*

And in that moment, Luke fully realizes he has truly become the Darkness he hates – and he throws his lightsaber away. "You have failed, Palpatine! I am a Jedi, as my father was before me!" [134] *And though this is shouted at Palpatine, his words are meant for Vader to hear as well.*

In throwing his lightsaber away and claiming his Inner Jedi, Luke has dug deep to find his salvation, and fully realized that the prize he's been after for so long – destroying Vader and the Death Star – is not the true prize. Killing Vader was not the way. The true prize is walking the path of the Jedi, connected to everything and everyone.

So he shouts the words to the Emperor, naming both himself and his father as Jedi – but of course Vader hears them, too. And it begins to reawaken that long-sleeping Jedi spirit within Vader.

Palpatine is enraged, though. And tells Luke, "If you will not be turned, you will be destroyed." [135] *He's had enough of this mealy-mouthed kid. He raises his spindly arms and begins hurling crackling lightning at Luke. "Blinding white bolts of energy coruscated from his fingers."* [136] *Over and over, sending Luke writhing in pain to the ground. And who can't relate with excitement to coruscating lightning?*

And Vader crawls, "like a wounded animal, to his Emperor's side." [137] *Vader, at his nadir, has come to rock bottom.*

This is perhaps the clearest moment – at least in retrospect – that this entire story has been Vader's Hero's Journey as well as Luke's. And for Vader, this is the end of his Act Two Collapse of the Hero's Plan. Everything he has worked for since Anakin became Vader has come crashing down on him, with seemingly no way out of his destruction. He will, of course, soon reach deep within himself and come to a short, unexpected, redemptive Act Three of his own.

Meanwhile, back on Endor, Chewie and the Ewoks commandeer an Imperial walker, and start blasting stormtroopers right and left, as

Han has one failure after another trying to breach the bunker door. Finally, Han and Leia find themselves surrounded by stormtroopers, who are about to kill them.

They look into each other's eyes – this is the end, and once again they express their love for each other – this time verbally. "I love you," Han whispers. "I know," Leia replies. [138] *This is, of course, the mirror image of the scene in The Empire Strikes Back, just before Han is about to be lowered into carbonite. They kiss passionately for the first time then, and Leia says, "I love you," and Han says, "I know."*

(NOTE: There are two stories about that first exchange, in *The Empire Strikes Back* – both possibly apocryphal. One is that Han's line, "I know," was ad-libbed by Harrison Ford. The other is that, after a long, dramatic pause, Carrie Fisher was feeding him his line – he was the one who was supposed to say, "I love you." And Harrison says back to her, "I know" – meaning he knows what his line is. Someone should ask Harrison someday.)

In any case, after the expressions of love now, a huge laser blast kills the stormtroopers, and Chewie emerges out of the top of his Imperial walker.

The tide of the battle for Endor has turned.

ROTJ – CHAPTER 9, PAGES 164-181

Up in space, the battle rages. The deflector shield remains up, so it looks like this will all end up a lost cause – but Lando still has hope that Han will come through.

In the throne room, Luke is nearly dead under the assault from Palpatine's energy blasts, which he continues to hurl. Finally, Luke is motionless – apparently lifeless. Definitely the Collapse of the Hero's Plan, as well as the collapse of his life force.

And that proves too much for Vader to endure. Digging deep within himself, feeling the remnants of good within, feeling his hatred for the evil that is the Emperor, and feeling anguish at seeing his son so brutally murdered... he rises up. Lifts the Emperor high above his head, and hurls him into the chasm that leads far down to the power core of the Death Star.

This is the same chasm I described back in Chapter Four, just to set up this moment. ("We open with Vader talking to Palpatine at his throne on the Death Star. In the second paragraph I go into some detail about the 'black chasm' that channeled down to the core of the battle station, to the power unit that 'reeked of ozone.'")

After Vader throws Palpatine to his death, he staggers back to Luke's lifeless body, and collapses beside him.

CHAPTER FOURTEEN
A COUPLE SMALL DIGRESSIONS

TIME FOR A BRIEF PAUSE in the Race for the Logo. Amazingly, in the script I was given from which to write the novelization, that's not how Palpatine died! In my script it was *Luke*, who, gathering all his last strength, charged at the Emperor, and threw him down the shaft to his death. So Vader didn't kill the Emperor in that script, Luke did. And that's how I wrote the novelization I sent in to be published. But when the book hit the stands, it read the way we see it in the movie – *Vader* kills Palpatine. Here's the section of the script page, 102, given to me to write the novel from, in which Luke kills Palpatine.)

102

CONTINUED   1

increases in intensity, the sound screaming through the room. Luke's body stops moving; it appears lifeless.

At this instant, Luke springs to life and grabs the Emperor from behind, fighting for control of the robed figure despite the young Jedi's weakened body. The Emperor struggles, in his embrance, his bolt-shooting hands now lifted high, away from Luke. Now the white lightning arcs back to strike at Vader. Luke stumbles with his load as the sparks rain off his father's helmet and flow down over his black cape. Luke holds this evil despot high over his head and walks to the edge of the abyss at the central core of the Throne room. With one final burst of his awesome strength, Luke Skywalker hurls the Emperor's body into the bottomless shaft.

The Emperor's body spins helplessly into the void

Luke kills Palpatine on original script page from Return of the Jedi *(Lucasfilm, 1983.) Photo of Author's copy courtesy of the Author.*

And here's my original handwritten version of that segment

Fragment of original handwritten manuscript of the moment Luke kills Palpatine in final draft of Return of the Jedi *novelization (Del Rey, 1983.) Photo courtesy of the Author.*

And here's my typewritten manuscript page, in case you weren't able to read my handwriting:

ideous barrage. He stopped moving altogether. At last, he

ppeared totally lifeless. The Emperor hissed maliciously.

At that instant, Luke sprang up and grabbed the Emperor

rom behind, pinning Palpatine's upper arms to his torso.

Ieaker than he'd ever been, Luke had lain still these last

Iew minutes, focusing his every fiber of being on this one,

:oncentrated act — the only action possible; his last, if

he failed. Ignoring pain, ignoring his shame and his weaknes

ignoring the bone-crushing noise in his head, he focused sole

and sightlessly on his will — his will to defeat the evil

embodied in the Emperor.

Palpatine struggled in the grip of Luke's unfeeling embr.

his hands still shooting bolts of malign energy out in all

Fragment of original typewritten manuscript depicting Luke killing Palpatine, with publisher's mark-ups, of Return of the Jedi *novelization (Del Rey, 1983.) Photo courtesy of the Author.*

Later on, at the 1983 Fourth of July party up at Skywalker Ranch, I asked Lucas why the discrepancy. Did he put misleading plot twists in different versions of the script, so if some false plot element was leaked, he'd know who the leaker was? Or did he originally plan to have Luke kill the Emperor, but then changed his mind at the last minute – just as he'd changed the title of the film at the last minute.

He just smiled at me, though, and said he always knew what the ending was going to be. And that's all he said.

But now, briefly back to our intrepid heroes in the published novel, as a segue into the second brief digression.

CHAPTER 9, CONTINUED

Down on Endor, Han and company dress up as stormtroopers, trick the guards inside the bunker into opening the doors, rush in and over-power them, plant charges, and blow up the generator – crashing down the deflector shield that surrounds the Death Star!

The Rebel fleet sees the deflector shield come down – their final assault can begin. Lando, in the Millennium Falcon, zooms down to the surface of the Death Star, accompanied by his wingmen, to begin his approach to the reactor core, through well-defended shafts, and pursued by TIE fighters – as Admiral Ackbar and team disable an Imperial Star Destroyer at close range – enough to crash it into the Death Star, setting off internal explosions all over the evil battle station.

At this point, I thought it might be helpful if I talked a bit about my thought processes surrounding the upcoming, emotionally cli-mactic moment of Luke unmasking his dying father.

The handwritten page below is the *verso* blank script page, the backside of page 103, and opposite page 104 of the screenplay – the script page in which Luke removes the mask from Vader. These are the notes I wrote to myself with thoughts about those first unmasked moments – possibly the key visual of the entire tril-ogy – as well as my thoughts about the nature of their relationship, and how that might unfold over the course of Vader's death scene.

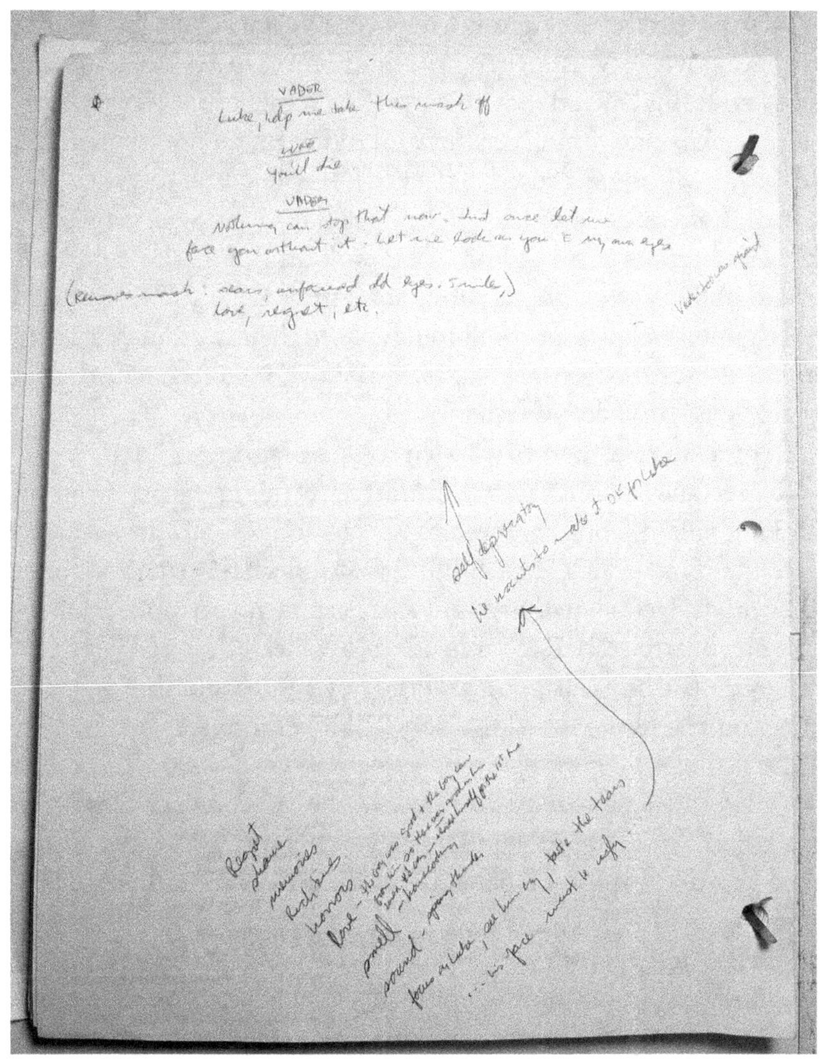

Notes to myself on back of script page 103, with thoughts about Luke removing Vader's mask during Vader's death scene. Photo courtesy of the Author.

The first few lines at the top of the page contain the dialogue leading up to the unmasking, followed by my first note, in parentheses:

(Removes mask: scars, unfocused old eyes. Smiles, love, regret, etc.)

And then in the margin:

Vader too was afraid.

We've heard about the duel between Anakin and Obi Wan at the lava flows of Mustafar, so it was important to see some of those scars now. But beyond that, this was the moment of Vader reclaiming the Anakin within him, now an old man. Gentle, vulnerable, regretful, with "unfocused old eyes." The line about Vader also being afraid referred to Luke's previous line of dialogue expressing his fear that Vader would die if he took off the mask. Vader isn't afraid of dying, though; he's afraid of letting Luke see his true self.

The notes below that speak to how I see their relationship being revealed over the next few pages, as the two men reconcile during the process of Vader's death.

Regret, shame, memories, rich lives, horrors –

Regret and shame are two feelings we might expect from an atoning villain – but I wanted to inject specifics into the scene, to give them memories of each other that reflected both good times they might have shared had they not been torn apart, and the horrors surrounding Anakin's transition to Vader.

Love – the boy was good and the boy came from him so there <u>was</u> good in him – loved the boy – & loved himself for the first time

Vader felt so guilty about the person he'd become, he needed to start finding shreds of evidence that he wasn't 100% evil to the core. If Luke was a good person, and Luke came from Vader, there must be good in Vader too.

smell – homecooking
sound – spring thunder

I wanted to give specific sense memories to them, as well. Elements they might have shared even briefly after the twins' birth, even if there was no direct communication between them and Vader. Sense memories that made this more than a generic death scene.

focus on Luke, see him cry, taste the tears –

Luke is moved to see his father in such a diminished state, this weak, pale, shriveled old man. I think most people feel this way at the bedside of a dying parent, and I wanted to make these real people that we could all relate to. Tasting his tears is another physical sense I wanted to give Luke, to take this out of the realm of abstraction, to make this a real human experience.

... his face must be ugly... > he wants to make it ok for Luke > self-deprecatory

This is back to Vader's feeling so ugly inside, and how that ugliness must be reflected in his newly revealed face. He feels shame that Luke has to see that, he wishes he could soften that blow, and self-deprecation may be how he tries.

In the scene itself, Luke lifts off the mask with some difficulty – I think physically representing the emotional difficulty he's feeling about actually looking at his father's face – physicalization of the subtext. And after disentangling the complex breathing apparatus, Luke gets his first look. "It was the sad, benign face of an old man."[139]

I go on to flesh out my notes as the scene unfolds, describing the scars, the pallor, the unfocused, tear-glazed eyes. A "face full of meanings,"[140] including regret, shame, rich times, horrors, and love. Straight from my notes, which I then elaborate on over the next several pages. It was "a face that hadn't touched the world in a lifetime." And they try to repair the damaged soul behind that face in the time it takes Vader to die in Luke's arms.

For me, this scene was all about The Masks We Wear. Close to my heart.

Okay, end of digressions. Onward to the Race for the Logo.

CHAPTER FIFTEEN
THE END IS HERE

CHAPTER 9, CONTINUED

At this stage in Chapter 9, with explosions rocking the entire Death Star, after the Star Destroyer had collided with it, Luke stumbles through his own personal hell of "electrical fires, steam explosions," and the rumblings of continued Rebel attacks now that the deflector shield is down – he stumbles, carrying the deadweight of his mortally wounded father. Until he can go no further, and rests Vader on the ground.

So not only was his original goal not what he thought it was – it was the opposite of that. Now he's struggling not to destroy Vader, but to keep him alive, to save him in body, as he's just saved his soul.

Barely alive, Vader whispers, "Luke, help me take this mask off." And Luke protests, "You'll die." And Vader responds, "Let me look on you with my own eyes." Not the synthetic, bionic eyes he's used since becoming Vader; but the true, human eyes of Anakin Skywalker. And when they remove the mask together, Luke sees "the sad, benign face of an old man." They're finally reconciling here, reaching a place of peace neither of them – and no one in the audience – would have thought possible. [141-144]

Just as most of us, I think, after decades of struggles with our fathers – sometimes loving, sometimes acrimonious – allow ourselves to see something more of our parent's true nature in the hours and minutes before they die. Maybe see the young man inside the old, when there was hope and aspiration, and before all the slings and arrows of outrageous fortune twisted and complicated things. I know I had those feelings sitting at my father's deathbed.

Luke and Vader share memories, tears, grief, hope, reconciliation, and ultimately, redemption. Vader now wants the best for his son, and doesn't want him to be afraid for either of them. "Luminous beings are we, Luke – not this crude matter." [145] This, a foreshadowing of the last moments of the book and movie. And now Vader tells Luke to leave him.

But Luke insists he'll save Vader, Vader won't die. And Luke won't leave.

And as Vader lies there staring into his son's eyes, there's a moment of serenity. Of understanding the ways they'd saved each other's lives.

Almost inaudibly, Vader says, "Luke… you were right about me. Tell your sister you were right." [146] *So there <u>was</u> good in him. He finally felt that in the end, and used it to save his son's life.*

And Vader dies.

X

Leo was a juvenile-onset Type I diabetic, with every known complication, in the hospital for a downhill month. That night in the ICU, hooked up to every line possible, febrile, absent his right leg, kidneys shot, unresponding peritonitis, lingering pneumonia, one week postmyocardial infarction, blind and battle-weary, he asked me to stop the torture and let him coast. He said: "No more IV's, no more tests, no more medicines, no more bloods drawn. Can you live with that? Not doing anything to me?"

"I can," I said, "but you can't."

"That's OK," he said, "I'm sick of this bullshit. Just for God's pity sake, let me go."

My shift was over, though, so I went home and collapsed in bed, exhausted. Too torn, myself, to sleep. Had a drink and lay there in the dark. In the morning I walked into the ICU and found him beginning his exitus. Labored, agonal respirations, thready pulse. I held his hand.

Breen, the chief resident, entered, looked at Leo's numbers, made a quick assessment, and said, "This guy's going down the tubes. Get some blood gasses."

That was my job as the intern on the service, to draw bloods and do scut work. I just shook my head No, though.

"What do you mean?!" demanded Breen. He wasn't used to any kind of subordination. "Look at him. He's gonna need a respirator for sure, just look at his breathing."

"He asked me not to," I said. "He wants to call it quits."

"Well he's not the doctor, and if you won't get the bloods, I will. We'll talk about this later." He opened a packet, got a glass syringe, brought it near Leo's femoral artery.

I grabbed his wrist and pulled it away from the patient. "No," I said.

We struggled. I pushed him against the wall. The syringe fell to the floor and broke. He threw me against the door. Leo's wife, Amy, walked into the little room. We all stood, looking at each other. My fists were gripping, my chest tight, my breathing irregular. Breen's face was red. I wanted to punch him.

Amy walked to the bedside and held Leo's hand. His breathing became quiet, then shallow; then it stopped. Amy looked at me.

"It's over," I said.

All over but the explosions, the misunderstandings reconciled, the dancing, and of course, the requisite funeral pyre.

So, elsewhere on the Death Star, destruction all around, Commander Jerjerrod, in a final act of spite, has his gunner turn the Death Star ray on the planet Endor itself – if he's not going to survive, then neither will this lush, harmless oasis in the sky. The Dark Side is like that.

Fortunately for Han, Leia, Chewie, and the Ewoks, Lando finally navigates the Millennium Falcon to the Death Star's reactor core, looses his concussion missiles into the reactor, and beats a hasty retreat, barely ahead of the massive explosion and shock wave that obliterates it before it can destroy Endor.

Leia and Han watch the fireworks from Endor – and Leia knows Luke got off the Death Star in time. She can feel it, because she's Force-connected to Luke. Han mistakes her relief for a different kind of feeling for Luke, and gallantly offers to stand aside, to let them be together. He loves her so much, he can be selfless in that way. Leia laughs, though, and tells Han it's not like that. She and Luke are siblings. Han is gob-smacked. And the two of them embrace, the beginning of a long romance.

This is the final triumph in the Hero's Journey. The Death Star and the Emperor are destroyed, Han and Leia are in love, Luke redeemed his father and is safe.

That night, there's a huge victory celebration on Endor, with dancing, singing, and bonfires. Off in the woods by himself, Luke has brought his father's body back down here in a shuttle, and places it on a funeral pyre, for a last good-bye.

Then he joins his friends at the Ewok party, and they embrace joyously. This is the final beat in the stopping points of the Hero's Journey. Bringing it all back home. In some stories it's the gold you were seeking, in other stories it's the magic elixir. In this story it's satisfaction that the galaxy has been freed from the horrors of its tyrannical Emperor; and the triumph of Luke's soul searching, bringing him at last to a reconciliation with his father, and into the way of the Jedi.

So (in a shot called in to me after the novelization was finished, to be added on after the fact, both on the page and in the film) *– only Luke can see, shimmering in the flames of a bonfire, the spirit images of Yoda, Obi Wan… and Anakin. Just as Vader had told him. "Luminous beings are we, Luke. Not this crude matter."* [147]

That is the prize Luke brought back home from his Journey. The jewel he found in the darkest cave and returned with. It's the understanding that we are luminous beings.

So it's also a triumph over Death, since we go on to be luminous beings in the weave of the Force.

Except for the Empire. The Empire was dead.

Long live the Alliance.

APPENDIX A
TOUCHED BY THE FORCE

OVER THE YEARS, fans have asked me if I believe in the Force. I didn't used to. But as I reach Act 3 of my life and reflect on the myriad strange and wondrous things that have occurred, I find my mind changing. What follows is a kind of rambling account, with seemingly unrelated side stories, of a memory that left me feeling connected to *a* Force, if not *the* Force. I'm certainly no Jedi; but maybe I'm just a little Jed-*ish*.

The Force is, among other things, at least a metaphor. It's a metaphor for an energetic field of connectedness in the universe. Religions call that God, though I personally don't think it has anything to do with received rules of behavior by an omniscient overlord. Yet sensing its effects, people have sought organizing principles to its nature for millennia. Such organizing principles are beyond my grasp, but I have had glimpses of that connectedness over the course of my life. Encounters with a shadow of the thing itself. Like gravity – which we can't see, understand, or characterize, except indirectly, by the effect it has on things – so has this Force, or the field for which it is a metaphor – touched me in my life. The "poltergeist" experiences I mentioned earlier in this memoir are a couple freaky examples. Likewise my near death experience. Here is one last example, kind of a long, roundabout story that touched me more deeply, because of its personal meaning for me.

I was doing a fundraising party at Kalyra Winery in Santa Ynez, to raise money to produce a small film I'd written called *Wrongside Bob*. I put together a band, we had a silent auction for some of my *Jedi* and *Star Trek* memorabilia, there was face painting for kids, posters all over for the film, with my name prominent on the posters, when…

This guy walks up to me and says, pointing at a poster, "Hey, I *know* James Kahn." I smile back and say, "Hey, I *am* James Kahn." He goes on to say, "Well, we don't look the same, but I've always remembered sitting next to you on a flight from New York to LA, like 30 years ago, and we had a great conversation; I was at Warner Brothers, you were, I think, at Universal, I never forgot."

I vaguely remembered the conversation. Rex said he wasn't even here at the winery for my event, he was here because his girlfriend was face painting the kids, so he thought it was fate that we met again, and asked me to come visit him on the reservation. He was part Algonquin, but said he'd been adopted by the elders of the Chumash tribe here, because of some things he'd like to show me. And because of his "special gifts."

So I went to his place, a little house on the rez, filled with fossils – fish fossils, trilobites, mammoth jaws – and he told me he was a state certified paleontologist, that's what he'd gone into after he left Warner Brothers. When developers or oil companies wanted to dig on land, Rex was hired to make sure no Native artifacts or fossil beds were being disturbed. And that's what led him to what he wanted to talk to me about now.

He said that some years ago, he'd been surveying a large ranch for the owner who wanted to cut it up into parcels, when he came upon a huge, ancient oak tree, hundreds of years old by the size of it – and carved on the north side of the tree was a figure, an arboglyph, covered with moss and lichen.

The rancher said it was an old cowboy carving, but Rex recognized it as an Indian carving. So he took a picture with his phone, showed it to the elders of the tribe and asked them about it. And they said go back there on the night of the winter solstice, then come back and tell them what he saw.

He went, and as the stars came out and rose above the tree, Rex had a revelation. The head of the figure on the tree was the Big Dipper, rising above the tree, to the north; the collar under the figure's head was Cassiopeia, risen just below the Big Dipper; and the gouge above the figure's head was the North Star. He told the elders, and they told him that was a good start, but he should study it some more. So he read old journals, and listened to tapes made

Rex and the 200+ year old oak tree arboglyph he discovered. Photo courtesy of Rex Saint Onge.

a hundred years ago by the anthropologist Harrington interviewing elders back around the turn of the century. And this is what he learned.

If a flat stone is set in the ground, facing north, with a stake set vertically at the south end of the stone, the "head" of the figure is composed of the constellations he saw, on the rise at night, drawn at the other end of the stone. The arms of the figure are traced by the course of the shadow cast by the stake, over the span of one day – the winter solstice. And the legs of the figure are the tracing of the stake's shadow over the course of the summer solstice. Rex calls these shrines "flatstones."

Flatstone facing north, set in my front yard, with spike shadow pointing to early afternoon (the noon vertical line representing the body of the image of Siwut), a few weeks before the spring equinox (horizontal line being what the spike shadow will trace on the equinox.), all beneath the fiery red ball representing the position of the North Star rising above the flatstone. Art by Rex Saint Onge, photo courtesy of the Author.

Close-Up of the head of the image of Siwut, *mimicking the Big Dipper/Ursa Major rising in the northern sky above the flatstone. Art by Rex Saint Onge. Photo courtesy of the Author.*

Rex laid a large, level flat stone in my yard, oriented it due North, and drew the figure, returning 4 times over the course of a year, to trace the shadow of the sun across the stone – though he always insisted he wasn't drawing it, merely transcribing the picture that was being drawn by the sun and stars. The name given to this figure by the Chumash is *Siwut*, which means "it is my body." In their religion, Creator makes this image every day, everywhere on earth, the same way we humans were made, and how we look – proof we were all Creator-made.

Rex shows up at my place now and then, sometimes to perform little ceremonies, burning sage, chanting the Old Songs, sometimes telling stories about Coyote or Snake. He was adopted by the Chumash tribe because he's known to have a special connec-

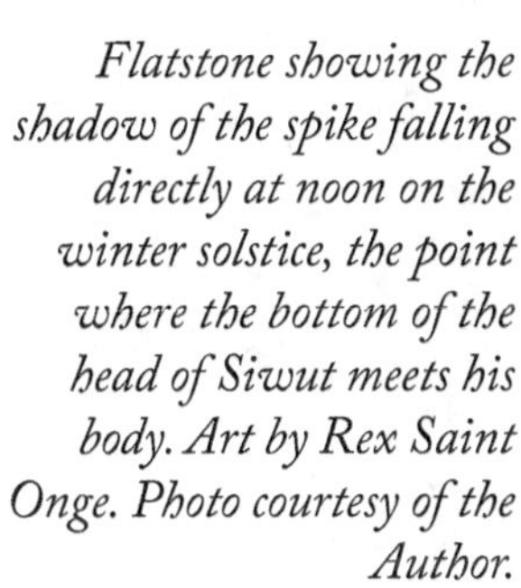

Flatstone showing the shadow of the spike falling directly at noon on the winter solstice, the point where the bottom of the head of Siwut meets his body. Art by Rex Saint Onge. Photo courtesy of the Author.

tion to the spirit world – he knows things about people living and dead he has no reason to know; he's rediscovered graves and caves all over the territory containing long lost petroglyphs. Sometimes Rex has said things I'm skeptical of – but later they pan out.

For instance, after telling me about various "light snakes" he's seen, he once took me to a cave in the back country, on the spring equinox. It was a deserted area of scrub and rock, on a rancher's land that was gated, but the rancher had given Rex permission to look around. We had to climb boulders up a 20-foot ladder to access a small cave opening, just big enough to crawl through. At 10 a.m. a beam of light shot through a hole in the ceiling, hit the wall, and over 45 minutes turned into a snake that crawled down the wall, across the floor, and then disappeared in a spot of light in a small cupule that had been dug into the stone floor. Here's a photo as it was heading toward the stone cupules.

Lightsnake cast by sun through a small hole in roof of cave, crawling down the wall and across the cave floor, where it will disappear into the carved cupule. Snake courtesy of Creator. Photo courtesy of Rex Saint Onge.

And he discovered this cave intuitively, "sensing" it was there, though it was marked on no map, and he had to get permission from the cattle rancher who owned the acreage to let him nose around, to "dowse for the light," until he found it.

So that's my friend, Rex.

Meanwhile, I'd been getting back into recording music after a one-year hiatus. Writing music is closer to my soul than any other writing I do – it moves me more than any scripts or novels I've ever done. It makes me feel whole. The way I can let melodies, images, rhymes and feelings bubble up is so intuitive, it's very different from most of my other writing, which is more intellectualized.

In the months before the end of 2017, my music producer and multi-instrumentalist, David West, said, "You ought to do an Irish song. You've done some nice ones before, and I know this guy in town who does beautiful Irish flutes, he'd be killer on backup." So

I thought okay, I do love Irish folk tunes; I'll try to put something together.

Around the same time, my wife, Jill, said, "You seem kind of depressed lately, J. Maybe you should give Tom a call." Tom is the therapist I sometimes touched bases with back then. My response to Jill was mixed bafflement and annoyance. "I'm not depressed. I'm having a great time in my life, doing all the things that I love – making music, writing my novel, working in the garden, going to the gym, hanging out with you – everything is copacetic." Jill said, "Okay. I'm just sayin'."

In my mind I rolled my eyes, and thought no more about it. I was actually kind of excited about writing an Irish-y song. So I picked up the guitar and noodled around with some progressions, until I came up with a chord structure that sounded like a nice refrain, kind of melancholy Irish.

What was the song going to be about? No idea. But a couple of the chords sounded a little reminiscent of a chord progression in an Irish song I used to sing the kids to sleep with, called *Autumn to May*. I heard it done by Peter, Paul and Mary back in the 60's. It was a kind of sweet jokey song, this Irish guy singing about a frog he used to know in a red vest, who sailed in a shoe, and the ditty went on from there, each verse more confabulating than the last, ending up with something like if anybody told a better story than that, it would have to be a lie.

So I thought maybe I could make a song like that, and the phrase that came to mind that fit into the chord and melody structure I'd come up with was "*Oh, the things that I've seen.*" Like I saw a frog in a red vest, and a swan that sat on an oyster bed – like the old Irish folk song. But I didn't want it to be exactly the same, I wanted it less fantastic, more real, with my own memories of the wild things that I've seen in my life. I wrote the first verse:

"I used to think I'm all that, used to watch my back, Was a real cool cat, 'til I kinda lost track, But you shoulda seen my fine hat, boys, shoulda seen my fine black, hat, Now that was a hat to be seen."

I quickly realized I was talking about my wild and woolly days back in Hollywood in the late 70's and early 80's, a time I'd left far behind. (Joan Didion has said she writes to find out what she's thinking, and that's often the case with me.) So I played around with that idea for a few days, but nothing really rose to the top. And while I didn't want to write the same song of wild stories as *Autumn to May*, I didn't really know what my song was about. So I left it alone for about a week.

Until I woke up one morning from a dream I couldn't remember, but I knew, I just knew, what the song was about now. It was about a man lying on his deathbed, saying good-bye to all his friends, telling them about his life, and all the things that he'd seen. *Oh, the things that I've seen.*

Then I thought, "Hnh. A man on his deathbed. Maybe Jill was right. Maybe I *am* depressed." Then I remembered my 70th birthday was coming up in a couple months, so that was the reason I was depressed, and the reason the song was about a man on his deathbed. I was suddenly feeling very mortal, in a very vulnerable, soul-exposed place.

But now that I knew what the song was about, I wrote the whole thing that day, it just flowed out of me. Kept the first verse, which seemed more than ever to me now to be about all those 20 years in Hollywood back in the day, my salad days now long wilted, like that's how my story started – before I went on to the rest of the song for the more meaningful things I'd seen in my life, sharing those memories and emotions with all my friends and family, living and dead, standing deathwatch at my bedside, singing to them, "Oh, the things that I've seen."

I recorded it, and it was quite moving for me – the idea of it, the writing of it, the singing and playing of it. Brian Mann came in on Irish accordion and Adam Phillips on flutes and pipes, and Shawn Thies with some beautiful vocal harmonies. *O, The Things That I've Seen.* Here's the link to the music video:

https://www.youtube.com/watch?v=KSZP6X4m_Rg

Then one day, unannounced and unrelated, after not having come by for half a year or so, Rex showed up with a couple friends, on the winter solstice, a week before my 70th birthday, to do a ceremony at the *Siwut* stone.

He did it, with some Chumash chanting and songs, some burning sage, which he calls "clouding," some stories about Coyote. He showed us two eagle feathers he'd collected – which is permitted for Native Americans, as part of their religion. It was a moving ceremony, and I felt honored to be included in it.

Then, at the end of the ceremony, he told me to stand at the head of the stone. He stood behind me, holding an eagle feather in each hand, and he reached around and placed the feathers over my eyes, so I couldn't see, and he said: "This is for the things that you've seen."

I nearly fell over. I asked him why he said that. Was it part of the ceremony? No, it just came to him, he said – it was "for all the things that you've seen."

Had the words come to him in a vision? How could he know that was the name of my song? And what the song was about, and how intensely I'd been connected to it for weeks, how it was entwined with my own 70-year-old feelings of mortality, and legacy, and loss? I hadn't told anybody about my song, except the few people who helped me produce it. Did Rex have the same dream I did, on the same night? Did I transmit the words to him through the ether?

My science friends would call it coincidence. Jung would call it synchronicity, J. B. Rhine would call it ESP, physicists might call it quantum entanglement. The Chumash elders would probably say Rex is just in touch with the spirit world.

But the Jedi would say the Force was strong in him. And maybe in that moment, the Force connected us.

APPENDIX B
SOME FALSE STARTS IN REVIEW

A FEW MONTHS after the release of the movie and book, the publisher – Ballantine – returned to me the finished manuscript I'd sent to them the year before. They had no more need of it, and it was mine now. This is the note that accompanied the manuscript:

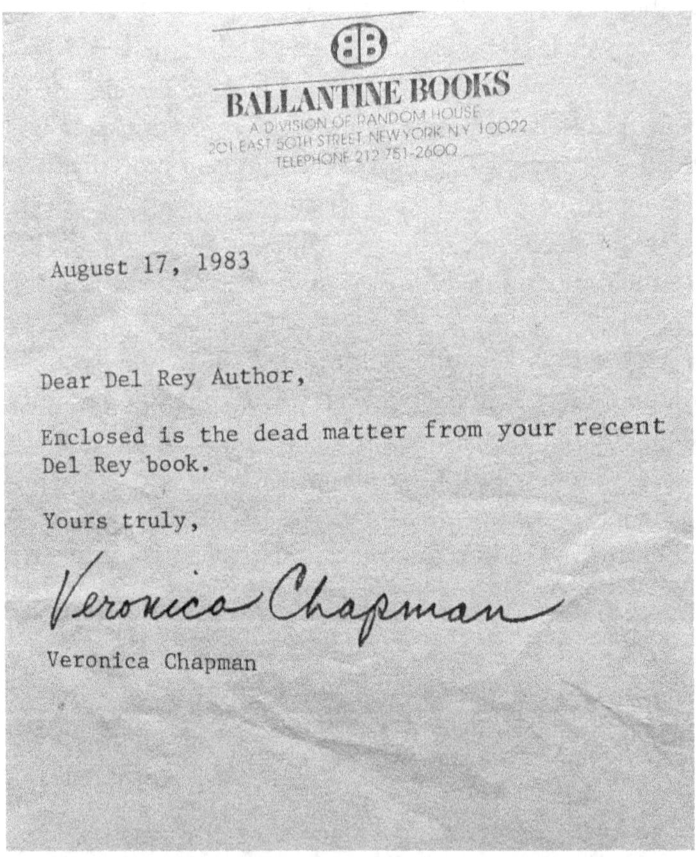

Cover page of manuscript returned to me by the publisher after publication of Return of the Jedi *novelization (Del Rey, 1983.) Photo courtesy of the Author.*

Seriously? I gotta say, it felt anticlimactic at best, and rather dismissive – though I'm sure "dead matter" is simply a term of art in the publishing trade. You never know who's secretly in your corner and who's not in this business, though.

One time, a producer I'd worked with on one of my shows – who always professed loving my work – told me I could use her as a reference any time when applying for future projects. I did use her name, several times – and then learned, again, two years after the fact, that when any showrunner called her to ask about me, she told them I was poison, that I shouldn't be hired for anything. Just part of the "In Hollywood your friends are the ones who stab you in the front" story. These were painful years for me, I'd fallen and I couldn't get up, filled with storms of betrayal and bad luck. Poor me.

But of course I had moments of extreme good luck, as well – like when, out of the blue, I got to work on the set of *ET*, meet Spielberg, and kick off a novelization career. An average writer's career in Hollywood runs 15-20 years, and mine went from 1983 to 2002, so I fit snugly into the norm. Some successes, some beat-downs, and a lot of fun memories. Still, when I stopped getting work, I felt crushed. For two years, I was depressed and directionless.

And then Jill said – as she'd said many times in the past – fuck Hollywood, make your own damn movie.

So I did. I co-founded the Santa Barbara Community Film Studio. Based on the template of Community Theater – all local volunteers, except instead of producing local plays and musicals, our mission was to produce feature films. We advertised for actors on Craigslist, we put out announcements for scripts to anybody in town who'd written one they wanted to see made. We registered as a 501(C)3 nonprofit organization, got funded with donations, assembled a crew of volunteers; and we made a feature film titled *The Bet*, which won Best Feature at the 2013 L.A. Femme Film Festival. Our hope was to spread this idea all around the country – the notion that any community could organize a film crew, get a script, and make their own movie. The franchise never took off, but it was a good idea.

Aside from producing that one feature film, none of my feature screenplays have been made into movies. I've pitched them, had them rejected over and over, put them aside, rewritten them, and written new ones. Pitched movie ideas and scripts to countless producers and development executives, only to have them nod blankly and say, "What else do you have?"

Over the years, I generated interest in 20 or so of my film scripts off my pitch, and sold half a dozen screenplays, three of which made it as far as pre-production, but fell apart just before filming started, on the shoals of producer/studio conflicts, financial shenanigans, leading cast scheduling conflicts, or political intrigues (in the case of a Chinese co-production).

Of course, writing and pitching a movie are two completely different exercises, but there's one thing that links them, if both are going to be successful. And that is, you have to know what the movie is <u>really</u> about. That's often what some executive or producer in the room is going to ask you when the pitch is done: "Yeah, but what's it <u>really</u> about?" If you were pitching *Star Wars*, you could condense the plot, and describe some of the characters, but then when somebody asked what it was <u>really</u> about, you'd want to say it's really about the coming of age of a young farmboy during an interplanetary rebellion, as he comes to learn his father is the Military Commander of the Evil Empire. You have to know this cold before you pitch. And you have to know it cold while you're writing it, or it will never be a compelling film.

The other thing you need to remember as you construct the story is that you have to decide what your main character's wound is. Everybody's wounded in some way, and in a good film you have to keep returning to your main character's wound and mine it, dialogue with it, wrestle with it, write it a satisfying outcome. The theme of your story is resolving that wound.

Those are the two core anchors of any good movie – understanding the main character's wound, and knowing what the story is really about. After that, the writing is all craft – quirks and subtext in dialogue, individuating voices, how to start and end scenes, internal scene structure, overall script structure, how to create a few great Moments, a thousand little details. But that's all a subject for a different book, about which many have been written.

These are six screenplays I've either optioned or sold, and why they didn't get made.

1. Pearl Hart. This true story was brought to me by producer Lee Caplin, who then optioned my script and thought he had a studio buyer, but he was wrong. (When a producer *options* a script, it's for a set period of time – 6 months, a year – during which he pays a small amount for, and owns the rights to it. At the end of the option period, either the rights return to the writer, or the producer *exercises* the option, and buys the script outright, for a full fee.) Pearl Hart was originally a Canadian debutante in 1892 when she decided that life wasn't for her, so she headed south and west, where she became a stagecoach bandit, ultimately committing the last recorded stagecoach robbery in American history. She went to prison, got pardoned, and became a champion of women's rights.

2. Deadpoint. Classic noir/insurance fraud/murder thriller in the *Double Indemnity* mode, this one was optioned by Victor-Grais Productions. It made it to being all cast and ready to shoot, with lead actor Pierce Brosnan attached – until he backed out at the last minute because he got an offer from some unknown movie about a character named James Bond, some kind of spy thing. So the *Deadpoint* deal fell apart.

3. The Transplant. Comedy-horror script, in tone like *Shawn of the Dead*, about a mad scientist/surgeon who transplants one patient's brain tumor into another patient's abdomen, and the tumor takes on a life and mind of its own, with the transplant patient going on a killing spree around the hospital. This one was optioned twice – once to Hannibal Pictures – but it all fell apart 2 weeks before shooting when there was a screaming fight money disagreement between the producer and the production company.

4. Wiz Kids. Originally titled *Merlin Cuts Class*, bought outright by Fireworks Studios. Concerns a 12-year-old 6th century Merlin, who gets magically transported to the contemporary Glendale Galleria, where he hooks up with some middle school kids to find where Excalibur was hidden, bring it back to put it in the stone where it belongs, and save his new friend Artie's mom's life along the way. Kind of Goonies meets Arthurian legends in Los Angeles. Fireworks Studios went belly up and nobody bought it out of bankruptcy.

5. *Lost Vegas*. Producer Lee Caplin said he had access to a bankrupt, vacant, Las Vegas casino and a $1 million German investor for 6 months, if I could write a small Vegas crime story in 6 weeks, with that budget. I did, he optioned it, but then the investor bailed during the savings and loan collapse in the '80's, and then the casino got torn down.

6. *Shanghai*. This last one was a Chinese production, and not only of historical note, but interesting as an example of what it's like to develop and write a script having to take notes from Chinese censors and government hacks, instead of just studio hacks. Based on a true piece of history, when, during World War II around 20,000 German and Polish Jews fled to Shanghai, the only city in the world that didn't require an entrance visa. Once there, they were given safe haven until eventually rounded up by the Japanese for a final solution. This project made it to four weeks from production in Shanghai, casting nearly done, John Avildsen attached to direct, me with an appointment at the Chinese consulate in L.A. the next day to get a visa to fly there for a press junket… and then I got an email to wait. And never heard from them again. And they didn't answer my emails. Well. That's show business!

APPENDIX C
AFTERTHOUGHTS

LOOKING BACK on my life in Hollywood, there are things I miss about it – the Writer's Room, the collaboration, the camaraderie, the flashes of glamor, writing a tasty script, seeing my name in the credits, rubbing elbows with entertainment giants and consummate craftspeople. But leaving L.A. also opened up a whole new world to me. Instead of writing everyone else's stories, on their shows, I could finally go back to writing my own stories again. Back to writing novels – my first love – and increasingly writing music. Folk music mostly; story songs.

I've released six albums, and those songs are the closest connection to my soul, of any writing I've done. Songs of the heart, and of the spirit. One of the songs on my *Matamoros* album, has the line, "The world keeps spinnin' 'round and 'round and 'round, and I just keep fallin' down and down and down." It's taken me a lot of falling down and getting up to get here, but maybe that's what the Hero's Journey is about.

In another way, it has something to do with a race against death. Like there are so many things I want to do before I die, but that train just keeps coming, and sooner or later it's going to hit me before I've finished doing everything I wanted to do. So if I keep writing about it, maybe those stories will keep me alive a little longer.

That scenario was brought home day after day in my work as a doctor. Contemplating mortality all around me laid the table for me to confront my own – which sometimes I did, and other times I denied. But I've certainly been in conversation with Mr. Death for a long time.

The end of the Journey comes together when the hero brings a prize back home from the conquest. The prize can be anything – gold, true love, triumph over evil, insight into life's meaning. So I look at myself and wonder: what are the jewels I'm bringing back from the guarded cave? After all the conquests, beat-downs, disappointments, joys, prides, wounds, friends, enemies, and revelations… what have I brought home with me?

I've brought it *all* home. Good and bad, joy and grief, anger, frustration, ecstasy and heartache – it was all a grand prize. All of it shaped me, deepened my soul, enriched my memories. What a treasure it's all been. I'm so grateful.

So maybe gratitude is the very prize. Conscious, profound gratitude. How lucky I've always been – to grow up in middle class affluence to parents who loved me, to be smart and driven enough to go to med school, to love and play music, to find joy in writing, to have found love with a woman, and then our children, to have stumbled into my dream job of writing television, to find public success in writing, to find deep peace in writing music, in family, in friends, in life. An unbelievably privileged life.

And then in the midst of that to be plagued by worry, insecurity, shame, anger, despair, financial fears, world destruction fears, rise of fascism fears, blame and prejudice, illness – the richness of the good and the bad together – until, at last, as the journey tumbles into its third act, to remember. How lucky I am. How grateful I am.

I don't always remember that. I'll go days or weeks feeling lousy, or depressed, or frustrated over some life stress, personal, cultural, or political. But then I catch myself, and remember how unbelievably fortunate I am, what a gift my life has been. So let me take a few pages to contextualize this whole wild ride. All the unlikely things that had to happen to get me to this place.

It was my wife, Jill, who suggested I pause and contemplate all my peregrinations, the context of my life, the miracle of how I got to be here. It begins in my ancestral memories of how my grandparents came to this country from Russia. Two stories, really, about my father's father and my mother's father. I wish I had stories from my grandmothers, too, but they weren't storytellers the way the men in my family were. My grandmothers – like most grandmothers, I think – stayed in the background making meals, taking care of all the kids, holding the home together, listening and smiling and shaking their heads when the men told their tales.

But my grandfathers' tales always filled me with wonder. My dad's dad, Joseph Kahn, and my mom's dad, Ben Pesmen.

Joseph Kahn Comes to America

Joe Kahn grew up near a little village about 500 miles north of Moscow called Cherevucha. They lived on a big farm they took care of for a non-Jewish landlord; it had about 200 cows, 40 horses, chickens, and geese. Joe remembers being 7-years-old, grabbing a horse by the mane, pulling himself up, and riding it all around ("I did whatever I wanted to, the horses understood I was in charge.")

There was also a lake on the farm, where they fished (which is why he decided, decades later, to build Paradise Villa on Lake Michigan – he loved being next to a lake and fishing). Then on the weekends they would take a wagon or a sled for a one day ride into town, to sell the geese and fish. One day a pack of wolves followed them, and they had to throw fish and geese off the sled one at a time as they went, to keep the wolves occupied, so by the time they got to town, there wasn't much left to sell. Another time when Joe's father was driving the empty sled across the frozen lake, the ice broke, and everything dumped into the freezing water. Joe's dad pulled himself out, grabbed the horse by the bridle and pulled the horse out, and then the horse pulled the sled out.

They let the horse sleep in the house that night to warm up, but the next day it got put in the barn. By the day after that, all four of its feet were dead from frostbite, and they had to kill it. And then his father developed pneumonia, and died 2 weeks later. Joe was 15, and as the oldest son, took over running the farm.

When he was 20, he got called up for the draft. When the Cossacks drafted Jews into the army, it was for a 30 year tour of duty, and they were sent immediately to the front lines – in this case, the war between Russia and Japan. But Joe's uncle taught him a trick to dodge the draft (which he initially wouldn't talk about to my father, he was too embarrassed). He leapt repeatedly from a chair to the ground, landing with a hard stomp onto one foot... until his hip dislocated. Then he would pop the hip back in, and do this over and over, until he could dislocate his hip at will. Then he went to his draft appointment, where they rejected him for having a dislocated hip.

All was well until one of the fish mongers in the market wanted to pay him 50% less for that batch of fish. When Joe refused, the guy turned him in to the police, telling them the trick he'd used to avoid the draft. The Cossacks came to the farm and got him and brought him back to the police station to get pressed into military service. But as he was being processed in, there was a brouhaha outside – another farmer riding into town, yelling bloody murder, there was a fight and a killing at some other farm 10 miles away. Everyone rushed out of the police station to see what was going on… and Joe tiptoed out the back.

He remembered he had a friend who lived on the second floor of the building next to the police station, so he went in the back door of that building, and stayed with his friend for 2 days. It was the beginning of shabbat when he arrived, so he wasn't going to go anywhere all day Saturday anyway. When things had quieted down, he borrowed his friend's horse and rode back to his farm to say good-bye to his family – he obviously couldn't stay there. His mother gave him the 300 rubles she'd saved, and a pouch of food, and he took a train, a wagon, and walked, crossing Poland until he got to a friend of the family who lived on the German border. His friend took him to an easy spot to cross that night, and from there he made his way to Hamburg and Bremen, where he bought passage on a ship to Baltimore.

From there he took a train to Chicago, where his Uncle Paulson had come 5 years earlier. By this time he'd gone through 200 of his 300 rubles, so he sent 100 rubles back to his mother, leaving himself $3, and set off to find Uncle Paulson, speaking no English. But the area around Maxwell Street was full of Yiddish-speaking immigrants, and when he had $1 left, he finally found Paulson. Joe was beside himself, having found no way to make any money, and just about out of cash. Paulson told him, "This is America. Anybody who wants a job can get work." So Paulson took him to a tavern on Madison Street run by a friend of his, and Joe got a job as a janitor.

He collected not only his wages, but all the spare change he found sweeping up – lots of it in the bathroom where men lost coins from their pockets when they lowered their pants. Eventually he tended bar as well, and picked up extra being a bouncer, until he had enough money to buy the place, and that was the start of his American dream.

He kept the tavern income as cash under the bed, until he had enough to start buying properties – the main one being the land in Union Pier that he turned into the 26 vacation cottages of Paradise Villa. In the beginning, the whole family worked at the tavern, though. Uncle Lorry was the bouncer. Lorry once cold-cocked a Chicago cop for picking the pockets of an unconscious drunk on the floor – so Joe had to pay off an alderman to make sure the cops didn't retaliate. My father – the intellectual of the family – only had two jobs. In the early days he had to deliver one case of whiskey to the alderman's house each month. And later, when Paradise Villa was a going concern, he ran the milk wagon that delivered fresh milk every morning to the guests – driving the car when he was 12-years-old.

Years later, when my father was 15-years-old, and all he'd ever seen Joe do before that was sit at his big rolltop desk doing the paperwork necessary to run his businesses, he was out walking with his father. One of Joe's cousins trotted up the dirt road on a cranky, snorting horse, barely able to control the beast. Joe told him to get down off the horse and let him give it a try. My father was thinking, Yeah, right, like my father can tame a wild horse. But Joe vaulted up onto the horse, pulled the beast's head around by the reins, and took off at a furious gallop down the road, until they disappeared. When he came back ten minutes later, the horse was as calm as could be, and the cousin thanked him and trotted off. My father said he never looked at his father the same way again.

Joe Kahn on a horse at Paradise Villa, Union Pier, Michigan, 1935.

Ben Pesmen Comes to America

Ben was born in 1886 and grew up in Panoruvka, near the Ukraine border. His grandfather, who lived in Castebaubber, was, among other things, a scribe who wrote most of a Torah scroll before he died. Never finished it. Ben's father, Abraham, did a little of this, a little of that. He sold fish at a market in Velizh, he was a store clerk, he fixed things. Ben's mother's maiden name was Chya Dolginov. And Ben's father had 3 brothers – Hyman, a tailor in Panoruvka; Isaac, a bookbinder in Lugansk; and I think another named Itzhak, but he may have confused that with Isaac in the telling.

When Ben was 12, he started painting signs for spare money. He remembers painting the sign for a doctor's office, but spelled the doctor's name wrong, so he didn't get paid.

When Ben was 14, he and his father were visiting his Uncle Isaac in Lugansk, when Isaac suggested Ben stay with him to apprentice. His father was reluctant, but Ben made a strong case, so his father left him there, where he learned the bookbinding trade for 4 years. He also learned secularism – he'd always worn *tallit* and *tfilin* and lived orthodox growing up, but Uncle Isaac didn't believe in any of that. So once Ben moved in with his uncle, he lost all the religious aspects of life, except going to temple on the High Holidays.

He remembers the day Uncle Isaac got a powerful cutting machine to cut through reams of paper; and the day Ben sliced through half his finger with it. At one point Isaac had the portion of the scroll that his father had written, shipped from Castbaub- ber to Lugansk, so he could start binding it. That project was never completed, though, because…

In 1904 there was a big pogrom in Lugansk, and Uncle Isaac told Ben to go hide under the barn. He took his one good coat, with a hidden pocket that held a bankbook showing 100 rubles in the bank. From under the barn he watched his Uncle Isaac get murdered, and buildings burned all over the village. He remem- bers taking out his pocketknife, and resolving to cut his own throat if he was discovered there – he knew what would be done to him if he were taken alive. He half-laughed when he mentioned this memory to my father, and said, "Ez retzach chazay." My father repeated it, also laughing, like they were repeating an old adage. I don't know what it means in Yiddish, but *retzach* means to kill in Hebrew, and *chaza* means "to behold, in a vision." So there's maybe a sense of what the idiom is about – "Look at me, I'm gonna kill myself." He stayed there under the barn 2 days, until things quieted down and until he got too hungry to stay where he was. At that point he took his coat to the bank, withdrew his 100 rubles, and took a 2 day train back to his parents' home in Panoruvka – he thinks it was hundreds of miles away, but not sure any more. My guess from Google Maps is around 600 miles.

When he got to Panoruvka, his family was gone. Turns out there'd been a pogrom there, too (maybe it was Easter, a favorite holiday for pogroms?) He stayed hidden at home for a few days until his mother and siblings (Lou, Sarah, Ruth, Bill) returned. Their story was that they fled when the pogrom started, and a peasant woman let them hide in her attic for one night only, then kicked them out from fear of getting in trouble. The next day they had to hide in the forest of birchwoods, until they found a farmer's barn, and hid there. Once, when voices could be heard outside, 1-year-old Sarah started crying, and Ben's mother (Chya – who was pregnant with Pete at the time) – had to smother her with a blanket to keep her quiet, nearly suffocating her until the voices outside went away. But baby Sarah survived. The next day, when the farmer found them, he kicked them out too.

When they got back to Panoruvka, Chya sold their one cow to their landlord, and moved to Novordik, where they all stayed in one room of a friend's house. That's where Pete was born. Ben and his father Abraham then took half the family's money to go to America.

They went to Vilna first, which was on the water, and they could book passage somewhere. They met a girl who asked if she could go with them as Abraham's wife, so she wouldn't need her own passport, and they said yes. But when they booked passage on a boat to Finland, the authorities found her to have the disease Trachoma, so they wouldn't let her proceed. She gave Ben and Abraham $40 as a thank you, and went back to Novordik. They took the boat to Finland, and with that $40 Ben was able to take another boat to Copenhagen, with plans to meet his father in America after he made more money in Denmark.

Ben made his way to Denmark, where he worked for another bookbinder for 8 months, until he made enough money to book passage on a ship over here. Made it to St. Joseph, Missouri, where he reconnected with his father and another family member, who got him a job in a meat packing house. They eventually made enough to bring all the rest of the family over here – except Uncle Hyman, the tailor, who decided to stay in Russia and nobody knows what happened to him.

So they got here, got married, started their families, and made sure their kids had a better life than they'd had. My father went to medical school at the University of Chicago ($125/semester tuition) and my mother went to the Art Institute of Chicago. They both had siblings, so I had lots of cousins, and we all grew up in the suburbs of Chicago.

I went to Maine West High School, which, as mentioned earlier, was a two-edged sword of random, hurtful anti-Semitism as well as some lifelong friends. Memories include setting elements colorfully afire in Qualitative Chemistry lab (Potassium flamed purple! Who knew?!), with cohorts Dave Thinnes and Al Ripperger, feeling like modern day alchemists; playing music with Thinnes, Ripperger, and Mark Sorensen in groups like Johann and the Pacemakers; reading wonderful, and sometimes boring, literature; going to the movies, playing ping-pong and poker and bridge, being shy at school dances, and eating pizza and watching a hundred TV Western dramas, *Gunsmoke, Have Gun Will Travel, The Rifleman, Cheyenne, The Rebel, Wanted Dead or Alive, Wagon Train, Rawhide, Bonanza, Laramie, Tales of Wells Fargo, The Adventures of Jim Bowie, Bat Masterson, Wyatt Earp, Yancy Derringer, Maverick, Tales of the Texas Rangers, Tombstone Territory, The Lone Ranger, Lawman, The Gray Ghost, Wild Bill Hickock, The Restless Gun, Broken Arrow, The Cisco Kid, Sugarfoot, Trackdown,* the list goes on, and I ain't kiddin'. Generally doing all the things suburban kids did in the 50's and 60's.

It strikes me that Steven Spielberg's origin story is extremely similar to mine, he even made a couple movies about it – *Fievel: An American Tail*, and then The *Fablemans* – and how random, but not, it is for our paths to have crossed in the way they did. His journey took him directly into film, while mine meandered from college, and protest marches, to medical school and the sorcery of lifesaving, to marriage, to 1970s Hollywood abandon, to writing novels, to having kids, to working emergency rooms… to the set of *ET: The Extra-Terrestrial*, where our strange, wandering roads, having split up in the Pale of Settlement, re-crossed on a sound-stage at Laird Studios. Highly unlikely.

It's a miracle, really.

So thank you to my grandparents who overcame torment to emigrate here, to my parents who struggled upward into the great American middle class, to my beautiful, talented wife, my beloved kids, my grandchildren, my cousins, my aunts and uncles now long gone, my friends, my enemies, my teachers, my readers, my fans, my champions, my denigrators, my life, the universe, music, pain, grief, jokes, sex, weeping, sneezes, thrills, outrages, books, words, movies, cold, night, flowers, obstacles, broken toes, water balloon fights, hunger, food, song, loss, beauty, stuffed animals, love, heart-break, babies, peace, weather, whiskey, community, harmony, tira-misu, Doritos, yes - even Doritos, and all the rest.

Thank you. Thank you. Thank you.

Appendix D
My Exegesis/Memoir of Writing *Return of the Jedi*

Reprised En Bloc

I've reprised all the disparate segments of the novelization commentary *en bloc*, below, to connect them into a single document, for ease of reading and referencing.

For attribution of Fair Use quotations, please see numbers listed in the Footnotes section, which refer to the numbers 1-44 and 59-147, previously noted in the segmented version of this exegesis scattered throughout the text of the memoir. All those citations listed earlier apply to the following, combined, text.

PROLOGUE, PAGES 1-5

My handwritten manuscript begins with the iconic line, "A long time ago, in a galaxy far, far away..." – of course, how else could it begin? – followed by the notation of the day of commencement of writing, Monday, July 19, 1982. Two weeks after my meetings with George up at Skywalker Ranch, one week after my unanswered letter about changing the ending. (What hubris I had!)

I wrote the first line, "The very depth of space," as my emotional reaction to the visual opening of the first film, and how impacted I was by that similar opening of all three films. Deep black space, the stars giving it a depth of field, and just pausing on that for a long chunk of screen time, letting the fact of it sink in, before the first spaceship enters the picture. The very depth of space. It's all I could think of to say, and I wanted the reader to dwell on that conceptually the same way I'd dwelled on it visually and emotionally that first time, in the 3rd row at the Chinese Theater.

(Not long after the book came out, an irate Texas elementary school librarian wrote to me complaining of my use of sentence fragments,

setting a bad example for young, impressionable minds. I replied with a kind of smarmy explanation of the difference between creative and expository writing, corrected a typo and some syntax in her letter, and felt quite smug with my cleverness. With the perspective of years, I wish my reply had been kinder, or gentler, or more generous. More Jedi-like. What an asshole I was sometimes, and too clever by half. Or maybe by three eights.)

In the next paragraph on page 1, I refer to the fate of Endor's planet, which had "long since died of unknown cataclysm." Endor was always referred to as a moon, which implied there must have been a planet to which it was attached. But we never see a planet. So I figured it must have had a planet once, and that planet got somehow destroyed by "unknown cataclysm." So that was my reference. I remember thinking at the time that when I was all done with the book, and before I submitted it, I'd come back to this spot, or find a better spot, to go into the specifics of the demise of Endor's planet.

But I forgot. Always seemed like a good idea to make a whole book or movie about that someday, though. The destruction of Endor's planet.

This leads to Vader's opening appearance in ROTJ – on page 2, arriving at the Death Star on an Imperial Star Destroyer. The security shield engulfing both Death Star and Endor goes down as his ship arrives – freaking out the officers on the Death Star, because they realize only one person could have lowered the shield from a spacecraft. Vader. Evil arrives before anyone else. Like since God made the animals before he made people, that snake had to have been waiting in Eden before Adam and Eve even existed. Evil waits.

It's also a foreshadowing of the fact of the security shield, which becomes such an important element at the end of the film.

Right from the start we see Vader's power, and the fear he instills, even in his followers. Establishing the enemy from the outset, seeing how powerful his forces are, tells us exactly what our heroes are going to be up against. Not that we don't already know. But the previous movie had come out two years before, so this is a good reminder.

Mof Jerjerrod, the overseer of Death Star Operations, along with the Imperial Troops, assemble to await Vader's arrival. When his shuttle door opens on the Death Star, I wrote "Only darkness glowed…" because

Vader always struck me as a radiant force of darkness, as opposed to a black hole, for example, that only absorbs light.

He tells Jerjerrod that the Death Star's construction is not happening fast enough, the Emperor will not be pleased – and furthermore, the Emperor is on his way. The Emperor, a still darker force than Vader, scares Jerjerrod even more – but on the other hand, his coming arrival heralds the total destruction of the Rebellion, "in a single blow." So way more powerful than Vader.

The specter of this excites Vader so much, the last sentence of the Prologue, on page 5, says, "For the briefest second, Vader's breathing seemed to quicken…"

This was something unimaginable, that his machine respirations could be affected by his emotions. But it was an intentional paradox. It was, in fact, the first tiny clue that there was yet a flicker of humanity in Darth Vader.

ROTJ, CHAPTER 1, PART ONE, PAGES 6–12

We shift the scene from Death Star to desert. "The sandstorm wailed like a beast in agony, refusing to die." Giving the desert the characteristics of a writhing beast was setting the stage. This is the Ordinary World of the First Act.

In a desert hut of nuance and shadow, unknown hands fashion a light saber, and call R2D2 over to get it. We might make the assumption that the mysterious figure is up to some dark deed; or we might assume the figure is Luke, himself now a man of shadow and nuance, burdened by the knowledge of who his father is. Either way, the setting asks us to expect a surprise.

For the first time here, we see Artoo's vocalizations written out. "Vrrrr-dit dweet?" I got a world of shit from fans for trying to write the way Droids and Wookies sound. But that's what a writer does, tries to evoke visual, auditory, olfactory and emotional moments with words on a page. I try my best.

In the next segment, where the winds of Tattooine "seem to come from everywhere at once," creating a sense of chaos, we get to learn about Jabba the Hut – "the vilest gangster in the galaxy," a creature who both "collected and invented atrocities." Every adventure has bad guys, I was just trying to elevate this one to the next level. C3PO and R2D2 are on their way to see him at his palace — a castle of evil at the center of nature's chaos.

The fussy Threepio does not want to be delivering the message they've been tasked with giving Jabba — but then, "No one worries about Droids," he complains. Developing Threepio's personality and inner life was an integral part of the book as well as the movie. And he was a fun character to make fun of, but always affectionately, never meanly.

When they reach the compound, Threepio "musters his resolve" because that's all he could do in this situation — resolve was a "function that had been programmed into him." I was always trying to reconcile the computer system that he was with the human feelings he exhibited. And felt. Now, in 2025, we're only just beginning to explore these same dichotomies as Chat GPT and other AI programs are being developed into sophisticated "companions." C3PO is the granddaddy of all that.

When they knock, an Eyeball sticks out of a small opened hatch, and says, "Tee chuta hhat yudd!" Threepio, who has been programmed to understand 6 million languages, responds in Eyeball. And the two Droids are admitted through the iron door, which grinds shut behind them. No escape. Abandon all hope, ye who enter here. (BTW, nobody ever gave me grief about writing out Eyeball dialogue. I guess I was more fluent in Eyeball.)

They're escorted through the corridors by Gamorrean guards, and we learn it is Artoo who's been programmed with a message from Master Luke, to give to Jabba. Threepio is quite nervous, and just wants to get out of there. I'm not sure why anxiety would have been programmed into him. Maybe it just arose out of a self-teaching algorithm. I know I'd learn to be anxious flying around the galaxy in the midst of a rebellion.

They're soon joined by Bib Fortuna, Jabba's major-domo, a humanoid from whose head emerged "two fat, tentacular appendages that exhibited prehensile, sensual, and cognitive functions." Seeing pictures of Bib made me wonder just what those tentacles did, and those three functions seemed likely. After I came up with that, I always wanted to do a book about that race of aliens. Threepio tells Fortuna they have a message for Jabba. Artoo "beeped a postscript," and Threepio translated, telling Fortuna, "And a gift." But this is the first time C3PO has heard about a gift, and it worries him. With good reason.

So much so, that as they approach Jabba's chamber, he whispers to Artoo, "I have a bad feeling about this." This is a recurring joke – Han has said the same thing in other circumstances – so it's a bit of a wink to the audience. Threepio is saying it to Artoo, but really telling the audience, that difficult challenges are coming.

C3PO and R2D2 are brought before Jabba the Hutt, having been instructed by Luke to give Jabba a message and a gift. Threepio is freaked out at being here – and we see why in our first introduction to the Hutt.

He was huge, his eyes were yellow, and his reptilian skin (I surmised) was "covered with a fine layer of grease." Yuck. I was trying to come up with the most disgusting physical attributes I could. Stunted arms, sticky fingers (Great Rolling Stones album!), and no hair – it had "fallen out from a combination of diseases." I particularly liked that notion, that he had syphilis, ringworm and scleroderma among other things, causing his hair to fall out. (I always enjoy bringing my medical interests into my novels.) His plump tail was like "a tube of yeasty dough," and he "drooled continuously." (Again inspired by some of my ER patients.)

"We're doomed," says Threepio, "wishing for the thousandth time that he could close his eyes." It occurred to me, looking at one of the production stills of Threepio, that his eyes were always open – and what a horror it would be if I could never close my eyes, never shut out the thing that I didn't want to see. In that moment, I shared C3PO's horror.

With Jabba, we meet Oola, his dancing girl chained at the neck, soon to meet a sad fate; and Salacious Crumb, a giggling "monkey-like reptile" who fed off the "food and ooze that spilled" out of Jabba's mouth. I was thinking a little bit of the remora, whose diet is mostly the feces of the shark it's attached itself to.

As the droids stand before Jabba, Threepio urges Artoo to give him the message, so they can get out of there – and Artoo projects a holographic image of none other than Luke Skywalker.

Luke introduces himself as a Jedi Knight – and this is the first time we learn Luke is now a full-fledged Jedi. He requests an in-person meeting with Jabba to bargain for the life of Han Solo – and the entire court bursts into laughter at the idea. Contemptuous laughter is probably the strongest form of insult and power differential.

But Luke's hologram isn't done making his proposal to Jabba. To sweeten the bargain, and to show good faith, Luke offers these two droids as unconditional gifts. Threepio totally dithers now, at the idea that Jabba will be his new master. Bib Fortuna, Jabba's major-domo, is sycophantishly contemptuous of Luke – telling Jabba that if Luke would rather bargain than fight, he is no Jedi.

Jabba agrees, there will be no bargains: "I have no intention of giving up my favorite decoration." And with that cue, he indicates the alcove where the carbonized form of Han Solo hangs, "his face and hands emerging out of the cold hard slab, like a statue reaching from a sea of stone." A sudden reminder of the thing we've all been waiting to see, but had forgotten about in the moment.

This is the first time we've seen Solo since his carbonization in the last movie, and it's a stark image – this living bas relief on display for the voyeurism and ridicule of Jabba's entire court. And we are invited to be part of that rogue's gallery, looking on with a kind of morbid fascination.

ROTJ, CHAPTER 1, PART TWO, PAGES 13-15

This section of the novel is all about pure power struggles. And a peek into self-identity. After this first glimpse of the carbonized Solo, we change settings to explore torture chamber tropes, as a way to get into the "minds" of our droids – again, presaging Artificial Intelligence issues that have come to the forefront so recently. As our droids are taken to the reassignment room, "Artoo beeped pitifully" in response to what he saw. So even Artoo has an inner life of feelings and fears. But the psychology we have much more access to is Threepio's.

C3PO looks for an existential cause of how he could possibly have met this horrible fate – so unfair, so without reason. And what a human emotion that is! More human, paradoxically, than the slight tinge of emotion we saw Vader experience when his breath merely quickened with excitement at the prospect of the Rebellion's total annihilation.

It's also an emotion that traditionally has seen many people turning to religion for the answers to these questions revolving around life's meaning – which becomes an interesting turnaround later in the story, when C3PO is viewed as a god by the Ewoks. Also interesting in light of the recent massive gains in AI technology, which make Threepio's *existential ruminations as much science as fiction. Who knows when AI will achieve the same level of introspection we claim to have ourselves?*

Once inside the torture chamber, "an agonized electronic scream, like the sound of stripping gears" draws C3PO's attention to EV-9D9, the Grand Inquisitor droid of this chamber of horrors – a droid with "some disturbingly human appetites." So now we're learning the possibility that all droids have feelings, and some of them are kinda psycho. Legs are being pulled off one droid, as "red-hot irons" are applied to another one's feet. There is no functional reason for such inducement of gratuitous pain - Jabba has simply programmed Ninednine to be a sadist. And no reason to have programmed pain into the feet of the torture victim. But the torture 9D9 oversaw being inflicted actually melted the last droid's circuits – whereupon Threepio's wiring "sympathetically crackled with static electricity." More of C3PO's quasi-human inner life.

As Threepio starts elaborating on one of his responses the way he is wont, 9D9 tells him, "a simple yes or no will do." He surmises 9D9 is the kind of droid who has to prove herself "more-droid-than-thou." Threepio has attitude, and we hear it from the viewpoint of his own inner workings – something the book was able to do that the film wasn't.

But when he pridefully tells her he's fluent in over 6 million forms of communication, he quickly realizes his mistake – for now he's to be stationed at Jabba's side, as the official translator. And the last protocol droid doing duty at Jabba's side, he is informed, was disintegrated for displeasing Jabba.

Threepio's anxiety plunges to ever greater depths. As he is taken away to have a restraining bolt installed, R2D2 lets out "a long, plaintive cry" – more of Artoo's childlike character – then he turns to Ninednine and "beeps in outrage." She laughs at his feistiness, and says he'll do well on Jabba's sail barge.

That's a little convenient (for the writer), since Artoo's presence on the barge is essential to Luke's plan for escape. Seems like a big coincidence that 9D9 assigned him there. But I like to think Luke was able to distantly Force-alter one of Ninednine's circuitry pathways just slightly – enough to influence her assignment of Artoo to the sail barge, and Threepio to the throne room.

And "the droid on the torture rack emitted a high-frequency wail" – as if to punctuate the fate of C3PO and R2D2.

ROTJ, CHAPTER 1, PART THREE, PAGES 15-22

A lot of things are going on at once here.

Threepio is brought to Jabba's vile court to begin his job as official trans-lator. He "hovers warily near the back of Jabba's throne," trying to stay as low profile as possible. Because Threepio has such human attributes programmed into his "personality," it was hard not to project onto him my own fears and insecurities. I think we all responded to that in him.

Oola, the dancing girl, refuses Jabba's disgusting sexual advances. I'm definitely getting a Harvey Weinstein vibe here, though I never could have imagined the physical resemblance between Jabba and Harvey back when I wrote this. In response to Oola's rejection, Jabba has a trap door opened in the floor, and Oola falls through it to her death — "a terri-ble shriek, followed once more by silence." Similar subtextually, I guess, to what was experienced by actresses who rebuked Weinstein and saw their careers dumped into the abyss. We'll soon come to learn the specifics of Oola's fate, when Luke meets the Rancor in the dungeon below.

C3PO continues ruminating nonstop, as the bounty hunter, Boushh, brings in the captured Chewbacca, in chains and on a leash. I used the term "leash" specifically to emphasize Chewie's canine aspects, to suggest he was being humiliated, beyond just the fact of his capture.

When Threepio sees the mighty Wookiee warrior in irons, he gives up all hope: "The future was looking very bleak indeed." It was impor-tant to keep his speech — even a description of his internal feelings — in the cadence of his formal speech patterns. This bounty hunter, who'd been able to accomplish such a feat as to best the great Chewbacca, "was humanoid, small, and mean," whose helmet had an eye-slit "that gave the impression of being able to see through things."

These were meant to be hints that the bounty hunter was, in fact, Princess Leia — humanoid, small, and possessing special insights due to being strong with the Force. Not that we know that she's strong with the Force yet, but suggesting this bounty hunter has the appearance of "seeing through things" is a subtle clue to what we'll learn later about her.

I think in the film it was more obvious — Boushh looked the size and shape of Leia — but I had to give more subtle suggestions in the novel.

Besides which, really – who in the galaxy could possibly subdue the great Wookiee except a close friend?

Boushh speaks in native Ubese – a metallic language – and Jabba calls for Threepio, his new talkdroid, to translate. Jabba asks the mercenary Boushh his price for the Wookiee. Boushh demands 50 thousand, which enrages Jabba, who makes a low counteroffer – until Boushh activates a thermal detonator, discombobulating Threepio and the entire court – and the negotiators settle on a compromise price for Chewbacca.

I wondered, at times, if a chronic anxiety disorder had been programmed into Threepio at his inception, or if that was simply a function of malware and circuitry glitches from his hard knock life.

As Chewie is escorted out to a cell, he spies Lando Calrissian in the crowd, and we come to learn Lando has infiltrated Jabba's court with the intention of helping to try to free Han – for several personal reasons: guilt over getting Solo into this mess, an urge to join the Rebel Alliance and give the Empire some payback, warm feelings for Princess Leia, and a bet with himself that Han could not be rescued.

Max Rebo starts wailing his jizz-music again, and the ongoing party resumes. Boushh surveys the crowd – and locks gazes with Boba Fett, the bounty hunter who put Han in carbonite and sold him to Jabba – and the two mercenaries size each other up. This is the first appearance of Boba Fett since he captured Solo and embedded him in carbonite – and we definitely get the feeling he's a force to be reckoned with.

The final segment of Chapter 1 begins with Chewbacca being led to his cell and unceremoniously thrown in, the door slammed – whereupon he lets out a long howl that "carried through the entire mountain of iron and sand up to the infinitely patient sky." The juxtaposition of the sky's patience lends weight to the lack of patience Chewie – and we – feel in this situation. His howl is the physicalization of the subtext of all our inner outrage.

We move from there to the throne room, now dark and silent, where "shreds of tattered clothing hung from the fixtures, unconscious bodies curled under broken furniture. The party was over." In 1982, the year I wrote this, a lot of Hollywood parties ended this way. I was just drawing on personal experience.

The dark figure of Boushh moves among the shadows. We don't know why at first. He goes to the alcove where Han hangs frozen in carbo-

nite. Does he mean to steal Jabba's treasured possession? This is the first clear close-up we have of that iconic image: Han, reaching out from the carbonite in which he's been frozen.

It was unclear to me, when I began writing, how much time had passed since the end of The Empire Strikes Back *– and how long Han had been frozen in Carbonite. I called some of my contacts at LFL, and got someone to relay the question to George, but nobody had a clear idea. And George never responded. I said I thought it must have been at least some months for our team to retreat, go into hiding, and come up with the rescue plan. Nobody could nail it down more specifically than that.*

I decided to say it was 6 months – though I intentionally left some wiggle room, as Han was waking up: "He was, understandably, disoriented, after having been in suspended animation for six of this desert planet's months—a period that was, to him, timeless."

By saying "this desert planet," I left open the question of how long a month actually was on Tatooine. Recent canon has suggested the actual timeline was closer to a year – an interpretation I allowed for with the leniency of my phrasing.

In any case, Boushh now deactivates the force field around the carbonite trophy and lowers it to the ground. Then "after one last, hesitant glance at the living statue before him," he throws the decarbonization lever. I added the hesitation to reflect the deep feelings Leia has for Han – and the fear in this moment that something could go wrong, that the decarbonization might actually kill him.

Referring to Solo as a living statue evoked Pygmalion for me – the sense that the passionate feelings Boushh had for this inert form were so strong, they could bring it to life. Han's upraised hands fell "slackly to his sides." His face eased into a death mask – then a life mask – and then his "eyes suddenly snapped open, and he began to cough." Prolonging the moment of awakening, starting with a death mask to suggest the possibility that Han might never wake up. (Of course we all know he will, but you try to create tension where you can.) Boushh tries to silence him, so as not to arouse the guards. To keep this moment private – both for purposes of escape, and personal intimacy.

But Solo was disoriented and blind, after having endured what seemed like an eternity "trying to draw breath." I was trying to imagine the torture of what it would be like to be frozen in carbonite and con-

sciously trying to breathe, feeling you had to breathe, but being unable to. And now suddenly he's overwhelmed with all sensation rushing back, along with every memory — "from his childhood, from his last breakfast, from twenty-seven piracies… Men had gone mad, in these first minutes following carbonization." But Han just wasn't that kind of guy, is what I'm trying to say.

He was able to focus down on a few simple questions. Where was he? Where was Lando, who had sold him out? And where was Boba Fett, who had carbonized him?

Boush tries reassurance first. "You're free of the carbonite and have hibernation sickness." The logical, rational explanation. And btw, let's get the hell out of this place. But Han isn't ready for logic yet. He starts to fight his savior, whose mask he feels with his hands — he doesn't know who this is, and isn't about to jump from a frozen frying pan into an unknown fire. His last view before carbonization was of Boba Fett, and this figure above him wears a similar metal mask. "Who are you, anyway?" Solo demands. Not where, or why — but "who" is the most important referent for Han.

The bounty hunter, removing her helmet, reveals herself to be Princess Leia. "'One who loves you,' she whispered, taking his face tenderly in her still-gloved hands and kissing him long on the lips." And they kiss. Ahhhh. Forget all those geographical and analytical explanations. Time to cut to the emotional chase.

End of Chapter One.

ROTJ – CHAPTER 2, PART ONE, PAGES 23-27

Han and Leia reconnect as soon as she's released him from the carbonite. He can't see, though, and he wants to know where he is. "She looked at him a long moment… Tears filled her eyes. 'We'll make it,' she whispered." She knows full well that she's risked everything to save him, including losing time from her duties with the Rebellion — but she just flat out loved the big lug too much to stay away.

Han, too, "was flooded with emotion all at once." Which is, of course, so uncharacteristic of Han. Fortunately for the reputation of his gruff exterior, "a repulsive squishing sound" reveals Jabba and all the "most disgusting miscreants of Jabba's court." The exact opposite of the love we've just been watching. One of the axioms of screenwriting (and its amplification in novelization) is to begin a scene with one emotion, and leave the scene with its opposite.

Jabba cackles. His gathering mocks the lovebirds, as Han and Leia both offer Jabba riches to let them go. He scornfully rejects that, though, and has Han taken off to a cell – while he has Leia brought to him.

Lando steps up – disguised as one of Jabba's guards – and takes Leia's arm, as a prisoner. She whispers to him not to worry – even though their plan is going awry.

What I liked about this scene was the way it kept alternating, not just from the opening moment to the exit, but from hope to despair and back again. All looks lost – then the heroes have a plan – the plan goes sideways – but they think on their feet and come up with a new plan. That's what makes them heroes.

Standing defiantly before Jabba, Leia offers carrots and sticks – lots of money to let them go, but if he doesn't, she tells him she has powerful friends. Jabba is unimpressed. He pulls her to him until "her belly [is] pressed to his oily snake skin." I wanted to drill down on this moment, this image that's so disgusting, even Threepio says, "Oh, no, I can't watch." The idea of something so gross it even offends the sensibilities of a droid, takes it to a new level. Until…

"Jabba poked his fat, dripping tongue out to the princess, and slopped a beastly kiss squarely on her mouth." Turning it up to eleven. I tried to imagine myself in Leia's position. Gag.

My hope is that moments like this, coupled with Jabba's ultimate fate at the hands of Leia, instilled in a young, impressionable female audience the notion that, when they grew up, they didn't have to take this crap, #metoo.

After being released from carbonite by Leia, but immediately recaptured by Jabba, Han is taken to a dungeon cell, still blind. As he tries to organize his thoughts in darkness, it all comes rushing back to his disoriented mind that he was saved by Leia, and he has to get out of here. The dungeon walls are solid rock, though, so he can think of nothing he has to bargain with.

And suddenly, as if things could get no worse, he hears a growl – and "the hairs on Solo's arms stood on end." All at once a wild creature bellows and grabs Han "ferociously around the chest… squeezing off his breathing." Once again, all seems lost – but Han knows that voice:

"Chewie, is that you?" And "For the second time in an hour, Solo was overcome with happiness." Again, the back and forth emotions – and again, Han is so uncharacteristically overcome with emotion.

Chewbacca says, "Arh, arhaghh shpahrgh rahr…"

I was criticized in some quarters for trying to write the sound of Chewie's speech, as I had been criticized for aping Artoo's beeps and whistles. But I loved writing those transliterations, evoking on the page the sounds we all know so well from the films. If someone hadn't seen the movie, these quotes might not have much meaning – but the people complaining about it had seen the film often, so as far as I'm concerned, they have little justification for dismissing my Rosetta Stone attempts. Or if they do feel justified, well, so be it.

And Han understands Chewie perfectly – learning that not only is Leia here with an escape plan, but so is Lando, and so is Luke! And Luke is now a Jedi Knight!

Han scoffs at that, saying, "Come on, I'm out of it for a little while and everybody gets delusions." Chewie protests. Han says, "I'll believe it when I see it."

Whereupon he walked "stoutly into the wall." (Inspired by my own misadventure walking into a wall.)

ROTJ – CHAPTER 2, PART TWO, PAGES 27-31

Jabba's palace gate scrapes open to reveal, making his unshadowed appearance in this episode, Luke Skywalker – "clad in the robe of a Jedi Knight." I didn't say definitively he was a Jedi – just clad in Jedi robes. Leaving a little room for doubt. In any case he's here to rescue Han, we know not how.

He's older now, and defined by his losses – lost illusions, dependency, friends, sleep, laughter… and the loss of his hand. He's grown more powerful, too, of course. He has a Jedi's patience and perspective, as well as Force control. And there's a darkness to him now, that "gave a depth to his personality where before it had been thin, without dimension – though such a suggestion probably would have come from jaded critics."

I was getting kind of meta here, with a double meaning for the movie critics who'd rolled their eyes at Luke's character in the first Star Wars film, as "thin, without dimension." I was putting those "jaded critics" on notice that this Luke had real depth.

Luke strides into Jabba's lair, Force-chokes two Gamorrean guards, and works his Jedi mind trick on Bib Fortuna: "You will take me to Jabba now." And Bib replies, "I will take you to Jabba now." We hadn't seen that done since Obi Wan told the Stormtrooper on Mos Eisley, "These aren't the droids you're looking for," and the Stormtrooper nodded and echoed him in agreement.

When Luke arrives in the throne room, he sees Leia, dressed as a dancing girl, chained at the neck and leashed to Jabba. Luke has to shut out her pain, to focus on the Hutt – and Leia closes her mind as well, so as not to distract Luke from what he must do.

Threepio is thrilled to see Luke, his salvation from this dreadful place. Jabba scolds Bib Fortuna for allowing Luke in. Luke whispers, "I must be allowed to speak," and Fortuna tells Jabba, "He must be allowed to speak." Once again, using Obi Wan's mind trick. But when Luke tries the mind trick on Jabba, to release Han and Chewbacca, Jabba just laughs: "Your mind powers will not work on me, boy." Haughty and dismissive, he is unaffected by Jedi, or even human, thought patterns.

Luke speaks plainly, telling Jabba to release Solo or prepare to die. Again Jabba laughs. Threepio tries to warn Luke that he's standing on a… but Luke ignores the droid and Force-takes a guard's gun to point at Jabba.

That's when the grate Luke is standing on drops him into the pit below, where Oola had been dropped earlier. Just what Threepio was trying to warn him about.

So he may be a Jedi, but he still has some things to learn.

ROTJ – CHAPTER 2, PART THREE, PAGES 31-37

When Luke is dropped into the Rancor pit, we see a guard eaten right away, so we understand what Luke is in for. But he's up to the task, meeting the Rancor's brute strength with agility and inventiveness – I particularly liked sticking the long bone in the beast's craw, because I think we all know what it feels like to get even a small fishbone caught in our throat.

Of course, the Rancor's ultimate death is pretty much a foregone conclusion – so my favorite part of the scene is at the end, when the Rancor's keeper weeps. This man and beast had been each other's only friends for so long – and now the poor jailer's life would be an empty shell, devoid of companionship, as after the death of a dearly beloved pet. In the movie, that moment was played for laughs, but I genuinely felt for the guard, and tried to express that.

All of our heroes have been caught, now, and all are brought before Jabba: Luke, in chains, after killing the Rancor; Han, blind from the carbonite freezing; Chewie, led in by Lando impersonating a guard, the only good guy not yet discovered; Leia, tethered to Jabba; and C3PO, his restraining bolt keeping him close to the throne. Yet they remain their cavalier selves, despite Jabba's dire sentence – they'll be taken to the Great Pit of Carkoon, and thrown to the Sarlacc, who will digest them painfully for a thousand years.

Luke just smiles, though, threatening Jabba, "This is the last mistake you'll ever make." Luke, we infer from this, is not only looking forward to freeing his friends, but to killing Jabba, "to free the universe of this gangster slug." This prospect gives Luke a "dark satisfaction."

Hmm. "Dark satisfaction" isn't a very Jedi-like emotion. In fact, this installment of the series was originally titled Revenge of the Jedi, *but at the last minute, George Lucas decided revenge wasn't a Jedi-like emotion either, so he changed the title word to* Return.

But Luke's dark satisfaction at the anticipation of killing Jabba is no accident. Just as Vader's rapid breathing when he got excited at the end of the Prologue was a hint of a little humanity left in him… Luke's dark satisfaction foreshadows the presence of the Dark Side in him, which will grow as time goes on.

As the prisoners are taken away to their presumed fate, Leia watches them go – noticing Luke's face is fixed in a broad smile. She tries to let his demeanor "expel her doubts," but it feels like she's picking up on a perceived darkness in him.

That's how the section ends in the published book. But in my original manuscript I added one more line, that got cut. Leia: "Luke, old kid, she thought, you're either really brave, or you don't know what's going on."

The Lucasfilm book editor may have felt it was a better button on the scene to end on Leia expelling her doubts. Or possibly the editor didn't care for her flippancy in this grim situation. But for me, my original line kept the focus on Leia's feeling that Luke's smile was inappropriate. She can feel something is up with him, and it ain't good.

ROTJ – CHAPTER 2, PART FOUR, PAGES 37-51

This is the beginning of the first great all-hands-on-deck action sequence in the book/movie, the battle at the Sarlacc Pit. Jabba is on his sail barge, surrounded by his court, attended by Threepio, served by Artoo, and tethered to Princess Leia. Two gunboats accompany the barge, one with the prisoners – Luke, Han, and Chewie – surrounded by their guards: Barada with the long gun, the top-knotted Weequay brothers, and Lando Calrissian, still undercover as a guard.

Han is keeping up a continuous patter of "reckless disregard," to get his guards used to him talking and moving, in case an opportunity for escape presents itself. Reckless disregard is Han's defining characteristic. And Luke uses this time to remain silently introspective – to prepare for the fight ahead, and to remember his youth here on this desert planet. The place he'd first met Obi Wan Kenobi, who'd first shown Luke the way of the Jedi. The beginning of all he'd gained and all he'd lost.

Lost his uncle and aunt here, lost his way of life, lost his innocence. And Ben had taken him to the pirate city of Mos Eisley, where he'd met Han and Chewbacca, deepened his newfound bonds with the droids, Threepio and Artoo, and gone on to save Leia, and lose Obi Wan, and… it all comes rushing back to him now, floating above the sands of Tatooine. "I grew up here," he says simply to Han. Grew up in so many ways. It's a poignant moment, in such a few words that say so much. "And now we're going to die here," Solo replied. Always the cynic.

Luke is confident, though. "Just stay close to Chewie and Lando. We'll take care of everything." Han knows this kind of bravado – in fact, it's the kind of thing he might well have said himself in other circumstances. But it gives him a sinking feeling, here, if everything depends on a kid who thinks he's a Jedi who can wield a Force Han doesn't even believe in. "A fast ship and a good blaster" are all Han believes in, and he wishes he had them now.

But it won't be long before he gets his wish.

"Blood lust and belligerence were testing new levels" on Jabba's Sail Barge, as the party grows more out of control before the execution of the prisoners. It brought to mind, for me, what were called "Celebration Lynchings" in the South, in the '20's and '30's – grand, often drunken picnic events, where innocent Black men were hung before a crowd of thousands. Those death parties were also "a long time ago," but not long

enough, and bloodlust in the world doesn't seem to get much tamer as time goes on.

Threepio is being forced to translate an argument between Ephant Mon and Ree-Yees, with Salacious Crumb kibbitzing. It ends in a fist-fight that Threepio uses as an excuse to fade into the crowd — where he bumps into Artoo, who's serving drinks. Threepio is surprised to see Artoo here, but Artoo seems confident, even nonchalant. Which annoys C3PO, who's quite upset at the prospect of Master Luke's imminent execution.

Jabba, further excited to see the fistfight unfolding before him, tugs on the leash that holds Leia by the neck. Pulls her close to him, and forces her to drink from his glass. It's disgusting, but Leia closes her eyes and tries to appear obedient — waiting for her moment. She consoles herself that there are worse things than touching this creep.

This leads her to think about some of those worse things. Like the night Lord Vader had her injected with chemicals by his pain-droids, and tortured her to get information about the location of the Rebel base. She'd almost broken, but she'd endured those agonies and degradations — just as she can endure Jabba.

Leia senses the Sail Barge stop, and looks out the slatted window to see the convoy paused over a giant sand pit — at the bottom of which is "a repulsive, mucus-lined, pink, membranous hole" surrounded by "rows of inwardly-directed, needle-sharp teeth," with a "black cavity at the center."

"This was the mouth of the Sarlacc."

And this is where our heroes are about to be thrown. All I had to work from was a black and white photograph of the Sarlacc pit, but I imbued it on the page with the most graphic, physical, colorful, horrific prose I could come up with.

I have so much fun writing creepy creatures.

"An iron plank was extended over the side of the prisoners' skiff." Thus begins the first move in this battleground game of chess. Walking the plank, of course, is the hallmark of the pirate adventure, putting this chapter of Star Wars firmly in the continuum of great buccaneer tales. In this case the guards untie Luke's hands, the reasons for which are obscure

to me. Maybe Jabba wanted to see him flailing? Certainly, he needs his hands for what comes next – so maybe Luke mind-tricked the guards into releasing his bonds. In my mind, that's what happened.

He takes a moment to let the desert "warm his soul" – for, as mentioned earlier, this would always be his home. He winks at Leia on the Barge, and she winks back – they must be Jedi-mind connected by this point – and Jabba has Threepio make a speech, hoping Luke will die honorably. This statement coming out of Threepio's mouth doesn't scan well for him, it's against all his programming to speak happily of his master's death.

Jabba informs them he will entertain pleas for mercy, and Han shows his characteristic bravado. But Luke is calm. "Jabba, this is your last chance… Free us or die." It seems like a hopeless threat, given the circumstances. But as earlier, it seems like an un-Jedi-like sentiment, again suggesting Luke hasn't realized his full Jedi potential. Jabba's court laughs – but Artoo secretly rolls up to the top deck of the Barge. Something is afoot.

Jabba gives a thumbs down. Luke gives Artoo a signal, and Artoo ejects an object in a high arc toward Luke. Luke jumps off the plank – catches it on the way down – lets the rebounding plank spring him high in the air – where he catches what Artoo has thrown. Luke's lightsaber. Game on. And now it's full ahead war.

This is Luke's own lightsaber, that he made himself in Obi Wan's old hut on the other side of Tatooine – and which we realize now is what we saw him inserting into Artoo at the very beginning of this story. And he wields it "as if it were fused to his hand."

As in any war, once the first shot is fired, all plans are moot. A lot of things are happening at once. As Lando grapples with a guard, the helmsman falls over the side into the Sarlacc's mouth – with a horrific scream. Another guard falls to the side of the sand pit – and an oozy tentacle darts out of the Sarlacc's mouth, pulling the soldier to his thousand years of digestive doom. Showing us physically exactly what the stakes are.

As Jabba shouts orders to his minions, Leia sees her chance. She jumps behind him, grabs the chain that tethers her to him, wraps it around his many-chinned throat from behind, and pulls with all her strength. "The small metal rings buried themselves in the loose folds of the Hutt's

neck, like a garrote." I wanted to give Leia a little help with the strangulation, and help the reader feel Jabba's death struggle.

He almost breaks her grip, with his huge mass. Yet Leia ignores her
pain, and focuses "all her life-force… into squeezing the breath from
the horrid creature." Jabba's "reptilian eyes began to bulge from their
sockets… his oily tongue flopped from his mouth… until he finally lay
still – deadweight." I really wanted to make this a testament to Leia's
strength of will.

Leia will soon sever the chain, but in this moment, she's freed herself
from this despicable monster. As I mentioned earlier, it's my deepest hope
that thousands of young girls who read this in the book, internalized it,
and grew up with the strength of knowing they didn't have to take the
kind of sleazy, power-mad depredations men like Jabba dole out.

As Luke grabs his laser sword to ignite the battle at the Sarlacc Pit,
Boba Fett quickly goes into action. We haven't seen the famous bounty
hunter fight before, we've only heard about his exploits, and watched
him load the carbonited Han onto his ship in the last episode. We see
him now, but it's so chaotic on the skiff, it's hard to keep track of all the
things going on.

Boba Fett flies down to Luke's skiff from Jabba's Barge, and aims his
gun at Luke – but Luke cuts it in half with his light saber. Fett wraps
Luke in a cable, but Luke cuts it free and knocks Fett unconscious. So
maybe Fett wasn't such a formidable foe after all.

Meanwhile, a cannon blast from the Barge throws Lando overboard
into the sand pit, where he slides slowly toward the Sarlacc's mouth.

The other skiff attacks the prison boat, and Luke jumps into the midst
of a dozen guards, taking a page from Boba Fett's opening maneuver,
and following a Jedi rule-of-thumb: "When outnumbered, attack."

Han, still blind, grabs a spear to hold down to Lando, to pull him
back up on board. But now Boba Fett is back up, taking aim at Luke,
who's decimating the guards on the other skiff. Chewie barks at Solo to
swing his spear at Fett, but Han swings it the wrong way. Chewie yells
again, Han course-corrects – and hits Boba Fett in the back, igniting
his rocket pack.

The jet shoots Boba Fett over the skiffs, ricocheting him into the side of
the sand pit – and straight into the mouth of the Sarlacc. Chewie tells
Han what happened, and Han wishes he could have seen it. It surely

was a satisfying moment, to see the bounty hunter who froze Han in carbonite meet his just desserts.

Of course, Boba Fett will return in another book, another movie, and ultimately his own TV series — so he did manage to escape from the Sarlacc's belly. But for now, it's just another passing moment in the fog of war.

More chaos in the battle at the Sarlacc Pit. A deck gun on the Barge hits the prisoners' skiff, knocking it on its side and sending Han over the edge, where he dangles from the rail by his foot. Chewie is tangled up in debris elsewhere. Luke wipes out the guards on the second skiff, then begins hand over hand climbing up the wall of the main Barge, to dismantle the deck gun that's doing so much damage.

Leia is assisted by Artoo's cutting tool, to sever the chain tying her to the dead Jabba. They run out together, but pause when they see Threepio lying on the floor, his eyeball getting pulled out by Salacious Crumb, the reptile-monkey. Artoo gives the monkey a zap, as Leia helps Threepio up, and the three of them run out the door.

The barge deck gun hits the tilting skiff again, knocking it even more sideways. Chewie is jolted loose, but he manages to hang on with one hand, while he grabs Han's leg with the other — as Han tries to reach Lando, who slides a little further down the sand pit every time he tries to move.

The tricky part in all this is maintaining a sense of comedy in the midst of thrilling battle. It's a little easier because we know the characters, and we love to see them laughing in the face of long odds — and as Han always says, "Don't ever tell me the odds."

Luke reaches the deck gun just as the gunner is about to let off the coup de grace on the dangling chain of Chewie to Han to Lando. One of the gunners shoots the light saber from Luke's hand, though — exposing his artificial hand that replaced the one Vader had cut off. It gives him pause — again to reflect, even momentarily, on all he's lost.

The main gunner shoots at the prison skiff again — tipping it further down. Far enough that Han is able to actually grab Lando's outstretched wrist. Solo yells at Chewbacca to pull them back up — but at that moment one of the Sarlacc's tentacles slithers out of its mouth and grabs Lando around the ankle.

Again, the situation has gotten even worse — but we can somehow create a comic element out of it, because it's so <u>much</u> worse. Wounded comrades, tipping skiff, hanging on for dear life, slipping down a sand pit, deck cannons shooting at them… and now a Sarlacc tentacle? It's deadly… but laughable.

The deck gunners line up their sights for the final kill shot — but Leia has commandeered the deck gun at the other end of the Barge — and she wipes out the main deck gun with a single blast. Leia rocks! And it's nice to see her save the others for a change.

Which brings us to the end of the battle at the Sarlacc Pit. Using one of the big deck guns, Leia blasts the other big gun that's about to destroy the skiff where Chewie and Han are trying to pull Lando from the clutches of the Sarlacc's tentacle. As she does that, Luke Force-grabs his light saber from the deck and decimates the guards surrounding him. He shouts at Leia to point her gun down toward the deck.

Artoo knows what this means. I think Luke must have pre-programmed him for this moment. Artoo beeps instructions to Threepio, who refuses the order. But Artoo just bumps him off the Sail Barge, down to the sand, and jumps down after him.

Meanwhile, the Sarlacc tentacle is pulling on Lando's leg, while Han still holds on to him. Chewbacca grabs a laser pistol to shoot the tentacle, but it's too far for accuracy. So Han tells Chewie to give him the gun. Lando protests: "I thought you were blind!" Solo reassures him: "I'm better." Cracking jokes in the face of death.

Somehow this doesn't reassure Lando, but he doesn't have a lot of say in the matter. Han gets the gun from Chewie, squints, pulls the trigger, and hits the tentacle — which lets go of Lando and slithers back into the Sarlacc's mouth. The mighty Chewbacca pulls Han back onto the skiff — along with Lando, who Han is still holding on to.

Back on the great Barge, Luke gathers Leia up in one arm, and grabs a rope dangling from the rigging. This is a wink to the audience — a callback to the same maneuver in the first movie, when Luke threw a grappling hook to the rafters, grabbed Leia, and swung them to safety by rope. It's a classic pirate movie trope - which connects it to the earlier moment at the start of this battle, when Luke was made to walk the plank.

As Luke leaps off the Barge, he kicks the deck gun trigger – and the blast goes straight down through the deck, where Leia had aimed it. The Barge starts massively exploding, while Luke and Leia swing on the rope to the skiff where their friends await them – and Chewie, Han and Lando help them aboard.

They sail the skiff over to where C3P0 and R2D2 are half buried in the sand, and haul them out with a giant electromagnet. And as Jabba's Barge continues to explode and burn, our heroes have "a great, long moment of hugging, laughing, crying, and beeping." The catharsis after the crisis.

As the Sail Barge erupts in conflagration, they sail off into "the scorching afternoon light of Tatooine's twin suns." Like they've been in hell, and now they're leaving.

ROTJ – CHAPTER 3, PAGES 52-67

So begins ACT 2 (of the film), moving to different locations, and refocusing on the ultimate challenge – blowing up the Death Star.

With Jabba and his court dead at the Sarlacc Pit, our companions walk through a Tatooine sandstorm to get to the Millennium Falcon and Luke's X-Wing. Han's vision is returning as the carbonite sickness wears off, and he finds himself deeply grateful that his friends would risk so much to save him. He's usually such a sarcastic cynic, this feeling is new for him, and it makes him a little uncomfortable, and a little confused.

But it also makes him humbled in a way he's never been. Always before, he was the loner, the cowboy, the rogue. But now: "Once, he was alone; now he was a part." A part of something bigger than himself.

The others all see the change in Han as well. It's a gentle moment for everyone – the recognition of a friend who is evolving.

Then it's all business, and they're anxious to get to the Rebel Base – except for Luke, who tells them, "I have a promise I have to keep first… to an old friend." He doesn't say who that is, but we all know he means Yoda.

So the group splits up – Han, Leia, Chewie, Lando, and Threepio in the Millennium Falcon, to get back into the rebellion; and Luke in the X-Wing with Artoo, where he pauses to look at his damaged hand: the exposed wires and titanium bones replacing the hand Vader cut off. It's a reminder of what the stakes are, and also of the deeper meaning this conflict has for Luke than for the others. On the one hand (pun intended) he sees the beginnings of his terrible transformation to becoming his father, sliding into the Dark Side. On the other hand, this is about bringing down his father.

He pulls a glove over the damage – he doesn't want to think about all those implications right now – "And for the second time in his life, he rocketed off his home planet, into the stars." Like the beginning of his Act Two.

At this point we return to Vader, the object of Luke's ambivalent ruminations. Always good to touch bases with the main antagonist, to see what our heroes are up against, to keep reiterating just how evil this foe is. Vader is on the Death Star, awaiting the arrival of his master, the Emperor, now approaching on a shuttle from a recently arrived Destroyer. Once more I brought in inklings of Vader's still-human emotions – his excitement at Palpatine's visit. "A feeling of fullness, of power, of dark and demon mastery – of secret lusts, unrestrained passion, wild submission." There's an almost sexual component to the power dynamic, as if Vader is in the thrall of his first desperate love affair. An intrinsically human emotion.

Yet physically, the Emperor was "shriveled with age and evil." A master Svengali, yet with something of gentle regard for his acolyte, Vader. So when Vader kneels before him, he says, "Rise, my friend. I would talk with you." Trying to draw a paradox between Palpatine's evil and camaraderie. Trying to make him a little more complex, like we all are.

And as they walk, we reveal that Vader isn't quite such a naïve flower after all. His secret plan is to learn all he can from Palpatine, hone all his mastery of the Dark Side – then usurp the Emperor's throne, destroy him, and rule the universe with his son at his side; his son in whom he'd already sewn the seeds of darkness, his son whom he would shepherd fully to the Dark Side, to rule the universe together. His son, Luke.

The Emperor knows nothing of the specifics of Vader's plan – but he, too, wants to corrupt Luke to the Dark Side, and he senses Vader is eager to make that happen himself. He cautions Vader to have patience. It's a challenge Vader and Luke share. But it's a trait Vader must clutch, if he's to complete his ultimate betrayal of Palpatine.

Meanwhile, we find Luke on Dagobah, Yoda's home planet. Luke has mixed feelings about being here — there's that ambivalence again — for though this is the home of his mentor, the place also holds a dark piece of Luke's soul. This is where Luke once had a vision of his own Dark Side — a vision of decapitating Vader, only to find out it was his own head he'd cut off. In dreamspeak, he was telling himself that he and Vader were one.

He finds Yoda waiting for him in his small hut — and Yoda is frail, now, his voice weakened. At 900 years old, his life force is fading. He tells Luke there's only one more thing Luke must do in order to become a full-fledged Jedi — he must confront Vader.

Luke wants to know if Vader is truly his father, and Yoda confirms it — though he's upset by the fact that Luke has already rushed to confront the Sith Lord before his own Jedi training was complete.

"Beware of anger, fear, and aggression," Yoda tells him. (This tenet is so central to the Jedi philosophy, it's what caused George Lucas to change the original title of the movie from Revenge of the Jedi to Return of the Jedi. Revenge is so not a Jedi-like emotion. And this is Yoda's core truth.)

As Yoda lies on his deathbed, he tells Luke that when he is gone, Luke will be the last Jedi. But he urges Luke to pass on his knowledge. "There... is... another... sky..." And then he dies. Disappears. His dying words foreshadow the next revelation, though it's couched in the poetic phrasing of "another sky." Maybe he was just talking about Jedi Heaven; but then Luke's last name is Skywalker, after all.

So Yoda is gone. Luke is grief-stricken and hopeless, with no one to turn to for guidance — until, of course, the shimmering image of Force-Ben shows up.

Force-Ben tells Luke his father, Anakin, betrayed his Jedi training and was seduced by the Dark Side of the Force, becoming Darth Vader — and Obi Wan takes the blame of that transformation on himself. He feels that his pride at the belief that he could train Anakin was what allowed Anakin to be seduced.

Luke is stunned by this story, and his first response is to think there must still be some good in Vader — that small kernel that was once Anakin. Obi Wan doesn't believe it, though. To him, Vader has become the epitome of evil. But Luke is horrified by the implications: "I can't kill my own father," he says. This is Luke's bottom line, and for everyone paying attention, this isn't just foreshadowing – he's telling us how this is going to end. Or at least how it's not going to end.

Obi Wan describes his own plight at first trying to lure Anakin away from the Dark Side, until they had to battle over the molten fire pits on Mustafar (though that specific locale had not yet been named by George Lucas – he only described to me the broad outline of the light saber fight, and Anakin falling into a lava pit, his legs destroyed.) "He is more machine, now, than man," Ben tells Luke – Luke, whose own hand is now a machine. But just as Luke is now part machine, Obi Wan is telling us Vader is still part human, somewhere deep inside.

But Obi Wan also tells Luke that though Vader defeated him once, he hopes Luke has learned the lesson of patience, and that will serve him when he has to confront Vader for the final time. Luke reiterates that he can't fight his father. Obi Wan says, "You were our only hope." Really putting a lot of weight on Luke's shoulders.

"But Yoda said I could train another," Luke protests. He's looking for any way out of this mess.

And now Obi Wan reveals the last secret he's always kept so close: "That other is your twin sister."

Wait... what? This is the big revelation. Luke and Leia are siblings! They were separated at birth to protect them from the Emperor, who feared their double Jedi power. But it's a secret Luke must never reveal, or Leia will be in terrible danger.

Obi Wan goes on to explain to Luke that when Anakin left for the final time, he didn't know his wife, Amidala (not yet given a name in this trilogy,) was pregnant. (This storyline changed as the prequels emerged, but for now, this is the story I was given from George.) So the twins were separated and hidden to protect them.

Leia was taken to Alderaan, to be brought up as the daughter of Senator Organa. And Luke was taken by Obi Wan to Tatooine, to be raised by Obi Wan's brother, Owen.

On Alderaan – Obie Wan continues his story to Luke – when Leia became part of the Rebel Alliance, she'd always been told by her adoptive parents that if she were ever in mortal danger, to contact Obi Wan on Tatooine. And that was the beginning of reuniting the twins. And though she's not a Jedi, the Force is strong in her, as it is in Luke. Obi Wan tells Luke it is Leia's destiny now to grow into her power – but it is Luke's destiny to face Darth Vader. A destiny he cannot escape.

ROTJ – CHAPTER 4, PAGES 68-82

Chapter 4 resets all the characters, everyone poised to plunge into the next element of the dramatic arc. Luke. Han, Leia, Chewy, Lando. The Rebel Alliance. Vader and Palpatine.

We open with Vader talking to Palpatine at his throne on the Death Star. In the second paragraph I go into some detail about the "black chasm" that channeled down to the core of the battle station, to the power unit that "reeked of ozone." This is, of course, the abyss into which the Emperor is thrown at the end of the story, and I wanted to bring it up here so it didn't just feel like a convenient manhole at that final climax.

There's some backstory about Senator Palpatine's political maneuvering that catapulted him to the position of Emperor, using all the Dark forces at his disposal. So "his soul was the black center of the Empire." The bad guy can be complex, even nuanced, but in the end he's gotta be the really big bad guy. Content in this position, Palpatine now tells Vader they will soon destroy the Rebel Alliance, and bring Luke over to the Dark Side.

Meanwhile, the entire Rebel fleet is gathered at the edge of the galaxy, led by Mon Mothma, herself once a Senator of the Republic, even as she was secretly organizing Rebel cells to resist the emergence of the Empire. Now the upper echelon of the Rebels – including, of course, Han, Leia, Chewie and Lando – get their marching orders from Mon Mothma about the attack on the Death Star. The smuggled plans have revealed a weakness – and furthermore, intelligence suggests the Emperor is on the battle station now. So destroying it could bring an end to the Empire.

Smuggled plans demonstrating a weakness in the Death Star's defenses that will allow it to be destroyed by lobbing a missile into its core is the same story that led to the destruction of the first Death Star in Episode IV. The element that raises the stakes in this narrative is that the Emperor is on the battle station, so he'll be destroyed as well, and with that, it is hoped, the Empire itself will collapse.

The Death Star is protected by an energy shield generated from the moon, Endor. The shield must be deactivated, and then the Death Star main reactor must be obliterated by a small attack force, to be led by Lando. The commando team going to Endor to take down the generator includes Han, Leia, Chewie, and, just for giggles, C3PO.

That's when Luke shows up, back from Dagobah, to say he'll join the commando team going to Endor. Leia hugs him, relieved at his safe return — but she senses something is up with him. And he's not ready to tell her yet that she's his sister. A lie of omission.

So off they all go, to their appointed assignments. As the stolen Imperial shuttle approaches Endor and requests clearance from the Death Star to lower the shield so they can land, tensions are high among Han, Chewie, Leia and Luke. They're not sure the stolen clearance code still works, and they're nervous about all the Star Destroyers and TIE fighters flying around. In typical Han fashion, he tells Chewie to "fly casual." That was just a brilliant scripted line, embodying the entirety of Han's character in those two words. So thank you, Lawrence Kasdan (or George Lucas, if that was you).

The code works, the shield goes down, and the shuttle makes its way toward Endor. But Luke realizes that his Force-connection to Vader is a huge liability: Vader knows he's here, and Luke's presence could endanger the entire mission. "I shouldn't have come," he says. It's the beginning of his realization that his destiny is diverging from that of his comrades. They have to destroy the shield generator. He has to destroy Vader.

And he's not wrong. Because Vader, on his Star Destroyer does sense a presence — and sets off to fly back to the Death Star, to tell the Emperor. Luke is here. It's time to bring him over to the Dark Side.

These two beats — Luke's realization that Vader is here, and he has to face him; and the mirror of that, with Vader realizing that Luke is here, and he has to tell the Emperor so they can bring Luke over to the Dark Side — constitute the mid-ACT 2 turning point, the midpoint crisis, the point of no return. The stakes are raised, and the goal no longer quite the same. Luke is no longer here just for the Death Star. Now it's personal.

ROTJ – CHAPTER 5, PAGES 83-103

As the second half of ACT 2 really kicks in, the obstacles become greater, as battalions of Stormtroopers show up in increasingly greater numbers to thwart our mission.

We see Endor for the first time. Lush, verdant, rippling ferns – the exact opposite of the emptiness of space, the deserts of Tatooine, the high tech corridors of the Empire, and the gritty, dented hardware of the Rebel Alliance. In this bucolic Eden, our commando squad hides their stolen Imperial shuttle under a canopy of mulch and dead branches. Leia, Chewie, Han, Luke, Threepio, R2D2, and a handful of nameless supernumeraries. I referred to these Rebel commandos as "elite ground-fighters," though most of the fan world knows their kind as Redshirts. The group's mission is to destroy the Imperial field generator at its bunker some miles away, so the Rebel fleet can mount its Hail Mary attack on the Death Star. Someone's going to have to die, and these thankless souls have targets on their backs.

Before our heroes can even start out, though, they spot two Imperial scouts in a glen. Impetuously, Han runs out to take them down, with Chewie not far behind. Han is just so happy to be back in the fight, he's unrestrainable. Unfortunately, after a brief combat, two more Imperial scouts appear, and take off on their speeder bikes to warn the garrison. Leia grabs the bike of one of the two fallen scouts, and sets out in pursuit – with Luke hopping up behind her.

This is another great Star Wars chase scene, high speed at ground level, weaving between trees, roots and vines, under low bridges, and over branches. The descendant of the American movie car chase scene, and nobody does it better. As they catch up with one of the scouts, Leia pulls alongside him and Luke jumps off her bike and onto the scout's bike, knocking him off, to his death. Imperial Redshirts have an even shorter life expectancy than Rebel Redshirts.

Two more scouts on bikes show up in pursuit. Luke tells Leia to stay on the tail of the one in front, and he'll take the two behind them. Alas, Leia gets in trouble with her quarry, but manages to jump clear of her bike just before it crashes and explodes. Leaving her unconscious, and the scout thinking she must be dead.

Luke dispatches his two scouts, in skilled and clever ways more fun to watch than to talk about. Still, it was fun to write (and, hopefully, to read.) His bike got wrecked, though, so he was left to walk back to his commando unit.

And while Vader goes to tell the Emperor his "sense" of who he thinks was on that stolen shuttle on Endor, the Rebel commando unit awaits Luke and Leia's return. When Luke finally does make it back, they're all concerned that Leia didn't. It's decided that Luke, Han, Chewie, and the two droids will go search for Leia, while the rest of the unit proceeds to the field generator to hide, awaiting further instructions.

Around this time, Leia wakes up under a fern. Groggy but seemingly okay. She looks around to get her bearings, and sees for the first time – as do we – an Ewok. Wicket. He looks like a furry little teddy bear – but he has a knife, and she's unclear about his intentions. To me he looked like a small Wookiee, and I wondered about making a connection between their two species. But George said they weren't related, and after my flights of fancy about Leia's backstory that had gotten cut, I didn't want to push my fantasy agenda about Ewoks any further.

Wicket threatens Leia with a spear, but she's not having any of it. This little guy doesn't scare her in the least. And when she scratches him between the ears, he purrs like a kitten. Unfortunately, her guard was down when a laser bolt hits nearby, scaring Wicket into the underbrush. An Imperial scout appears and trains his gun on Leia. But Wicket stabs him in the leg, Leia grabs her gun, kills the scout – and now she and Wicket are best friends.

The Ewoks are a whole new set of Threshold Guardians – characters who may turn out to be friends or enemies, it's not always clear which – but who hold the key to the next level of our quest.

This encounter felt like it was about Leia bringing her best feminine energy to the initial encounter, being kind to Wicket, which enlisted his help when it was most needed. Had Han been in the same position, you gotta think he'd have just bopped Wicket on the head as soon as the spear came out.

As Wicket escorts Leia off to safety, she submits to a sense of awe and oneness with the magnificent splendor of this natural realm – the giant trees, lush foliage, sweet furry creatures – she feels somehow part of it all. Almost as if she were connected to it by a living… Force. She felt as if she were a part of this forest, these trees, a "part of them across time, and space, connected by the vital, vibrant force, of which…" Which, we will come to learn, is strong in her. Foreshadowings like this are some-

times better expressed in print than on the screen, where elements like pacing prevent such introspection or insight.

Meanwhile Vader has his audience with Palpatine, and tells him a Rebel force has penetrated the force shield and is on Endor. The Emperor just nods and says he knows. Vader goes on to say his son is with the Rebels. Palpatine is curious about that revelation, and surprised he was unable to sense the boy's presence. He orders Vader to go down to the moon, and is certain Luke will come to him, "Of his own free will… His compassion for you will be his undoing."

This trope shares a lot with numerous mythologies Lucas is drawing from. Vampires, for example, in the Bram Stoker version, can only enter your premises if you invite them in, of your own free will. A strong soul cannot be coerced, only seduced – and the Emperor is intent on seducing Luke to the Dark Side.

Down on Endor, the search party finds Leia's wrecked speeder bike and a torn piece of her jacket – but no Leia – which is of concern, though both Luke and Han are trying to act too macho to reveal just how worried they are.

Chewie, on the other hand, is distracted by a wonderful smell – fresh meat. He sniffs out the raw food, and grabs at it before the others can race over to stop him – and they're all hoisted up in the net that the meat was baiting. After a lot of grumbling and blame throwing, they cut their way out, crashing back down to the ground – only to be surrounded by a hostile party of Ewoks brandishing spears.

Han is about to shoot his way out with his blaster, but Luke stops him – he has a feeling about these furry little guys. The Ewoks gather our heroes' weapons, and tie them up, chattering away as they do – until they get a closer look at Threepio. They prostrate themselves before the droid, and begin chanting. When Luke asks Threepio – who is, of course, fluent in over 6 million languages – what they're saying, he explains that he thinks the Ewoks believe he – C3PO – is a god. Chewie and Artoo think that's hilarious, and Han demands that Threepio use his "divine influence" to get them out of this. But Threepio says he can't – it's against his programming to impersonate a deity.

This has resonance with the scene in Chapter One when C3PO is taken into Jabba's torture den. So unfair, so without reason, he felt in that moment. A moment in which he searched for his life's meaning, as do all who turn to religion for that answer. And now he's being regarded by the Ewoks as their god — the entity who gives meaning to their lives. All very puzzling for the protocol droid.

So the captive entourage proceeds to the Ewok village — Han, Luke, Chewie, and Artoo hanging upside down on poles — and Threepio borne on a litter, like a royal potentate. The lowly Threepio can only savor this moment of elevation above his owners, who so often treat him so dismissively. It's a feeling we can all relate to. Viewing the majesty of the approaching village, content for the moment to bask in his new role, he simply thinks, as any god might, "And it was good." A biblical thought, for a newly biblical entity.

ROTJ – CHAPTER 6, PAGES 104-124

We pick up at our intrepid adventurers' arrival in the Ewok village — unceremonious to them, though they are soon to be at the center of an Ewok ceremony. And in contradistinction to all the back and forth action scenes in the previous material, nearly this entire chapter is set right here, in the village. After so much hubbub and criss-crossing narratives, we need a pause, to take a breath, to get our bearings, restate the story and the stakes, and get ready to launch into the next series of battles.

The village of "diminutive monkey-bears" — which is what they reminded me of — is a labyrinth of trees, vines, rope bridges, scaffolding, webbing and tunnels. Our heroes are tied to poles, carried upside down to the largest hut, where Han is put on a spit and suspended over a small fire, while the tribe decides their fate. With characteristic understatement, Han says he doesn't like the look of this. Han has a way of telling the audience how to feel.

The situation deteriorates when Chewbacca roars at an Ewok, and Artoo zaps another one. Luke tells Threepio, who knows their language, to calm things down — but Threepio apologetically explains Solo is going to be the main course for dinner tonight. As their deity, Threepio is obligated to preside over the ceremony. That's when Chief Chirpa enters with the village's new guest — Leia! She'd been brought here by her new little Ewok companion.

Leia demands her friends be freed, but the Ewoks have other ideas. Leia, worried, asks Luke what he can do. This is the first moment that Han is nettled by Leia's seeming closeness to Luke — a feeling that will be amplified later on.

Luke orders Threepio to tell the Ewoks that if his friends aren't freed, he'll become an angry god, and use his magic on them. Threepio protests, reluctant to violate the Ewoks' religious beliefs — but Luke closes his eyes and uses the Force to levitate Threepio. Threepio is surprised he has such power — but the demonstration works, and the Rebels are freed.

That night, Threepio tells the Ewok Elders the story of the Rebellion, in order to enlist their aid in the struggle against the Empire. They're fascinated — but their response is that the Empire is not their problem. Endorian isolationists.

Next, Han makes his pitch for their help, in his own inimitable fashion; and then Luke follows, pleading on behalf of the galaxy — which is just too abstract an argument for the Ewoks.

Finally, Leia tells them, "Do it for the trees." Wicket nods, and expands on her philosophy, telling his tribe they are all leaves on the great tree of life, all connected, and all must work together. It was basically an early eco-argument, set within the context of the Force as a counterpoint to Imperial colonialist exploitation.

Between Leia's strong-woman takedown of misogynist Jabba, and this rousing call for protecting the interconnectedness of all of nature, this is a pretty forward-looking space opera.

Our heroes are freed, amidst great celebrating and goodwill — though Luke stands apart, with an unexpected darkness in his heart — he senses Vader's presence not far off. When he wanders away from the bonfires and gaiety, Leia sees him and follows, and asks him what's wrong. She doesn't know yet why she feels so connected to him.

He tells her he senses Vader's presence on Endor, and he has to leave his friends before he endangers their mission. And he has to face Vader. Leia wants to know why. Isn't it more important just to destroy the deflector field generator?

First Luke stuns her by confessing Vader is his father – and as if that weren't enough, he tells her Vader is Leia's father, too. So Luke is her brother.

Whoa! Before Leia can even digest this news, Luke tells her he can sense there's still good in their father, and he has to face Vader so he can save him. Luke and Leia embrace, and Luke goes off to face his destiny.

But Han has witnessed their embrace, and full of jealousy he storms up to her, wanting to know what that was about. She can't tell him now, she's had no time to assimilate all this news. All she can do is cry, and ask Han to hold her – which he does, now totally confused, the big lug.

The next morning, as Vader stands near the Imperial landing platform in a cleared space on the forest moon, overseeing the arrival of his stormtroopers, armored walkers, and weapons being deployed to protect the field generator, Luke is brought to him by a squad of guards to whom Luke has surrendered. The head guard gives Vader Luke's lightsaber.

Vader dismisses them and faces his son; and they both know this is the beginning of the final battle.

ROTJ – CHAPTER 7, PAGES 125-146

Luke tells Vader he knows there is still good in the Dark Lord. That's why Vader couldn't kill him earlier. And we've certainly seen evidence of this, from the climaxes of the first two movies. It always seemed like Vader should have been able to kill Luke when he was on his tail flying to destroy the Death Star in Episode IV; and then again when Vader cut off Luke's hand – that was a laser swordfight Vader ought to have won outright. So Luke's accusation of good in Vader now rings true – to us and to Vader, though he denies it.

In fact, it seems to anger Vader to be accused of still having any good within him. His self-identity is so wrapped up in being Palpatine's evil apprentice, anything that could diminish that just rankles him. This is known as Empty Unit Narcissism by some psychologists – a patient's belief he's not just a terrible person, he's the worst person ever, nobody is worse than he is. A kind of narcissistic pride in his own malevolence. So to have that belief challenged - it just steels Vader's resolve to kill his son if Luke won't be turned to the Dark Side.

Meanwhile, the Rebel fleet is planning its imminent lightspeed attack on the Death Star – its success dependent on the commando team taking out the field generator on Endor – followed by the attack squadron led by Lando, flying the Millennium Falcon, to destroy the Death Star at its core.

And we're into the back and forth now. Han and the commandos have made their way to the shield generator. Paploo the Ewok steals a guard's bike to draw the other guards away, and the commandos make it into the bunker with a stolen code, as…

Vader brings Luke to the Emperor on the Death Star. Luke is so full of rage, searching for a way to kill the Emperor – especially when Palpatine, like a benevolent master, has Luke uncuffed. The Emperor quizzes Luke about who continued his Jedi training after Obi Wan failed – and he sees in Luke's heart that it was Yoda, and Yoda is now dead.

Luke is furious he allowed the Emperor to read his thoughts this way, it feels like such a violation – but he gives himself up to the mental assaults, lets himself be buffeted, as Yoda had taught him: let your opponent waste his strength in his attacks, until he expends himself, allowing you to deal the victory blow.

But Luke also sees fear in the Emperor. And that lets him know he can win.

Palpatine takes Luke's lightsaber from Vader, and points out the moon Endor through the window. He tells Luke the Rebel attack is doomed to fail. Even now, his friends are walking into a trap in the bunker on Endor. And when the Rebel fleet gets here, they'll discover they've flown into a trap, as well; and Luke will get to watch them destroyed.

This feels like the end of ACT 2, the Collapse of the Hero's Plan. Luke has come so far, and it's all come to naught. Everything they've been struggling to achieve was engineered by Palpatine, who lured them here, and is now set to crush the Rebellion. With Luke forced to sit here and watch.

Luke is so distraught he almost Force-grabs his lightsaber – but stops himself. He must not succumb to anger, and to the Dark Side – as…

Han and Leia and the commandos make it past the first level of guards inside the field generator bunker, and move on to the inner core, as...

The Rebel fleet bursts out of hyperspace, going into attack mode on the Death Star – only to realize the deflector shield isn't down yet – it only looks down because the signal is jammed. And as Rebel fighters crash and burn against the shield, and Imperial Star Destroyers and TIE fighters appear, Lando and the Rebel Generals realize this was, indeed, a trap.

So the battle is joined, as...

Han and the commandos make it into the control room of the bunker, and start placing charges to blow up the field deflector generator – when they find themselves surrounded by dozens of stormtroopers, weapons aimed at them, and ordering them to surrender. The commandos are hopelessly outnumbered. They give up. As...

On the flagship Super Star Destroyer, an underling asks Admiral Piett for the order to start the all-out attack on the Rebel Fleet. But Piett says no – his orders from the Emperor are merely to keep the Rebels from escaping. Palpatine has something more sinister in mind for destroying them – as...

Palpatine, Luke and Vader watch the aerial dogfights from the throne room. Like a silent fireworks display. But now the Emperor reveals to Luke that the Death Star's weapon system is fully operational. He radios his control room and tells them to fire at will. And Luke can only watch in horror as the beam from the Death Star shoots out at a huge Reber Star Cruiser – and in the next moment, vaporizes it.

Luke's despair and anger overwhelm him. He sees his lightsaber lying on the throne. "And in this bleak and livid moment, the dark side was much with him." Embodied in the light saber. Luke is succumbing to the Dark Side of the Force.

Now that the Hero's Plan has collapsed, Luke can't see a way to win without succumbing to the very thing he's been fighting against. His own Dark Side.

ROTJ – CHAPTER 8, PAGES 147-163

General Ackbar and the high command of the Rebel fleet are stunned to see the Death Star operational, and vaporizing their Star Cruisers. He orders a retreat. But Lando convinces him they won't get a second bite at this apple. They have to press on with the battle, until the deflector shield comes down. Ackbar acquiesces – but he looks hopeless.

Back in the throne room, Palpatine points out the carnage to Luke, explaining the entire Rebel fleet will soon be destroyed, along with Luke's friends on Endor. Luke, angry beyond control now, Force-grabs his lightsaber from where it sits on the throne, and in a single motion, brings it down on Palpatine's skull. Luke is beyond Dark Side/Light Side philosophies. He's just in the moment now. And he wants Palpatine dead.

But Vader is right there, to block the blow with his own lightsaber. Father and son face off for the ultimate lightsaber duel, as Palpatine looks on with a smile, watching Luke's descent into dark anger.

On Endor, Han, Leia and the others are now prisoners in the clearing before the bunker, surrounded by hundreds of Imperial stormtroopers. With the end seemingly imminent, Han and Leia hold hands, allowing themselves to experience their love in these last moments. Maybe their warrior skills can no longer save them – but they can exit this life in the solace of their love.

Suddenly Threepio and Artoo enter the clearing – stop when they see the situation they've walked into – and turn around to run back into the woods. Stormtroopers chase them. But as they're about to be captured, 15 Ewoks drop out of the trees and take down the stormtroopers. Teebo blasts a loud note from a ram's horn – and that's the call to action to the whole Ewok nation. The Battle for Endor has commenced.

Hundreds of Ewoks descend on the battalion of stormtroopers, countering laser blasters with rocks and arrows. Chewie jumps into the bushes as Han and Leia shelter under the arches of the bunker. Han tries to open the bunker doors with the stolen code, but this time it doesn't work, the door lock has been reprogrammed. They need Artoo to hack it. Han contacts Artoo over the commlink, and tells him to get over here.

The battle rages all around them, high tech vs. low. Classic David and Goliath stuff. The Ewoks are getting laser blasted while they use their primitive weapons. Sometimes several Ewoks mob a stormtrooper to bring him down. And Chewie is right in the midst of the fray, protecting his little genetic cousins, as they protect him. (Even though George said Wookiees and Ewoks weren't related, I have to believe they shared some distant antecedent that even George didn't know about.)

Artoo makes it over to the bunker door, with Han and Leia giving him cover fire. He plugs into the lock – but a laser blast fries him, and he falls over, smoking. Han goes back to trying to hotwire the lock, as the fighting intensifies, the Ewoks hurling boulders with catapults at Imperial walkers, and dive-bombing stormtroopers from animal skin hang-gliders.

Meanwhile, up in the sky, the dogfights are escalating, and Lando devises a new, desperate strategy – having the Rebel Star Cruisers go head to head at close range with the Imperial Star Destroyers. "Like tanks at twenty paces." That was the visual I was trying to evoke from the production stills I had of the space fight. The Rebels aren't likely to win those confrontations, but better that than systematic annihilation by the Death Star.

And in the throne room, the lightsaber duel between Vader and Luke gets more intense. Vader is actually pleased to see Luke's skill level. He's already thinking that after Luke comes under Vader's wing, for further tutelage, they'll more easily be able to destroy Palpatine and rule the galaxy themselves, father and son, side by side.

But with a flurry of attacks, Luke actually drives Vader to his knees and stands above him, poised for the killshot. In that moment he even has the thought that he could kill Vader and take the Sith Lord's place at the Emperor's side. Momentarily, it makes him feverish with power.

Vader is stunned by his son's unexpected strength, and for the first time realizes Luke might kill him. Fury and revenge fill his soul.

But the Emperor, seeing all this, is filled with glee, watching the Dark Side energize both combatants. He shouts out joyfully, "Let the hate flow through you! Become one with it! Let it nourish you!" Like a man-

ager of a bare knuckle boxer in the ring, caught up in the screams of cheering spectators.

And that wakes Luke up from his fugue-state plunge into hatred. *What am I doing? What am I becoming?* He lowers his sword. "I will not fight you, father." He remembers who he is, and what he's promised himself.

Luke is wrestling so hard with the core of his own very being – must it always take violence and hatred to triumph?

Vader sneers that Luke is unwise to lower his defenses. But when Luke Force-connects his mind with Vader's, it makes him think of the times Vader could have killed him, but didn't – in the dogfight at the first Death Star, in the lightsaber duel on Bespin. And the time Vader could have killed Leia when she was first captured – but didn't. Luke says, "Your thoughts betray you, father. I feel the good in you." Luke says it partly to get under his father's skin – and who among us, as a rebellious teenager, hasn't wanted to do that? And that really pisses Vader off.

The Dark Lord throws his saber at a girder supporting Luke, sending Luke tumbling into the darkness, as Vader's lightsaber flies back into his hand. And now Vader must stalk Luke into the shadows. But Luke has pushed the notion of patricide from his heart, and rolls his lightsaber across the floor to Vader. Vader takes it, again exhorting Luke to come over to the Dark Side. He knows Luke's feelings are strong for his friends, but…

Suddenly Vader can see into Luke's heart, to his true feelings, to his concern for… his sister! Luke's feelings have betrayed him, and now Vader learns for the first time that Luke's sister – Vader's daughter – is alive. Vader smiles at Luke. "If you will not turn to the Dark Side, perhaps she will." Tables turned – Vader knows how to get under his son's skin, too.

And that's just too much for Luke. The last straw. "Never!" he screams, Force-grabs his lightsaber back into his hand, and redoubles his attack in a frenzy, blow after blow, finally forcing Vader to his knees – and cutting off Vader's right hand!

Just as Vader had done to Luke. The son overcoming the father, poised to kill him – until he looks at Vader's severed hand, the same as his own, and realizes once again how much like his father he's become, how he's become the very thing he hated.

And once again, in that moment, the Emperor is so overcome with excitement at all this hatred, he can't restrain himself. "Good! Kill him!" he shouts to Luke. "Your hatred has made you powerful!" Palpatine is speaking to himself with those words, as well as to Luke.

And in that moment, Luke fully realizes he has truly become the Darkness he hates – and he throws his lightsaber away. "You have failed, Palpatine! I am a Jedi, as my father was before me!" And though this is shouted at Palpatine, his words are meant for Vader to hear as well.

In throwing his lightsaber away and claiming his Inner Jedi, Luke has dug deep to find his salvation, and fully realized that the prize he's been after for so long – destroying Vader and the Death Star – is not the true prize. Killing Vader was not the way. The true prize is walking the path of the Jedi, connected to everything and everyone.

So he shouts the words to the Emperor, naming both himself and his father as Jedi – but of course Vader hears them, too. And it begins to reawaken that long-sleeping Jedi spirit within Vader.

Palpatine is enraged, though. And tells Luke, "If you will not be turned, you will be destroyed." He's had enough of this mealy-mouthed kid. He raises his spindly arms and begins hurling crackling lightning at Luke. "Blinding white bolts of energy coruscated from his fingers." Over and over, sending Luke writhing in pain to the ground. And who can't relate with excitement to coruscating lightning?

And Vader crawls, "like a wounded animal, to his Emperor's side." Vader, at his nadir, has come to rock bottom.

This is perhaps the clearest moment – at least in retrospect – that this entire story has been Vader's Hero's Journey as well as Luke's. And for Vader, this is the end of his Act Two Collapse of the Hero's Plan. Everything he has worked for since Anakin became Vader has come crashing down on him, with seemingly no way out of his destruction. He will, of course, soon reach deep within himself and come to a short, unexpected, redemptive Act Three of his own.

Meanwhile, back on Endor, Chewie and the Ewoks commandeer an Imperial walker, and start blasting stormtroopers right and left, as Han has one failure after another trying to breach the bunker door.

Finally, Han and Leia find themselves surrounded by stormtroopers, who are about to kill them.

They look into each other's eyes – this is the end, and once again they express their love for each other – this time verbally. "I love you," Han whispers. "I know," Leia replies. This is, of course, the mirror image of the scene in The Empire Strikes Back, *just before Han is about to be lowered into carbonite. They kiss passionately for the first time then, and Leia says, "I love you," and Han says, "I know."*

In any case, after the expressions of love now, a huge laser blast kills the stormtroopers, and Chewie emerges out of the top of his Imperial walker.

The tide of the battle for Endor has turned.

ROTJ – CHAPTER 9, PAGES 164-181

Up in space, the battle rages. The deflector shield remains up, so it looks like this will all end up a lost cause – but Lando still has hope that Han will come through.

In the throne room, Luke is nearly dead under the assault from Palpatine's energy blasts, which he continues to hurl. Finally, Luke is motionless – apparently lifeless. Definitely the Collapse of the Hero's Plan, as well as the collapse of his life force.

And that proves too much for Vader to endure. Digging deep within himself, feeling the remnants of good within, feeling his hatred for the evil that is the Emperor, and feeling anguish at seeing his son so brutally murdered... he rises up. Lifts the Emperor high above his head, and hurls him into the chasm that leads far down to the power core of the Death Star.

This is the same chasm I described back in Chapter Four, just to set up this moment. ("We open with Vader talking to Palpatine at his throne on the Death Star. In the second paragraph I go into some detail about the 'black chasm' that channeled down to the core of the battle station, to the power unit that 'reeked of ozone.'")

After Vader throws Palpatine to his death, he staggers back to Luke's lifeless body, and collapses beside him.

Down on Endor, Han and company dress up as stormtroopers, trick the guards inside the bunker into opening the doors, rush in and overpower them, plant charges, and blow up the generator – crashing down the deflector shield that surrounds the Death Star!

The Rebel fleet sees the deflector shield come down – their final assault can begin. Lando, in the Millennium Falcon, zooms down to the surface of the Death Star, accompanied by his wingmen, to begin his approach to the reactor core, through well-defended shafts, and pursued by TIE fighters – as Admiral Ackbar and team disable an Imperial Star Destroyer at close range – enough to crash it into the Death Star, setting off internal explosions all over the evil battle station.

At this stage in Chapter 9, with explosions rocking the entire Death Star, after the Star Destroyer had collided with it, Luke stumbles through his own personal hell of "electrical fires, steam explosions," and the rumblings of continued Rebel attacks now that the deflector shield is down – he stumbles, carrying the deadweight of his mortally wounded father. Until he can go no further, and rests Vader on the ground.

So not only was his original goal not what he thought it was – it was the opposite of that. Now he's struggling not to destroy Vader, but to keep him alive, to save him in body, as he's just saved his soul.

Barely alive, Vader whispers, "Luke, help me take this mask off." And Luke protests, "You'll die." And Vader responds, "Let me look on you with my own eyes." Not the synthetic, bionic eyes he's used since becoming Vader; but the true, human eyes of Anakin Skywalker. And when they remove the mask together, Luke sees "the sad, benign face of an old man." They're finally reconciling here, reaching a place of peace neither of them – and no one in the audience – would have thought possible.

Just as most of us, I think, after decades of struggles with our fathers – sometimes loving, sometimes acrimonious – allow ourselves to see something more of our parent's true nature in the hours and minutes before they die. Maybe see the young man inside the old, when there was hope and aspiration, and before all the slings and arrows of outrageous fortune twisted and complicated things. I know I had those feelings sitting at my father's deathbed.

Luke and Vader share memories, tears, grief, hope, reconciliation, and ultimately, redemption. Vader now wants the best for his son, and doesn't want him to be afraid for either of them. "Luminous beings are we, Luke — not this crude matter." This, a foreshadowing of the last moments of the book and movie. And now Vader tells Luke to leave him.

But Luke insists he'll save Vader, Vader won't die. And Luke won't leave.

And as Vader lies there staring into his son's eyes, there's a moment of serenity. Of understanding the ways they'd saved each other's lives.

Almost inaudibly, Vader says, "Luke… you were right about me. Tell your sister you were right." So there <u>was</u> good in him. He finally felt that in the end, and used it to save his son's life.

And Vader dies.

So, elsewhere on the Death Star, destruction all around, Commander Jerjerrod, in a final act of spite, has his gunner turn the Death Star ray on the planet Endor itself — if he's not going to survive, then neither will this lush, harmless oasis in the sky. The Dark Side is like that.

Fortunately for Han, Leia, Chewie, and the Ewoks, Lando finally navigates the Millennium Falcon to the Death Star's reactor core, looses his concussion missiles into the reactor, and beats a hasty retreat, barely ahead of the massive explosion and shock wave that obliterates it before it can destroy Endor.

Leia and Han watch the fireworks from Endor — and Leia knows Luke got off the Death Star in time. She can feel it, because she's Force-connected to Luke. Han mistakes her relief for a different kind of feeling for Luke, and gallantly offers to stand aside, to let them be together. He loves her so much, he can be selfless in that way. Leia laughs, though, and tells Han it's not like that. She and Luke are siblings. Han is gob-smacked. And the two of them embrace, the beginning of a long romance.

This is the final triumph in the Hero's Journey. The Death Star and the Emperor are destroyed, Han and Leia are in love, Luke redeemed his father and is safe.

That night, there's a huge victory celebration on Endor, with dancing, singing, and bonfires. Off in the woods by himself, Luke has brought his father's body back down here in a shuttle, and places it on a funeral pyre, for a last good-bye.

Then he joins his friends at the Ewok party, and they embrace joyously. This is the final beat in the stopping points of the Hero's Journey. Bringing it all back home. In some stories it's the gold you were seeking, in other stories it's the magic elixir. In this story it's satisfaction that the galaxy has been freed from the horrors of its tyrannical Emperor; and the triumph of Luke's soul searching, bringing him at last to a reconciliation with his father, and into the way of the Jedi.

So only Luke can see, shimmering in the flames of a bonfire, the spirit images of Yoda, Obi Wan… and Anakin. Just as Vader had told him. "Luminous beings are we, Luke. Not this crude matter."

That is the prize Luke brought back home from his Journey. The jewel he found in the darkest cave and returned with. It's the understanding that we are luminous beings.

So it's also a triumph over Death, since we go on to be luminous beings in the weave of the Force.

Except for the Empire. The Empire was dead.

Long live the Alliance.

APPENDIX E
OTHER WORKS

FILMOGRAPHY
https://bit.ly/JamesKahnIMDB

St. Elsewhere – Writer, 1984, 1 episode, "A Pig Too Far"
E/R – Writer, 1984, 3 episodes
Family Medical Center – Head Writer, 1989, 167 episodes
Beyond Reality – Writer, 1991-1992, 4 episodes
Star Trek: The Next Generation – Writer, 1992, 1 episode
TekWar – Writer, 1995, 3 episodes
Medicine Ball – Writer, 1995, 1 episode, "Sex, Lies, and Adhesive Tape."
Melrose Place – Writer 1995-1999, 20 episodes; Producer 1997-1999, 74 episodes
Xena: Warrior Princess – Writer, 1 episode, 2000, "The Abyss"
Star Trek: Voyager – Producer 2000-2001, 24 episodes; Writer 2000-2001, 4 episodes
Doc – Writer, 2002-2003, 3 episodes
All My Children – Script Writer, 2009-2010, 30 episodes
The Bet – Feature Film, Producer, 2013

MUSIC VIDEOS
https://bit.ly/JamesKahnMusicVideos

Dolores Quits Dancing
Workin' That ER
O The Things That I've Seen
So Long the River
No More a'Whalin'
The Risin' of the Seas
The Vast Infinity

In the Covid Times
Wrongside Bob
The Twelfth Elf
Waterline
Come Out and Play
Lost in the traces
O the Ocean Rolls

NOVELS
Diagnosis: Murder – Carlyle Press, 1980
World Enough, and Time – Del Rey/Ballantine Books, 1980
Time's Dark Laughter – Del Rey/Ballantine Books, 1982
Timefall – St. Martin's Press, 1986
The Echo Vector – St. Martin's Press, 1987
Incarnate – Premiere Press, 2014
Matamoros – Pen Wild Press, 2019
The Twelfth Elf (Children's Book) – Pen Wild Press, 2020
The Wake-Up Call (Graphic Novel) – Pen Wild Press, 2021

NOVELIZATIONS
Poltergeist – Warner Books, 1982
Return of the Jedi – Del Rey/Random House 1983
Indiana Jones and the Temple of Doom – Ballantine Books 1984
The Goonies – Warner Books, 1985
Poltergeist II – Ballantine Books, 1986

DISCOGRAPHY
Waterline https://bit.ly/WaterlineAlbum
Man Walks Into a Bar https://bit.ly/ManWalksIntoABarAlbum
The Twelfth Elf https://bit.ly/TheTwelfthElfAlbum
The Meaning of Life https://bit.ly/TheMeaningOfLifeAlbum
Matamoros https://bit.ly/MatamorosAlbum
By the Risin' of the Sea https://bit.ly/RisinOfTheSeasAlbum

ACKNOWLEDGEMENTS

I OBVIOUSLY couldn't have had the life I've been writing about without massive support from a thousand people. Starting with my parents, Al and Judy; to my brave grandparents Joe and Sarah Kahn, Ben and Goldie Pesmen, to the mythological Uncle Lorry; to my soul-mate cousins Doug, Andrea, Mitch, and Marc; high school friends Al Ripperger (RIP), Dave Thinnes (RIP), Mark Sorensen, Dawn Piotter, and Harriet Hall (RIP); college and med school confidantes Mark Tanz, Mike Glick, Art Reingold, Jesse Hall, Barbara Engel, Deborah Madansky, Bobby Berg; hospital, ER, and clinic foxhole mates Jerome Hoffman, Alex Lampone, Walter Theis, Bill Meller; TV show friend and mentor Chuck Pratt, who taught me how to write a television script; Kate Wallace, who championed my music, and David West, who took my music to a whole new level. To Rex Saint Onge, for windows into the Forces. And to John Scalzi, for skipping class to read *Return of the Jedi*.

Special call-outs to Jill Littlewood, my wife and partner, who kept me afloat all this time; to Laura, Jordan, and Eliot, my three amazing kids who made me not only a better writer but a better person, and kept urging me to do this memoir; to Matt Meisterheim, my 7th grade English teacher, whose discounted B+ sent me on to a life of writing.

And more recently, to Jeffrey Sher and Bob Brunner, who gave me critical notes on an early draft; to Lee Goldberg (another one of Shukri's writers back in my *Beyond Reality* days), who connected me with BearManor Media; and to Ben Ohmart, the connectee who consented to publish this stumbling stroll down memory lane.

Random Chronological Photo Ops

Grandfather Joe Kahn, grandmother Sarah Goldberg Kahn, and Sarah's father Morris Goldberg behind the counter at his butcher shop on Maxwell Street, Chicago, 1918.

Grandparents Ben and Goldie Pesmen at Seder with the Author as a Cub Scout, 1957.

Johann and the Pacemakers, playing "Twist and Shout," 1964. Mark Sorensen, recorders; Brian Dole, recorders; Al Ripperger, recorders; James Kahn, lute.

Cousins, 1967.

The Author and Jill reclining against LP collection, 1974.

Husband and wife, wild Hollywood days, 1977.

The Author in full, with his children, 2014. Life is good. Photo courtesy of LaurynSophia Photography.

Reissue of Star Wars Trilogy *(Del Rey, 2015), with my name misspelled on the front cover, "Khan" instead of correct "Kahn." Possibly meant to be a meta reference to feature film,* The Wrath of Khan, *from parallel franchise,* Star Trek, *in which William Shatner wails the name of his arch enemy, "Khaaaaaaaaannnnnnnnn!!!!" Flawed book recalled after 30,000 copies sent to bookstores. A junior editor did call me to apologize. Trilogy reissued with correct spelling. Uncertain how many copies of the flawed copies remain at large.*

Husband and wife in stylish lockdown masks, 2020.

The Author and a few good friends in Cardiff, Wales, 2017.

Jill, 2019.

The Author, in repose, 2024.

Photo Attributions

Photo of Queen 'Fabiola de Mora' courtesy of Enstropia, Photographer Lothar Schaak, (No Endorsement Indicated). License: https://creativecommons.org/licenses/by-sa/3.0/de/deed.en

Photo from *ET: The Extra-Terrestrial* courtesy of Universal Studios

Photo of Slim Pickens Public Domain

Photos of St. Charles Saloon courtesy of Dave Thorpe

Slim Pickens' boots photo courtesy of the Author

Photos of oak tree arboglyph and cave-dwelling lightsnake courtesy of Rex Saint Onge

Photos of *Siwut* flatstone created by Rex Saint Onge, courtesy of the Author

Flawed Trilogy cover photo courtesy of the Author

Family photos courtesy of the Author

Front cover photo by Jill Littlewood

Back cover photo by James Kahn

Endnotes

1-44, 59-147 - *Return of the Jedi*, Del Rey/Random House (1983)

45-49 – *Indiana Jones and the Temple of Doom*, Ballantine Books (1984)

50 – "Anything Goes," Cole Porter (1934)

51-57 – *The Goonies*, Warner Books (1985)

58 – "Hotel California," The Eagles (1976)

Index